# The Administrator's Handbook for Christian Schools

# The Administrator's Handbook for Christian Schools

Larry Stephenson

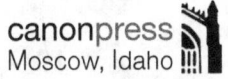
canonpress
Moscow, Idaho

*A dissertation submitted to Dr. Ken Talbot in candidacty for the degree of Doctor of Education from Whitefield Graduate Schools, Office of Academic Studies, Cary, North Carolina, Convocation 11, 2006.*

Published by Canon Press
P. O. Box 8729, Moscow, ID 83843
800–488–2034 | www.canonpress.com

Larry Stephenson, *The Administrator's Handbook for Christian Schools*
Copyright © 2006 by Larry Stephenson

Scripture taken from the New King James Version.® copyright © 1982 Thomas Nelson, Inc. Used by permission. All rights reserved.

Cover design by Rachel Rosales.
Interior design by Jessica Evans.

Printed in the United States of America.
All rights reserved. No part of this publication may be reproduced, stored in a retrieval system, or transmitted in any form by any means, electronic, mechanical, photocopy, recording, or otherwise, without prior permission of the author, except as provided by USA copyright law.

*Library of Congress Cataloging-in-Publication Data is available on the Canon Press website.*

12 13 14 15 16 17 18 19 20         10 9 8 7 6 5 4 3 2 1

I dedicate this book to my family:
Kelly, Audrey, Lesley, Ty, and Darcey.
Love you and thank you for
all of your sacrifices for my calling.

# CONTENTS

**Chapter 1: Biblical Mandate: The Administrator's Handbook** ............ 21

    Two Distinct Teams ............ 23

    Peer Pressure: The Power of Influence ............ 24

    School Culture ............ 25

    Determining Your Educational Philosophy: Evangelistic or Discipleship ............ 25

    School Wide Christian Goals and Educational Philosophy ............ 26

    Can Education Be Neutral? ............ 27

    Value of Biblical Application ............ 28

    Conclusion ............ 29

**Chapter 2: School Policies and Procedures** ............ 31

    Admissions ............ 31

        *Enrollment Process and Guidelines* ............ 32

        *Fees and Tuition* ............ 33

    Student Exit and Withdrawal Procedure ............ 33

        *Exit Procedure* ............ 33

        *Steps to Withdrawal* ............ 33

    Collections Policy ............ 34

    Grievance Guidelines ............ 35

        *Students/Parents to Teachers* ............ 36

        *Parents/Patrons to Administrator/Principal* ............ 36

  *Staff to Administration* ................................................................ 36

  *Volunteers to Staff/Administration* ............................................ 37

 Teacher Procedures, Policies and Guidelines ....................................... 37

  *Class Reverence Guidelines* ......................................................... 37

  *Classroom Management* ............................................................... 37

  *Lesson Plans* ................................................................................. 38

  *Grading Principles* ....................................................................... 38

  *Teacher Guidelines for Class Review* ........................................... 39

  *Grade Reporting* .......................................................................... 40

  *Exams* ........................................................................................... 40

  *Testing Schedule Guidelines* ........................................................ 41

  *Twenty Percent Rule* ................................................................... 41

  *Extra Credit* ................................................................................. 42

  *"F" Issuance Principles* ................................................................ 42

  *Grading Late Assignments* .......................................................... 42

  *Work Missed During a Suspension* ............................................. 42

  *Students Leaving Campus* ........................................................... 43

  *Sexual Harassment, Abuse, or Child Abuse Policy* ...................... 43

  *Movie Guidelines* ......................................................................... 44

  *Music Guidelines* ......................................................................... 45

  *Enrollment of Staff Children* ....................................................... 45

  *Supervision of Staff Members' Children* ..................................... 45

  *School Options for Staff Children* ............................................... 46

  *Obtaining Substitute Teachers* .................................................................. 46

  *Cell Phone Usage* ......................................................................................... 46

 Medical and Emergency Standard Operating Procedures ........................... 47

  *Medical Emergencies* .................................................................................. 47

  *Administration of Medication* .................................................................. 48

  *Fire Drill* ........................................................................................................ 48

  *Tornado Drill* ............................................................................................... 48

  *Lockdown Procedure* .................................................................................. 49

  *Lock-In Procedure* ...................................................................................... 50

 Conclusion ........................................................................................................... 50

**Chapter 3: Philosophies for Curriculum** .................................................. 51

 Aligning Your Curriculum with Your Goals .................................................. 51

  *Step 1: Review Stage* ................................................................................... 51

  *Step 2: Pilot Stage* ....................................................................................... 52

  *Step 3: Polish Stage* .................................................................................... 52

  *Step 4: Publish Stage* .................................................................................. 52

 Use of Secular Material ..................................................................................... 53

 Controversial Subjects ....................................................................................... 53

  *Doctrine Guidelines* .................................................................................... 54

  *Selecting Debate Topics* .............................................................................. 55

 What Is Classical Education? ........................................................................... 56

 Curriculum Recommendations ....................................................................... 56

  *Non-Denominational Guidelines* ............................................................. 56

*Recommended Curriculum Goals by Subject:* ......................................................... 56

 *Bible* ............................................................................................................. 56

 *English* ......................................................................................................... 57

 *Writing* ......................................................................................................... 58

 *Science* ......................................................................................................... 59

 *History* ......................................................................................................... 60

 *Mathematics* ................................................................................................. 62

 *Literature* ..................................................................................................... 63

 *Foreign Language* ........................................................................................ 64

Recommended Courses for Secondary Students ................................................. 67

 *Junior High School (Grades 7 and 8)* ............................................................ 67

 *High School (Grades 9-12)* ............................................................................ 67

Advanced Courses and Advanced Placement Program .................................... 68

Promotion Guidelines ............................................................................................ 68

 *Elementary Grades* ....................................................................................... 68

 *Secondary Students* ...................................................................................... 69

 *Academic Probation* ..................................................................................... 69

 *Guidelines for Retention* ............................................................................... 70

 *New Student Placement Guidelines* ............................................................. 71

Homework Philosophy and Guidelines .............................................................. 71

Honors and Awards ............................................................................................... 72

 *Honor Rolls* ................................................................................................... 72

 *Faculty Commendation Award* ..................................................................... 72

  *Perfect Attendance* .................................................................. 73

  *Valedictorian and Salutatorian* ................................................ 73

 High School Graduation Guidelines ............................................... 73

  *Credits Required for Graduation* ............................................... 74

 Conclusion ...................................................................................... 74

**Chapter 4: Student Discipline and Behavior Guidelines** .............. 75

 Effective Biblical Discipline ........................................................... 75

  *Consistency: Its Crucial Role* ..................................................... 76

 Basic School Rules ......................................................................... 76

 Additional Recommendations for Teachers .................................. 77

  *Controlling Student Talking* ..................................................... 78

  *Discipline as a Result of Student Talking* ................................. 78

  *Posture-Position Recommendations* .......................................... 79

 Uniforms and Dress Code .............................................................. 79

  *Enforcement* ............................................................................. 80

 Office Visits ..................................................................................... 80

  *Expulsion and Suspension* ........................................................ 81

  *Re-Admission* ........................................................................... 82

 Conclusion ...................................................................................... 82

**Chapter 5: Personnel Guidelines** ..................................................... 83

 Teachers—The Key Element ........................................................... 83

 Hiring and Managing Staff ............................................................. 84

 Staff Church Attendance ................................................................ 84

Staff and Student Relations ................................................................. 85

Dress Code for Staff Members .............................................................. 85

Guidelines for Staff/Teacher Evaluation ................................................ 86

Morale—Keeping a Healthy Balance ..................................................... 86

Training and Certification ..................................................................... 87

Compensation Guidelines ..................................................................... 87

Employee Leave of Absence Guidelines ................................................ 88

Family and Medical Leave Act (FMLA): .............................................. 89

Personal Leave Guidelines ..................................................................... 89

Sick Leave Guidelines ............................................................................ 89

Emergency Leave Guidelines: ................................................................ 90

Employment Separation/Termination Guidelines ................................ 90

Do's & Don'ts of Employee Dismissal ................................................... 91

## Chapter 6: Athletics ................................................................. 93

Athletic Philosophy ............................................................................... 93

General Objectives and Guidelines ....................................................... 93

*Participation* ................................................................................ 93

*Rules and Regulations* ................................................................. 94

*Classification and District* ........................................................... 95

*Sportsmanship Ideals* .................................................................. 95

*Try-outs* ....................................................................................... 96

*Academic Eligibility* .................................................................... 96

*Sunday or Non-School Day Practices* ......................................... 96

    Games and Practices Over School Breaks ............................................ 96

    Single Season Dual Sport Participation .................................................. 97

    Practice and Event Guidelines ............................................................... 97

Personnel and Volunteer Policies ..................................................................... 98

    *Coaches and Volunteers* ......................................................................... 98

    *Head Coach Job Description* ................................................................. 98

    *Team Managers and Assistants* ............................................................ 100

    *Code of Conduct at Athletic Events* ..................................................... 100

    *Athletic Expectations and Etiquette* ..................................................... 100

        Practice Attendance Policy ............................................................. 101

        Missed Academic Time for Athletics ............................................... 102

Awards Eligibility and Presentations ............................................................. 102

    *Award Schedule* ................................................................................... 103

    *Presentation of Awards and Certificates* .............................................. 103

Safety in Athletics ........................................................................................... 103

    *Safety and Risk Management* ............................................................... 103

    *Injury Related Unconsciousness* ........................................................... 103

    *Insurance* ............................................................................................. 103

Scheduling Updates and Notifications ........................................................... 104

Additional Guidelines ..................................................................................... 104

    *Inclement Weather Guidelines* ............................................................. 104

    *Athletic Fees* ........................................................................................ 105

    *Uniforms and Game Apparel* .............................................................. 105

  *Transportation* ................................................................................ 105

  *Equipment* ..................................................................................... 106

  *Public Relations* ............................................................................. 106

**Chapter 7: Finances** ............................................................................... **107**

 The Role of the Board ........................................................................ 107

 The Role of the Administrator and Business Manager ..................... 108

  *Administrator: Chief Budget Officer* ............................................. 108

  *Proposing Policies* .......................................................................... 109

 Budgets ................................................................................................ 110

  *Two Types of Budgets* ..................................................................... 110

  *Developing an Effective Budget* ...................................................... 111

  *Establishing Good Budgetary Standards* ........................................ 112

  *Developing Long-Range Plans* ....................................................... 113

  *Managing Deficits* ......................................................................... 114

  *FFNA: Assisting Families with Financial Hardships* .................... 115

  *Setting Up a Budget Calendar* ....................................................... 115

  *Presenting the Budget to the Board* ................................................ 115

 Billing .................................................................................................. 117

  *Sensible Billing Strategies* ............................................................... 117

  *Collections* ...................................................................................... 117

 Other Areas of Finance to Consider .................................................. 119

  *Accounting: Defining Its Function* ................................................ 119

 Conclusion .......................................................................................... 119

# Chapter 8: The Function Of The Board ............................................................ 121

## Purpose and Role of a School Board ........................................................... 121

### Appointments and Qualifications for Board Members ........................ 121

### A Board's Charge ........................................................................................ 122

### Governing Policies ..................................................................................... 123

### Board Member Code of Conduct ............................................................ 123

### Individual Board Member Responsibilities .......................................... 124

### Cost of Governance .................................................................................... 125

### Board Meeting Recommendations ......................................................... 125

## Two of the Board's Greatest Responsibilities ............................................ 125

### Hiring an Administrator: What Makes a Good Administrator? ........ 125

### Guiding Principles for an Administrator .............................................. 125

## Policy Governance Manual ........................................................................... 129

### Managing Your Administrator ................................................................ 129

#### Mission of Organization ...................................................................... 129

### Authority and Accountability .................................................................. 130

### Delegation to an Administrator .............................................................. 130

### Monitoring Administrator Performance .............................................. 131

### Communication and Support .................................................................. 132

### Administrator's Board Reports ............................................................... 132

### Executive Limitations ............................................................................... 133

### Compensation and Benefits ..................................................................... 134

### Treatment of Consumers .......................................................................... 134

*Emergency Administrator Succession* ........................................................ 135

Recommended Yearly Agenda for a Board ................................ 136

Conclusion ........................................................................................ 137

## Chapter 9: Organizational Calendar ........................................................ 139

Academic Administrator Calendar ............................................. 139

Events, Programs, and Holidays .................................................. 139

## Chapter 10: Frequently Asked Questions ............................................... 145

Public School ................................................................................... 145

Athletic Scholarships and Christian Schools ............................. 147

Bible in Math and Science Classes ............................................... 147

AP Exams in Math and Science .................................................... 148

Non-Christians at School .............................................................. 149

Secondary Doctrine ........................................................................ 149

Student Service Projects ................................................................ 150

Boys and Girls ................................................................................. 151

Proms or School Dances ................................................................ 152

Version of the Bible ........................................................................ 153

Winning and Losing ....................................................................... 153

Co-ed Sports .................................................................................... 153

Corporal Punishment .................................................................... 154

## APPENDIX A: Curriculum Charts ............................................................ 155

Scope and Sequences for Grades K-12 ........................................ 155

Scope and Sequence for Grades 3-5 ............................................. 156

  Scope and Sequence for Grades 6-8 .................................................................. 157

  Scope and Sequence for Grades 9-12 ................................................................ 158

  Bible Words for the Teaching and Learning Process ...................................... 159

**APPENDIX B: Student Report Cards and Transcripts** ...................................... **161**

  Elementary Report Card ................................................................................... 161

  High School Report Card ................................................................................. 163

  Student Transcript ............................................................................................. 164

**APPENDIX C: Parent Forms** ................................................................................... **165**

  Parental Accountability Agreement .................................................................. 165

  Membership Pledge .......................................................................................... 165

  Acceptance Letter .............................................................................................. 166

  Withdrawal from Applying for Enrollment ..................................................... 167

  Discipline Letter ................................................................................................ 168

  Academic Probation Letter ............................................................................... 169

  Uniform Violation Card .................................................................................... 170

  Tardy/Absence Notice ....................................................................................... 171

  Infectious Disease Parent Notification Letter .................................................. 172

**APPENDIX D: Personnel Forms** ............................................................................ **173**

  Employment Application .................................................................................. 173

  Reference Form ................................................................................................. 180

  Disclosure Form ................................................................................................ 182

  Pastor Reference Form ..................................................................................... 183

  Ministry Contract ............................................................................................. 184

Employment Denial Letter ................................................................ 186

Staff Evaluation Forms .................................................................... 187

Annual Teacher Evaluation Form ................................................... 187

**APPENDIX E: Medical Forms** ................................................................ **191**

Emergency Medical / Contact Form ............................................... 191

Record of Medication Given ........................................................... 192

Student Accident Report ................................................................. 193

Athletic Medical and Travel Waiver ............................................... 194

**APPENDIX F: Admission Applications and Re-Enrollment Forms** ............ **197**

Application for Student Admissions ............................................... 197

Student Re-Enrollment Instructions ............................................... 206

Student Re-Enrollment Form .......................................................... 207

Records Request for Student Admission ........................................ 210

Transfer Request for Student Records ............................................ 211

**APPENDIX G: Classical Methodology** ................................................... **213**

The Lost Tools of Learning by Dorothy L. Sayers ......................... 213

Lost Tools Chart .............................................................................. 229

**APPENDIX H: Financial Samples** ........................................................... **231**

Monthly Budget Report .................................................................. 231

Sample Yearly Budget Report ........................................................ 233

Six Year Budget .............................................................................. 234

Tuition Request Letter .................................................................... 235

Collection Letters ............................................................................ 236

*Withdrawal/Tuition Responsibility Letter* ................................................. 236

*Non-Sufficient Funds Letter* ........................................................................ 237

*Collection Letter* ......................................................................................... 238

*Year End Pledge Letter* ................................................................................ 239

**APPENDIX I: Athletic Samples** ............................................................... 241

Head Coach Job Description ....................................................................... 241

Application for Paid Coaching Position ....................................................... 242

Seasonal Evaluation of Coach ....................................................................... 243

Coaches Checklist ........................................................................................ 244

Volunteer Coaching Application .................................................................. 245

Driver's License Guidelines .......................................................................... 246

Driver's Application Form ............................................................................ 247

Transportation Policy .................................................................................. 248

Permission to Transport Students ................................................................ 249

**WORKS CITED** ........................................................................................ 251

# CHAPTER I

## BIBLICAL MANDATE: THE ADMINISTRATOR'S HANDBOOK

*"The end result of all education is a worldview...
That worldview is either man-centered or God-centered."*[1]

What is a biblical mandate? How does it impact us as Administrators? A biblical mandate is a "charge" from an *authoritative God*; a God who has called us to the task of educational leadership—specifically to future generations. The leadership we must provide is not understood by the world, but has been modeled for us by our Lord and Savior, Jesus Christ. As we faithfully respond to this call to imitate Christ, we must begin with a biblical premise in the education of all the students God has entrusted to our care. Scripture clearly and repeatedly indicates that children are to have a Christian education.[2] As parents seek to provide this, they entrust their children to our institutions where Christian principles, God's Word, and excellent academics work together in obedience to this command.

Martin Luther once conveyed, "I advise no one to place his child where the Scriptures do not reign paramount. Every institution in which men are not increasingly occupied with the Word of God must become corrupt... I am much afraid that schools will prove to be the great gates of hell unless they diligently labor in explaining the Holy Scriptures, engraving them in the hearts of youth."[3]

With this in mind, we must begin with a purposed mission to provide an excellent education founded upon a biblical worldview. To effectually attain this ideal, we must:

- Graduate young men and women, who think clearly and listen carefully with discernment and understanding; to reason persuasively and articulate precisely; to be capable of evaluating their entire range of experience in the light of the scriptures; and who do so with eagerness in joyful submission to God.

- Desire our students to recognize cultural influences as distinct from biblical, and to be unswayed towards evil by the former.

- Aim to find our students well prepared in all situations, possessing both information and the knowledge of how to use it.

---

1. Glen Schultz, as quoted in Tammi Reed Ledbetter, *"Christian Schools, Homeschooling Make Gains Among Southern Baptists,"* BPNews, March 12, 2003.
2. Eph 6:4. For this and all future scripture references, I will be using the New King James Version (NKJV).
3. David Feddes, "Christianity and Education," *Banner of Truth: Biblical Christianity Through Literature*, http://www.banneroftruth.org/pages/articles/article_detail.php?152/ (accessed November 18, 2006).

- Desire our students be socially graceful and spiritually gracious; equipped with and understanding the tools of learning; desiring to grow in understanding, yet fully realizing the limitations and foolishness of the wisdom of this world.

- Desire our students have a heart for the lost and the courage to seek to dissuade those who are stumbling towards destruction; that they distinguish real religion from religion in form only; that they possess the former, knowing and loving the Lord Jesus Christ.

- Desire our students to possess all of the above with humility and gratitude to God.

It is vital to hold true to a statement of faith containing the key elements of Christianity established as your school's primary doctrine. These elements are to be unapologetically taught in various ways through all grade levels. All corporation members, Board members, and staff should subscribe to these foundational principles:

- The Bible is the only inerrant, authoritative Word of God.[4]

- There is one God, creator of all things, eternally existent in three Persons: Father, Son, and Holy Spirit. He is omnipotent, omniscient, and omnipresent.[5]

- Belief in the deity of our Lord Jesus Christ, in His virgin birth, in His sinless life, in His miracles, in His vicarious and atoning death through His shed blood, in His bodily resurrection, in His ascension to the right hand of the Father, and in His personal return in power and glory.[6]

- For the salvation of lost and sinful men, regeneration by the Holy Spirit is absolutely necessary.[7]

- Salvation is by grace through faith alone.[8]

- Faith without works is dead.[9]

- The belief in the present ministry of the Holy Spirit, by whose indwelling the Christian is enabled to live a godly life.[10]

- Belief in the resurrection of both the saved and the lost, they that are saved to the resurrection of life, and they that are lost to the resurrection of condemnation.[11]

- Spiritual unity of all believers in our Lord Jesus Christ.[12]

Secondary or divisive doctrines and issues should *not* be presented as primary doctrine. Classroom discussion of secondary doctrine should be on an informative, non-partisan level. Teachers should be careful not to speak to the students regarding divisive doctrines in a manner

---

[4] 2 Tm 3:16
[5] Dt 6:4; Gn 1:1; 1 Jn 5:7
[6] Jn 10:30; Mt 1:18; Heb 4:15; Jn 10:32; Rom 3:25, Mt 28:6; Rom 8:34; Lk 21:27
[7] Jn 3:3-8
[8] Eph 2:8
[9] Jas 2:17
[10] Gal 5:16
[11] 1 Thes 4:16,17; 2 Thes 1:9
[12] Jn 17:20-23

that would cause offense to the parents. Presentation of all sides of an issue is encouraged. The teacher should encourage the students to follow up any questions they have with their parents and pastor. When these types of doctrine or issues arise, they should be referred back to the family and local churches for final authority.

## Two Distinct Teams

Teams are distinct and are different on the sidelines, in the stadium, and in the world. Scripture tells us to be "in the world but not of the world."[13] It confirms that those of darkness cannot discern things of the Spirit.[14] It is clear that with our children and the way we view education, we must recognize and discern these two teams. You can only wear one team's jersey. Those of the "world" will be antithetical and have inherent desires in regards to education and its purposes, whereas those "of Christ" will seek His will and His purposes. They are certainly different in regards to their objectives.

Christ tells us, "You are either for me or against me."[15] Education, therefore, has two distinct roads it may go down. It will either be with Christ or without Christ. The center of your universe, or for that matter the center of your curriculum, is either going to be *self motivated* which leads to self interest, or Christ-centered. The path of self-motivation has a purpose or objective that encompasses *your own* values or *your own* principles which manifests itself within *your own* humanism. Being Christ-centered focuses on something far greater than yourself, that being Christ, a standard higher than *self*.

The world will profess that *demos* or democracy is "of the people, for the people, and by the people." It will convey that its educational purposes are to *better society* by educating students to be tolerant; to comprehend all of education apart from religion. The Christian will say that it is not "of the people," it is "of Christ"; in *all* things it is Christ. It is His ways that are important; it is His ways that dictate our educational purposes. We, as Christian administrators, should follow Christ's ways and His premises, applying them to our individual lives through the outpouring of our individual standards and values.

I would like to discuss a conversation I once had with a father of one of my Christian school students. This particular individual was a significant leader in a local Christian ministry. He was very evangelistic in his approach and had a heart for the Lord. During a rather informal discussion he mentioned that he was trying to discern whether or not to continue to send his ninth grade daughter to our Christian school or to enroll her in public school. He felt confident that his daughter was prepared to be "salt and light" within the public school system and be able to win others to Christ. He attempted to ensure me that she would be a good influence on other students and even staff, thus impacting the school.

---

13  Jn 17:14-15
14  1 Cor 2:14
15  Mt 12:30-31

I responded quickly and directly stating that if he was truly considering public school, he needed to remember that this institution, by its very nature, has turned its back on God. Consider the modern humanist view as quoted by Charles Potter, "Education is thus a most powerful ally of humanism, and every public school is a school of humanism. What can the theistic Sunday school, meeting for an hour once a week, and teaching only a fraction of the children, do to stem the tide of a five-day program of humanistic teachings?"[16] The purpose of public schools is to teach and convince the students of ungodly values and morals, while infiltrating the core of Christian beliefs in its students. I further conveyed to him that if he was comfortable with such convictions, my preference would be for him to not re-enroll his daughter.

You might be asking, "Why so cold and direct?" Remember, your Christian school needs likeminded families with a wholehearted conviction that their children are to be immersed in the Word of God, especially as it relates to education. They must yearn for their children to have an attitude and desire to love and serve God, as well as their parents, while desiring to know more about God's creation and revelation. For in that study is "eternal life." Anything outside of that premise is "without Christ."

This particular minister was quite taken back and stated, "That is strong and very judgmental." I replied, "Yes it is, and it is *biblical.*" I went on to ask him to be in prayer about this decision for his daughter's life. After much prayer and seeking the Lord's will for his daughter, he decided to keep his daughter at our Christian school. Over the next few years, this family enrolled all their other children as well. This should be a reminder to us of the enormity of our responsibility as parents to seek God's will in every aspect of our children's lives; especially in regards to the teaching and influence they will receive for thirty hours a week within an educational institution.

## Peer Pressure: The Power of Influence

Before becoming a Christian school administrator, I held the dual role of public school principal and athletic coach. This enabled me to be involved with large groups of Christian students and athletes. Breakfast and lunch meetings permitted me to spend additional time and opportunities with students, allowing me to encourage them in their walk with the Lord. I found that in almost every one of those situations, young adults were greatly influenced by the popularity of other students and the culture around them. Sadly, due to ungodly influences, attributes that I respected and admired in many students during their family interviews had deteriorated before my eyes. To outsiders the change was slight, yet I noticed the purity and beauty of these students begin to diminish. To what end? At what point did these students begin to yearn for the world's acceptance and not desire to glorify God? When did their focus become *self?*

---

16  Charles F. Potter, *Humanism: A New Religion* (New York: Simon and Schuster, 1930), 128.

As these changes would develop and consequences would mound, many concerned Christian parents would ask to meet with me. They were discouraged and unable to understand the change in their child, as behaviors such as disobedience, disrespect, and rebellion had reared its ugly face. We would pray, troubleshoot, and brainstorm ideas of how to reclaim their child from the world that had successfully enticed them away from God. It was obvious to me during my discussion with these families that they had at some point compromised their values in a government system that eliminates Christ as its center—whether by omission or permission.

## School Culture

School culture refers to the culmination of values, policies, and organizational structures within a school. It is the shared convictions and morals of a particular school that affects the way in which it functions. Your school may be most known for its nurturing environment or its authoritarian structure, but what is critical is its reputation for being biblical in all practices and beliefs. Your school's culture and its methods will affect everything from the way you operate to the methods for administering tests; from the atmosphere in the halls, to the way a teacher relates to a student. It is imperative that Christian administrators mold the aspects of their school culture to reflect the shared biblical values of our God given responsibility in education.

## Determining Your Educational Philosophy: Evangelistic or Discipleship

As a Christian school, you will be faced with choosing one of two philosophical paths of education; one being evangelism and the other discipleship. These views should be firmly established in your school objectives and guidelines, as well as in your parent contract. The *evangelicstic* path will allow for non-Christian students to be enrolled and not denied admission as a result of their faith. By gaining admittance to your institution, the student will be exposed to other Christian students, parents, Christian curriculum, and scripture while they are being taught. This exposes them to the Word of God in an attempt to lead them to Christ, "faith comes from hearing the message, and the message is heard through the Word of Christ." [17]

If a Christian school holds to an evangelisticvision, its mission statement should specifically portray its intent to win the lost to Christ. How is this accomplished? It is accomplished through bringing the knowledge of Christ to the lost at their school. This philosophy will likely also provide additional emphasis on personal bible study (the gospel specifically and what it means to them individually), it may present tracts to students, offer up prayers for their salvation, and provide invitations at the end of chapel or bible class.

---

17  Rom 10:17

The second position is that of a *discipleship* school. A discipleship school immerses the students in the Word of God for the purpose of fully equipping them for "good work" in the kingdom of God.[18] They submit to parents, as the parents are submissive to their own church. It defers spiritual decisions in regards to the children back to their parents, and thus further back to their own pastor. This discipleship philosophy is an extension of the Christian home where parents desire their children to be educated in the fear and admonition of the Lord—all day long, everyday, seven days a week.[19]

Whether you are following an evangelistic approach or a discipleship approach, any allegiance to a particular denomination will also impact your educational philosophy. A school directly affiliated with a church—let's say hypothetically a Baptist church—will have a Baptist influence and potentially have a Baptist pastor on staff. That particular pastor would be teaching spiritual lessons that would understandably influence the students towards a Baptist vein. This influence will ultimately feed all the other parts of the curriculum. At a non-denominational school there is no particular emphasis, thus it protects the parents' views on any given subject from being compromised. This requires a school to take more of a neutral role. Christian administrators should also consider how many churches are represented within the families of their school and be respectful of those differences.

## School Wide Christian Goals and Educational Philosophy

In all levels, programs, and teaching, Christian schools must seek to teach all subjects as parts of an integrated whole with the Scriptures at the center. "All Scripture is given by inspiration of God, and is profitable for doctrine, for reproof, for correction, for instruction in righteousness, that the man of God may be complete, thoroughly equipped for every good work."[20] In order to be "Christ-centered," Christian education must be more than baptized secularism. It is not enough to take the curricula of the government schools, add prayer and a Bible class, and claim the result is somehow Christian.

Therefore, all Christian schools must strive to follow a "Christian educational philosophy" including but not limited to the following:

- The Bible clearly instructs parents, not the church or state, to "bring children up in the discipline and instruction of the Lord"[21]. Therefore, it should seek to teach and discipline in a manner consistent with the Bible and a godly home environment.
- God's character is revealed not only in His Word but also in every facet of the creation. Therefore, it should teach that all knowledge is interrelated and can instruct us about God Himself.

---

18  Tm 3:16
19  Eph 6:4
20  1 Tm 3:16-17
21  Dt 6:7

- God wants us to love Him with our minds, as well as with our hearts, souls, and strength.[22] Therefore, as Christians we should seek to individually challenge children at all levels and teach them how to learn, versus teaching them to learn by unthinking repetition.
- Parents should teach their children that all they do should be done "heartily, as unto the Lord."[23] Therefore, the school should seek to encourage quality academic work and maintain high standards of conduct. This includes biblical discipline principles.
- The school should believe that as long as a child is under the parents' authority and undergoing formal education, he should be trained biblically.[24]

## Can Education Be Neutral?

There is no such thing as neutrality in education. Every fact, every truth, will be understood in the light of a certain worldview. This means that history, art, music, mathematics, etc., must all be taught in the light of God's existence and His revelation of His Son, Jesus Christ. Because the Scriptures occupy a crucial role in teaching us about this revelation, they must also occupy a critical role in Christian education.

This is not to say that the Bible was meant to be read as a science or mathematics text. Contrarily, it provides the framework for understanding these so-called "secular" subjects. Without such a framework for understanding, all subjects will degenerate into chaotic absurdity. As R.L. Dabney stated,[25]

> Every line of true knowledge must find its completeness in its convergency to God, even as every beam of daylight leads the eye to the sun. If religion be excluded from our study, every process of thought will be arrested before it reaches its proper goal. The structure of thought must remain a truncated cone, with its proper apex lacking.

The universe is coherent, because all truth comes from God. Without God, particulars have no relation to other particulars. The universe must, under this understanding, be a multi verse: an infinite array of absurd "facts." In education, this position inevitably leads to the fragmentation of knowledge. History bears no relation to English and biology bears no relation to philosophy. A Christian worldview based on Scripture allows us to give the students a unified education. That unity is only possible due to the centrality of the Scriptures in the educational process. Without that centrality, true education will wither and die. With a Christian worldview, all subjects will be understood, and more importantly, they will be understood as parts of an integrated whole.

---

22  Mk 12:30
23  Col 3:23
24  Dt 6:6,7; Prv 22:6
25  R.L. Dabney, *On Secular Education* (Moscow, Idaho: Ransom Press, 1989), 16-17

## Value of Biblical Application

Deriving practical applications from and modeling God's Word are essential to completing a mission consistent with biblical truth. A Christian, faith-based education is essential to the achievement of our mission. Teaching God's Word, and teaching how to apply God's Word, is essential to education. Consequently we must strive to teach the following:

- All truth is God's truth.[26]
- It is important to have knowledge of and appreciation for the attributes of God.[27]
- The work of the Holy Spirit is significant.[28]
- Prayer is essential.[29]
- Every individual is of value; all are uniquely created in the image of God.[30]
- A personal relationship with Christ is essential.[31]
- Every aspect of curriculum should be permeated with God's Word,[32] including teaching on the natural world, human history and God's activity in it, humanity, its cultures, and how we are to live in the world.

Another essential goal we should strive for is to encourage every student to develop his/her relationship with God the Father through Jesus Christ.[33] Without regeneration, a Christian worldview and a Christian lifestyle are nonsensical impossibilities. For example, if a man is dead it is wasted effort to seek to revive him with a nourishing meal. If the life-principle is absent from the student, no amount of instruction and example on the part of the teacher will give that student life. We, as Christian leaders, have the responsibility to plant seeds of truth and to water. We also have the responsibility to recognize that growth comes from God, as He initiates growth in the life of the individual when he is born again. From that time on, any nourishment from instruction results in genuine growth as the Christian puts what he learns into practice.

It is not our role as administrators and educators to attempt to make God's work in human lives superfluous. There is no way to perfect human beings by means of instruction; even if that instruction is Christian in content. If the child already knows the Lord, the goal is to encourage him to develop that relationship. As he grows, the biblical education he is receiving will further that growth.

---

26  Ps 31:5; Is 65:16; Dn 10:21; Jn 1:17; Jn 8:32
27  Mt 22:37, Mk 12:30,
28  Jn 14:26
29  1 Thes 5:17, Js 5:16-18
30  Gn 1:27, Ps 139:13
31  Jn 1:12
32  1 Thes 5:21-22
33  Mt 28:18-20; Mt 19:13-15

## Conclusion

At every Christian school, students should be taught to master a subject in the effort to better equip themselves for the work God has planned for their life while desiring to work in harmony, and blessing others with their abilities. They should also be taught humility, recognizing that God has gifted all individuals differently, and for His purposes. This will be evident in how the Christian encourages or helps a peer whom he/she identifies is struggling while at the same time building them up in recognizing their strengths that God has given them. In a secular society that focuses on "of the people, for the people, and by the people," peers are focused on receiving human praise and attaining skills that will benefit themselves. In a godly society, our goal is to be used by God to be a member of a greater body. Encouraging, sharpening, and working as a team to build the body up as a whole. I would like to conclude this chapter with a quote from R.L. Dabney.[34]

> The education of children for God is the most important business done on earth. It is the one business for which the earth exists. To it all policies, all war, all literature, all money-making, ought to be subordinated; and every parent especially ought to feel every hour of the day, that, next to making his own calling and election sure, this is the end for which he is kept alive by God—this is his task on earth.

Dabney, in no uncertain terms, reminds us of the all-encompassing, spiritual responsibility administrators have been called to; perhaps the "most important business…on earth." Without Christ however, it *is* impossible; with Christ, with humility and with much prayer, we can fulfill one of the greatest roles of servanthood God has ever ordained. In it is the opportunity to sow millions of seeds, to water daily the work of the Spirit, and in obedience, to learn the true value of the greatest commandment: unconditional love for others.[35]

---

[34] Robert L. Dabney, Douglas Wilson, ed. *On Secular Education* (Moscow, Idaho: Canon Press, 1996).
[35] Mk 12:30-31

# CHAPTER 2

# SCHOOL POLICIES AND PROCEDURES

*"For the equipping of the saints for the work of ministry,
for the edifying of the body of Christ." - Ephesians 4:12*

Policies are plans of action. Procedures are the approaches used to implement these policies. Staff, students, and parents at your school need to have a clear understanding of the biblical philosophy and purpose of your institution. They should be willing to cooperate with all the written policies of your school. This is crucial in the area of discipline and schoolwork standards, as well as active communication with teachers and administration.

## Admissions

Establish clear parameters of how you will enroll and accept new students. Communicate these procedures in your school's admission statement that is included in your student/parent handbooks. (See sample in Appendix F). For example: "(*School name*) admits students of any race to all rights, privileges, programs, and activities generally made available to all students. We practice a biblical philosophy of admissions, not discriminating on the basis of race, sex, color, or national origin in the administration of its policies, admissions, scholarships, athletic, and other school-directed programs." You may also consider including a clause that allows you to select students on the basis of academic performance, religious commitment, philosophical compatibility, or their willingness to cooperate with your administration and abide by its policies.

- Require that at least one parent or guardian of each applicant give a credible profession of faith in Jesus Christ as Lord and Savior, as well as be a regular attendee or member of a Christian church.
- Students seeking admission should be evaluated on the basis of their report cards, achievement tests, references, admission questionnaires, interviews, and potential to perform satisfactorily at your institution.
- If you are not equipped with the resources required to serve children that require special educational programs due to learning disabilities.
- Students who seek admission directly following suspension, expulsion, or behavior problems from another school, should not be accepted until they prove themselves elsewhere, thus the first quarter should be considered a probationary period for all new students.

## Enrollment Process and Guidelines

Registration should be offered in the following order: current students, siblings, and then to the public. Screening and testing of prospective applicants is a process that is ongoing throughout the year. Test potential students to identify their skill set, as well as where they would successfully fit in your program. Interviews with students and families need to be scheduled with the appropriate principal, as he or she will determine final acceptance and grade level placement of the student. At this point, parents should be notified of acceptance or denial in writing, and a copy of this letter be filed with the original application. Once accepted, parents should receive a new student packet that includes material such as:

- Records transfer request form
- Emergency/Medical Contact Form
- Tuition payment forms and information from the Business Manager
- Student/Parent Handbook
- School Supply List
- Lunch order forms
- Uniform requirements and supplier information

Once a student is offered a seat at your school, the admission procedure should not be considered final until the following items are received:

- Tuition is paid in full or a completed automatic bank draft form is returned
- Permanent records are received from the child's previous school
- A health form is completed by the child's physician (including immunization records)
- A signed emergency contact form

As administrators, we must over-communicate to parents that school tuition is a financial obligation contracted for the *full* school year. Be sure to have parents sign their yearly financial tuition commitment, as there *will* be families that attempt to withdraw their child from your school and exempt themselves from the remainder of their tuition. Parents must understand and agree to support the policies of your school.

The following is a sample statement that can be applied for this purpose:

(School name) relies solely on tuition income to meet annual operating expenses. Therefore, it is necessary that the financial obligations of enrollment be for the entire school year. Once the student attends the first day of school, the financial obligation remains for the entire school year regardless of voluntary withdrawal or expulsion from the school. You are responsible for the timely payment of the full annual tuition and other fees due (school name). The only exception to this policy is if another student fills the vacated seat in a full class. If the seat is replaced in this manner, then the exiting family is only responsible for tuition through the last day prior to the new student's start day. All tuition and fees paid up to that date remain with (school name). In the event of demonstrated hardship, the administrator may consider an exception on a case-by-case basis. Please request a copy of the student exit procedure from the school office.

## Fees and Tuition

Determine what your base tuition will be per student and/or per grade level. Having an early, mid-year enrollment period will enable you as an administrator to get an idea of what the expenses will be for the upcoming school year. Does tuition cover all costs? Does it include books, personal school supplies, uniforms, school pictures, field trips and school lunch? Break it down and determine your cost.

New students should pay a non-refundable application fee and returning students pay a smaller re-enrollment fee. Following a formal notification of acceptance, a registration fee should be required within two weeks to your school. A non-response will enable you to offer this seat to another interested Christian family. Payment options can include an automatic draft over a determined number of months, full payment prior to the first day of school, or other options deemed financially sound by you.

## Student Exit and Withdrawal Procedure

### Exit Procedure

An exit procedure is a policy set for parents wishing to withdraw their students during the academic school year. Keep in mind that the family should be obligated to pay tuition for the entire school year once the first day of class has convened and the student was present for said day. The only exception to this policy should be if another student fills the vacated seat in a full class. If the seat is replaced in this manner, then the exiting family should only be responsible for tuition through the last day prior to the new student's start day. All tuition and fees paid up to that date should remain with your school.

### Steps to Withdrawal

- Parents should put their request for student withdrawal in writing. A letter addressed to the administratorshould offer details of the reason for withdrawal, as well as any requested special considerations. An anticipated time frame for withdrawal should also be included.
- The board and administration agree to pray with the family that God will provide a replacement student if there is not a waiting list.
- Once the principal has received this request, it should be presented to the administrator.

The administrator reserves the right to excuse a family as a compassionate service if the family can supply the school with a replacement student in a less than full class.

- The administrator determines whether there is a waiting list and begins the process of admittance for any available students.
- Until such time as the exiting student can be replaced in a full class, tuition payments for that student should continue on the regular schedule, even though the student may no longer be attending.
- If a student is identified by the administrator as a replacement and has begun classes, and your school has received its first tuition payment, the withdrawing family should be notified in writing of the replacement and released from contract with your school at that time.
- School records should be forwarded to the exiting student's new school upon written request and full payment of any outstanding account balance.

## Collections Policy

The book of Romans clearly charges Christians regarding their debt, "Render to all what is due them."[36] There will be times when your school attempts to collect on various account balances, including but not limited to, checks for payment due the school, automatic drafts returned from the bank, or outstanding tuition balances for families who have withdrawn from the school but were not released from tuition payments, (see Appendix H for sample letter.)

School records should never be forwarded to an exiting student's new school until written request is made and any outstanding account balance is paid in full.

- If you determine or have reason to believe that an account balance is un-collectible, the account may be submitted to a collection agency at the discretion of your administration (see the Appendix H for sample letter). Once submitted to the collection agency, your school should no longer deal with the account holder/debtor. It will be left to the account holder/debtor to deal directly with the collection agency. Any efforts on the part of the account holder to respond to follow up communication or to work out a solution for payment should be considered by administration in the determination of whether an account is uncollectible. You as the administrator should reserve the right to deviate from this policy based on a case-by-case basis.
- In the event your school receives a bank notice for a returned check, a letter should be sent to the account holder requesting a replacement check including any fees associated with the returned payment (see Appendix H for sample letter). If after thirty days there has

---

36  Rom 13:7

been no payment, a follow-up request should be made in writing. If after another thirty days there is still no response, your administration at its discretion may decide to submit the account to a collection agency.

- If your school receives a notice from the bank indicating a stopped draft payment by the account holder, or if you have reason to believe that regular payments have ceased, then the full outstanding balance of the account should become due and payable as of the due date of the last payment. If automatic draft payments have been stopped, the account should immediately be deemed as uncollectible. A two-week payment request notice should be sent to the account holder. If payment is not received during the two weeks, the account should be sent to the collection agency. If the automatic draft payment period for a particular school year has ended and there is an outstanding balance on an account, administration needs to follow up with a thirty-day notice, then a phone call. Depending upon response, or lack thereof to the follow up attempts, administration may, in its sole discretion, determine that the account is uncollectible and forward that account to a collection agency.

- Whenever an account is sent to a collection agency, the seat replacement policy should no longer be available to the account holder. The full balance is due with no options for refund or release should the seat be replaced at a later date. Once an account has been determined as uncollectible by your administration, the outstanding balance of the account may be classified as 'bad debt'. If the account is remitted to the collection agency, and the agency is unable to collect the funds, in all likelihood the credit bureau will be notified and the unpaid balance will remain on the account holder's credit history for seven years. Further legal action through a collection agency may be taken if necessary.

## Grievance Guidelines

Christian guidelines should be followed whenever there is a dispute or grievance concerning any aspect of the school's operations, or between any two parties connected in a direct way to the school. This includes students, parents, staff, volunteers, administration, and the Board. Follow the Matthew 18 principle in all dealings. "Moreover if your brother sins against you, go and tell him his fault between you and him alone. If he hears you, you have gained your brother. But if he will not hear, take with you one or two more, that 'by the mouth of two or three witnesses every word may be established.' And if he refuses to hear them, tell it to the church."[37] If any disputes arise that are not covered by your grievance guidelines, the board should decide what procedures to follow based on a parity of reasoning from those procedures established by these guidelines.

---

37  Mat 18:15-17

**Definitions:**
- Dispute: Any disagreement that results in broken fellowship or trust between the parties, or that disrupts the lines of authority in the school, or which (in the judgment of either disputant) threatens the successful implementation of the school's objectives and goals.
- Grievances: Any concern about any decision made by one in authority, where the concern is large enough to appeal the decision beyond that authority to the next level.
- Concerns: The substance and details of the dispute and/or grievance.

## Students/Parents to Teachers

- All concerns about the classroom should first be presented to the teacher by the parents, or if the student is mature enough, by the student himself. If the student presents the concern, a respectful demeanor is required at all times.
- If the problem is not resolved, the parents or student may bring the concern to the appropriate administrator. If the student brings the concern, he should have permission from his parents to do so.
- If the problem is still not resolved, the parents should appeal the decision to the administrator.
- If there is still no resolution, they should request a hearing *in writing* from the Board.

## Parents/Patrons to Administrator/Principal

- If parents or patrons have a grievance or dispute about the general operation of the school (apart from the operation of the classrooms), they should bring their concerns to the appropriate principal.
- If the situation is not resolved, they should present their concerns to the administrator.
- If there is still no resolution, they should request a hearing *in writing* from the Board.
- This procedure applies to board members who are acting in their capacity as parents/patrons, and not as representatives of the board.

## Staff to Administration

- All concerns about the standards of the school should first be presented to the appropriate principal. A respectful demeanor is required at all times.
- If the problem is not resolved, the staff member may appeal the decision in writing to the administrator, followed by a meeting to discuss the matter.
- If the problem is still not resolved, the staff member may appeal to the board in writing and request a hearing. The request will be passed to the board through the administrator. The administrator should pass on all such requests.

## Volunteers to Staff/Administration

- If any volunteer has a concern about the volunteer work, he should present that concern to the staff member responsible for his oversight (teacher, administrator, development or athletic director, etc.).

- If the problem is not resolved, then the concern should be presented in writing to the administrator, followed by a meeting with him to discuss the concern.

- If the problem is still not resolved, the volunteer may request a hearing from the Board in writing. The request should be passed through the administrator. The administrator is required to pass the request on to the board.

## Teacher Procedures, Policies and Guidelines

### Class Reverence Guidelines

In all areas of instruction, especially Bible classes and related activities, proper respect and consideration of God's character needs to be given and required. Specifically, class songs, skits, stories, and discussion that include references to the name and attributes of the Lord must be consistent with biblical principles. The following list is not meant to be all-inclusive, but it is characteristic of the kind of activities to avoid:

- Silly or trite references to Jesus Christ and His work on the cross.
- Implying, directly or indirectly, that all the students are Christians.
- Mockery of angelic powers, demonic or heavenly.
- Emphasis on good feelings or works instead of humble obedience and grace.

For the sake of the students' spiritual training and the school's work, joyful encouragement and instruction in reverential knowledge of the Lord is necessary.

### Classroom Management

Someone *will* be in charge of a classroom, whether it be a popular student or the teacher. Therefore teachers are to:
- Oversee all necessary day-to-day operations of the classroom.
- Keep all necessary records such as attendance and grades.
- Communicate effectively with parents as needed for academic or behavioral concerns.
- Contact parents after the student receives their *second warning during class*. Contact should be made by phone, e-mail, note, or in person.

- Field trips should be limited and pre-approved by the respective principal. Guest speakers should be approved as well.
- Keep homework to an *absolute minimum*. Writing should be done in the classroom. Reading should be done at home.
- Report cards should be prepared and sent out quarterly along with mid-quarter progress reports.
- Keep administration informed as to any student academic and behavioral concerns.
- Arrange parent conferences and inform administration of such meetings.
- Know the campus emergency procedures and how to implement them.
- Maintain a *neat*, *sanitary*, and *safe* learning environment.

## Lesson Plans

Weekly lesson plans should list each day's educational objective(s) and assignment(s) and should be submitted to administration when specified. Teachers should refer to the course objectives listed in your school's curriculum guide when preparing their lesson plans.

## Grading Principles

- Students should receive their graded tests/quizzes/projects/papers within one week of the test/quiz/due date.
- No single assignment should be worth more than 25% of the student's total quarter grade.
- A minimum of ten grades should be used to calculate the quarter grade. Bible and elective courses should have at least eight grades per quarter.
- Quarter grades should be based on various types of assignments. For example:

    <u>Tests/Book Reports</u>: At least three each quarter
    <u>Quizzes</u>: (Recommended) At least three quizzes
    <u>Homework/class work</u>: At least one graded assignment per week

- Semester grades are calculated by two quarter grades counting 80%, and the final exam counting 20% for that semester.
- If participation in class discussion is graded, consistent participation records should be kept.
- Projects, depending on the scope of the assignment, may be used in place of tests.
- There should be a variety in the amount and kind of testing, assignments, and homework.
- All grading should be criterion-referenced. Teachers should be prohibited from assigning grades based on a normal curve.
- Teachers may *not* use academic grades for discipline purposes.

## Teacher Guidelines for Class Review

### Beginning of Class:
- Build upon the lesson from the previous day. Start with the initial lesson and review its development, adding on the new lesson as it applies.
- Organize question-and-answer sessions at the beginning or end of class.
- Questioning: Teacher goes around the room during independent study time and questions students on the material they have been working on.

### During Class:
- Information journals: Students think through the lesson during the last five minutes of class and write down any questions they may have.
- Role-playing.
- Asking students to summarize or explain the material (orally).
- Study questions, provided by the teacher, to be answered in writing. Review the student's written answers during class discussion.
- Extemporaneous and impromptu speeches.
- English: Diagramming sentences on the board or asking students to use proper language at home.
- Math: Use similar problems from different sources (thus different wording).
- Bible: Start the year by giving the students a chart of biblical eras. Review at the beginning of the lesson, showing which era today's lesson fits into.

### End of Class:
- Last-minute questions: teacher asks individual students questions as they leave the room, attempting to tie material together.

### Before Quizzes and Tests:
- Before quizzes and tests, review the material to be tested by asking the students questions similar to those which will be on the test or quiz.
- Review games: trivia, bingo, "Bible jeopardy," "Around the world". (Have students prepare the questions for these games.)
- Add questions from old material to quizzes. This provides for ongoing review.
- Review the quiz or test together after it has been graded and discuss concepts again. (This is one of the best forms of review and is often neglected).

## Grade Reporting

Progress reports should be sent home at mid-quarter. Report cards are sent home with the students at the end of each quarter. There should be early and continual communication with parents of struggling students. Encourage your staff to contact parents during the year, keeping them abreast of any fluctuations in their child's grades. Parents want to know! Many parents request group parent/teacher conferences for direction on how to specifically help their child succeed. In regards to general communication, I have followed a simple but proven mantra: *"Over communication leads to success, under communication leads to a mess!"*

Oftentimes in Christian schools, teachers get into trouble when they overstep their boundaries by attempting to parent the student. The teacher is to simply provide their professional assessment and direction to the parent on how to help their child succeed. They should state to the parent, "Please encourage your child to ask me for clarification if he is confused about something. It is very important to me that he/she understands the lesson being taught."

## Exams

Exams are a way of measure and evaluation, not only for students, but for your staff as well. I always challenge and ask my teachers, "What is the most important thing that students need to know when they finish your course?" and "How will you know with certainty that they have mastered the things you determine to be most important?" I believe that continuous review is necessary in order to put emphasis on the most important information taught during the year. In the past, teachers have responded to my questioning by stating, "But, I taught that in the 1$^{st}$ quarter!" Logically, it is foolish to state that the material required on a first quarter test is not important enough for students to know on a year-end exam. Semester and year-end exams are not created for the purpose of belaboring students with two hours of questions. Alternatively, exams allow them to demonstrate their academic success for taking your class, as well as how well you have taught them.

### *What information should be tested on final exams?*

Review the course objectives. Use the course objectives to select test items (assuming that the objectives were taught accordingly). Test questions should reflect the relative importance of the course objectives. The more time spent teaching an objective, the more test items there should be related to that objective. Students should only be tested on the material studied during the semester.

*Preparing review sheets*

Review sheets should identify all of the information that will be included on the exam. Students will inevitably ask, "If we know the information on the review sheet, will we be ready for the test?" Review sheets also help parents identify the information they should review with their children. They should be handed out at least one week prior to the test. Review sheets should also identify any words that should be spelled correctly on the test, as well as identify any items that should be committed to memory (like specific dates).

*Principles of constructing quality test questions*

So called "trick questions" do not have any place on a quality test. Neither do extra-credit items. Do not allow teachers to prepare "power tests." Powers tests are specifically designed to take more time to complete than is allotted. Students who know the material should have plenty of time to complete all of the questions on the test. They should be given enough time to recheck some of their work. All students should receive the same amount of time to complete the test.

## Testing Schedule Guidelines

Table 1. Sample Testing Schedule

| MONDAY: | TUESDAY: | WEDNESDAY: | THURSDAY: | FRIDAY: |
|---|---|---|---|---|
| Math | Science<br>Logic | English/Literature<br>Foreign Languages | Bible/<br>Apologetics | History<br>Rhetoric |

Teachers should not randomly test any day of the week. They should follow a published test schedule. Such a guideline may be followed unless the teacher who has that "test" day grants approval. Teachers who want to test on a day other than the one that they have been assigned should check with the appropriate teacher to prevent students from having more that one major test per day. Exceptions to these guidelines may be made at the end of each semester when a separate finals schedule is arranged.

Follow a schedule such as this when establishing due dates for major projects or written assignments. Teachers should be required to record due dates for major projects and tests on their weekly lesson plans. They should give one test or quiz per week. A quiz should not cover more than a three day span of classroom material, and should not be worth more than twenty percent of a test grade.

## Twenty Percent Rule

If more than 20% of the students in a class fail a test, the teacher should inform the principal or administrator. They should meet together and attempt to determine the cause of the low student performance and then implement a plan for improving future performance. If deemed necessary, the entire class may receive the opportunity to re-take the exact test or a modified version of the test.

## Extra Credit

Extra credit should *not* be used in lieu of a failing or low grade on a test or assignment. An alternative assignment may be given to the entire class if a large number of students scored poorly or in the event the material was constructed poorly.

## "F" Issuance Principles

- One day each quarter should be designated as F-Day. It normally falls halfway between the midterm and the last day of the quarter. The purpose of F-Day is to formally alert/remind the teachers that they need to notify the parents of any student who will receive an F at the quarter's end.

- Respective principals or administrators should be made aware of any student receiving an F-Day warning.

- In the event of a student earning an F for the quarter in any class or subject, the parents should have received prior notification. That is, no quarter grade of an F is to be issued unless the teacher has ascertained that the parents and the student understand the reasons for the forthcoming grade. "Blind-siding," i.e. surprising the parents and student with an F at grading time, should be forbidden.

## Grading Late Assignments

Homework assignments should be collected at the *beginning* of the period. Any assignment turned in after the assignments are collected should be considered late. Students should not be permitted to complete assignments during the period and turn them in that same period for full credit. For each day an assignment is late, the grade should be reduced by ten percent. Assignments turned in more than two days past the due date should not receive credit. There are two exceptions to this requirement.
- If a student had an unplanned absence, the due date should be extended by the number of days he/she was absent.
- If a student had a planned absence of three days or more, the due date may be extended by half of the number of days they were absent.

## Work Missed During a Suspension

Students should be expected to complete all assignments given to their class during their suspension. (We will discuss reasons for suspension in the following chapter.) A reasonable timeframe may be established by the teacher. Assignments should be graded in a manner consistent with the procedure used for the rest of the class. Students should receive full credit for any work completed on time.

## Students Leaving Campus

If a student needs to leave school during school hours, a parent should notify the administration either by calling the office or sending in a note. For safety purposes, all students under the age of eighteen should be properly signed in and out of your campus.

- Sign in sheets, requiring a parent or guardian signature, should be positioned at the main desk(s).
- Students should be allowed to phone their parents if they are feeling ill.
- High school students wishing to drive off campus for lunch, should be required to submit a signed parent note at the beginning of the school year, allowing that privilege. Also require names of other students, if any, that they are permitted to ride with.
- Students who leave campus without permission need to be subject to discipline
- Teachers should never release a student to anyone before first checking with the office.

The teachers and administrator have the responsibility and custody of all the children while they are in school. A child is never to be released to a stranger until the office and parent(s) have been contacted and approval has been given.

## Sexual Harassment, Abuse, or Child Abuse Policy

Maintain a *zero tolerance* policy for any such abuse. Do not excuse, defend, or ignore any identified or unidentified case of abuse. Adhere to the following guidelines regarding any event or allegations of sexual harassment, abuse, or child abuse:

- All staff members, volunteers, parents and visitors, are requested to help identify and take care of any problem that exists or appears to exist.
- All staff should be requested to report to the administration any suspected or existing cases that may have slipped their attention.
- Encourage the victim, and the offender, to receive necessary professional help in order to deal with their pain, as well as to avoid the recurrence of the incident.

**Important Steps:**
- All cases should be immediately reported to the administrator.
- As soon as the administrator receives a report of an existing or suspect case, he documents the information, and prepares a detailed report of the incident after his own instantaneous preliminary inquiry.

- The administrator calls the Department of Social Services and makes an emergency appointment. He discusses the issue in person, not on the phone, so that confidentiality will be maintained.
- If the reported case is of a grave criminal nature, the administrator should immediately call the local police department and ask that an officer visit the site on an emergency basis. He discusses the case with the officer, maintaining confidentiality, and considers the officer's guidance.
- The administrator calls an emergency executive meeting with the Board.
- The administrator makes an incident report for file and, if the report is a genuine case, notifies the Division of Child Development.
- The administrator follows up the case with the parties involved and gathers information on the progress and the consequences. He maintains his report of the same in the new file opened on such a case.
- The administrator draws steps for action if a staff member or an individual from the institution is involved. All case decisions should be finalized with discussion, input and implements from the board at an emergency executive meeting. This includes preventive steps, if needed.
- Should the administrator be directly involved in a case, that case should be reported to the Board President, who will then follow the above outlined reporting procedures.

All actions, contacts, information, steps taken, and correspondence should be kept in a permanent file. The administrator, board members, staff, and others should maintain strict confidentiality about the case and those involved.

## Movie Guidelines

Any movies shown in classrooms should have an educational purpose rather than merely entertainment value. Teachers interested in showing students a DVD or video should always obtain administrative permission prior to making arrangements to show the film. The number of movies that the teacher has shown during the semester should be taken into consideration, as a classroom is for interaction and learning—not for entertainment purposes.

There is a variety of different movie standards that parents give to their children. To respect each the convictions of your school families, teachers should not recommend movies to students. You want to avoid a confrontation with a parent stating, "Well, my child's teacher said it was a good movie!"

## Music Guidelines

Lyrics are a major concern when selecting music, as you do not want students to memorize and present pieces in which the lyric content is evil, false, or unseemly. After considering lyrics, musical selections should be judged on the following bases:

- Does it have a pleasing melody?
- Do the dynamics and rhythm of the piece contribute to the entertainment or beauty of the piece?
- Will our students gain something musically by learning the piece?

A limitation to classical music should apply whenever students are in the classroom. History classes that are listening to the music of the period being studied are exempted from these guidelines.

## Enrollment of Staff Children

Your faculty or staff who are employed at least half-time, should be required to send their school-aged children to your Christian institution. You, in your discretion, may make an exception for compelling reasons such as disabilities or extra needs that are unable to be met by your school.

Your Christian staff should wholeheartedly believe what the Bible tells us about our children.

"You shall love the Lord your God with all your heart, with all your soul, and with all your strength. And these words which I command you today shall be in your heart. You shall teach them diligently to your children, and shall talk of them when you sit in your house, when you walk by the way, when you lie down, and when you rise up."[38]

If the teacher does not have a heartfelt passion for Christian education, it will be reflected in their classroom instruction. Doug Wilson states in his book *Recovering the Lost Tools of Learning*, "Not only are parents responsible to oversee the Biblical teaching of their children, they are also responsible to see that their children don't receive false teaching. Error is pervasive."[39]

## Supervision of Staff Members' Children

After school hours, unsupervised staff children tend to become a common occurrence. It is the continual responsibility of each staff member to supervise their own children.

---

38 Dt 6:5
39 Douglas Wilson, *Recovering the Lost Tools of Learning* (Wheaton, IL: Crossway, 1991), 51.

## School Options for Staff Children

Establish guidelines that maintain an educational standard of excellence for your staff and their children. As a condition of employment, the school-age children of staff should be enrolled in your school. School staff includes any teacher, development staff, or administrator who works for the school half-time or more. For the purposes of these guidelines, staff does not include janitorial/maintenance help, etc. Any staff member that wishes to educate their school-age children at home, should petition the board in writing annually for exemption from this requirement. Home schooling is any form of home education designed to serve the same function as the education your school would provide for that age level. Petitions for home schooling should be delivered to the administrator, including their main reasons for choosing this option.

## Obtaining Substitute Teachers

In the normal, unforeseen event that a teacher requires a substitute for any portion of the day, the following procedures should apply:

- The teacher should contact the administrator as soon as possible.
- The teacher should make copies of lesson plans and any other necessary materials available to the substitute. Administration should have current weekly lesson plans submitted by the teachers as well.
- If possible, the teacher should make arrangements for a substitute. In case of illness or emergency, the administrator will make arrangements for the substitute.
- Teacher assistants may be available to provide substitute coverage as needed. They do not normally receive additional compensation.
- It is the teacher's responsibility to inform the administrator/principal how long a substitute might be needed. Teachers should call prior to the end of the first day if the substitute will be needed the following day as well.
- The teacher should send the substitute(s) a written thank-you note after resuming work.

## Cell Phone Usage

Protect the academic environment in the classroom at all costs. Implement a policy that protects students from disruptions and distractions in the classroom. Though convenient and helpful, technology can become a vice. Any use of cell phones, laptops, I-pods, palm pilots and other electronic devices creates noise and becomes an interruption in the classroom.

Require that employees or any other school representatives use cell phones in a safe manner while being considerate of others. In order to achieve a balance between safety, need and productivity, I have previously instituted the following policy:

(School Name) has opted to follow a "Drive Now, Talk Later" policy. Because use of a cell phone while in transit has been found to increase the risk of involvement in traffic accidents, we prohibit use of any telecommunication device by a school staff member while driving a school-owned vehicle or on a school-related trip. This includes cell phones, whether hand-held or hands-free, PDAs, etc. and whether owned personally or by the school while doing any type of business for or related to school matters.[40]

## Medical and Emergency Standard Operating Procedures

Each administrator should prepare a comprehensive S.O.P. (Standard Operating Procedure) for emergency situations. We often wait until we are in a crisis before we seek knowledge of how to manage through one. It is not that most plans do not work, but rather that most people do not plan!

### Medical Emergencies

**Staff Procedures:**

- Notify the main office immediately!
- Assess the seriousness of the situation. If a life-threatening situation is taking place, call 911. A staff member should be sent to the school's main road entrance to flag down and direct the emergency vehicle to the right place on the campus. Another staff member should be stationed outside the building, to direct the paramedics to the correct door, elevator, floor, or room number.
- Parents should be contacted immediately.
- The administrator should remain with the student. He may also select an available, qualified, staff member to assist with the emergency procedures.
- A student should not be moved unless it is absolutely necessary and deemed appropriate.
- As necessary, teachers should quickly and quietly clear any students from the area of the medical emergency.
- If a less serious or minor incident occurs, the student should remain at the school office under observation. The parents should be notified for pick-up.
- The victim should be treated according to standard first aid procedures while waiting for further assistance.

---

[40] Taken from Cary Christian School Staff Handbook

## Administration of Medication

New general statutes for childcare facilities makes it a misdemeanor "to willfully administer, without *written* authorization, prescription or over-the-counter medication to a child attending a child care facility."[41] Be sure to communicate and review these practices with your staff. Written authorization *should* include the signature of the child's parent or guardian. (See Appendix E for sample form)

All school employees are vulnerable to a Class "F" felony if administration of medication results in a serious injury to a student. This prohibition applies to any employee, owner, volunteer or operator of a licensed or unlicensed childcare facility, including facilities operated by nonpublic schools. The only exception is the need for administration of medication in the event of an emergency medical condition, and if the medication is administered with the authorization of and in accordance with instruction from a bona fide medical care provider.

## Fire Drill

Should the need arise to exit the school building, all students and staff should be well versed in proper emergency procedures. Classes should be instructed to go to the primary exit depending upon their location within the school building. Planning and practicing these drills will eliminate confusion and form an orderly exit out of the school building. Include specific exit procedures for areas in your facility such as: staff workroom, art and music rooms, computer lab areas, library or other common areas. Students should move quickly and quietly from the school building. Once the drill is over, an administrator should dismiss students from the fire drill formation, and have them return to the building in an orderly way. Students should return to the building via the same, but reversed direction.

Reiterate to your teachers the following:
- Be familiar with the exit routes posted in the classroom.
- If an exit is blocked, use the closest exit available.
- If there is a fire just outside the classroom and there is no safe way to exit, raise the blinds, unlock the windows, and use a chair in front of each window to have the students exit the windows safely. Students are to move away from the building. This exit method is only to be used when individuals cannot safely exit the classroom by conventional methods.

## Tornado Drill

In the event of a tornado warning any students who are outside should be moved into the building as quickly as possible through the nearest entrance. This warning can be by word of mouth and repeated down the school hallways.

---

41 Law Academy for Independent School Leaders, *Senate Bill 226 - Administration of Medication* (Raleigh: Schwartz and Shaw, P.L.L.C, 2005), Section VII.

- Students should leave the classroom immediately in a quiet, orderly and calm manner in "fire drill" style (single file).
- Teachers are to close the doors behind them. No individuals should sit in front of the classroom doors, as they may contain a pane of glass. If absolutely necessary, adults may occupy this space.
- Everyone exits as per instructions from the administrator.
- Teachers should take their grade books with them. A roll should be taken to make sure all students are accounted for! Any problems should be immediately reported to the administrator.
- Students should sit with their backs against the wall, knees pulled up, heads bent down resting on the knees and arms hugging the legs. If the students are double stacked, then simply hugging their knees is fine. Teachers and assistants should be positioned such that they are strategically placed among the students.
- All individuals should remain in this position until the warning has been lifted or the practice drill is complete.
- An administrator or administrative assistant should check the bathrooms and help any students connect with their class.
- This procedure should be practiced and held five minutes for a drill, and longer if there is an actual warning. The administrator should notify teachers when they may return to their classrooms.

## Lockdown Procedure

For imminent potential danger inside the building, establish a code phrase for your "lock down" procedure.

**Teachers/Assistants should:**
- Close and lock the classroom door until further notification from administration.
- Close and lock all windows.
- Close all blinds tightly.
- Turn off the classroom lights.
- Move students to the interior corner/wall by the door, out of view from the windows and door pane. Everyone should remain still, seated and quiet until notified otherwise by administration.
- Remain calm—do not share details of circumstances with the students.

**Administration should:**
- Immediately notify the local police of the circumstances.
- Lock all exterior doors and hang signs (should time permit).
- Use discernment and prayer in confronting the perpetrator.

## Lock-In Procedure

For potential danger *outside* the building, students and staff should be in a heightened/potential emergency code. This means that there is something or someone in the community that poses a threat to the school, i.e. bank robbery, police chase, etc. All outer doors should remain locked, including the front doors. Students and staff may move around the building but should not go outside of the building. In both cases administration checks doors and puts up signs. Establish a verbal code phrase for this "lock-in" procedure. Administration should calmly instruct the staff of the "lock-in".

**Teachers and/or Assistants Should:**
- Close classroom doors and keep them closed until administration notifies otherwise. Everyone should remain inside the building.
- Close and lock all windows.
- Close all blinds tightly and avoid activity in front of the windows.
- Cancel all outside recess or P.E. (Any groups who are outside should return to the building immediately and calmly.)
- Remain calm—do not share details of circumstances with the students.
- Continue classes and daily routine as usual. If a class is off campus, the administration should call and have those students unloaded at a designated location.
- Drill often so the students will not know whether it is a drill or a real threat.

**Administration Should:**
- Notify the local police department if the circumstances merit.
- Lock all exterior doors.
- Hang signs on exterior doors notifying parents of "lock-in" status and require them to call the school office for admittance.
- If necessary, cancel or delay carpool and have parents come in to pick up their children.

## Conclusion

Plans and procedures are preventive measures for potential problems. You will not be able to predict every scenario. I have found it best to consider the worst-case scenario and plan accordingly. A plan poorly executed is still better than no plan at all.

# Chapter 3

# Philosophies for Curriculum

*"The goal of curriculum should be to prepare students to be soldiers and conquerors for the sake of Christ."*

Curriculum is the *means* of instilling in each student a love for truth, wisdom, discernment, and learning through the use of excellent materials. It is central for the implementation of your school's Christian vision and for educational achievements. Through a solid curriculum, students will develop the analytic, communicative, and physical skills that are essential for effective Christian service, both in the present and the future. As a Christian administrator, you should wholeheartedly seek to educate your students in God's truth enabling them to visualize and evaluate life situations through a Christian worldview.

If we view curriculum as the skeleton or the necessary backbone of a school, the importance of it is quite obvious. Without a solid, healthy core, the rest of the body will weaken and inevitably collapse. The skeleton, or curriculum as pictured in this analogy, is supported by the muscles—your teaching staff. Both parts must work together in unison for the optimal health of your institution and the realization of your vision. As an administrator, it is your responsibility to monitor and adjust your school's curriculum as needed. You should require it to meet standards of Christian excellence as well as have continuity and connectivity in your scope and sequence. Most schools go wrong by not connecting this map together within their student curriculum.

## Aligning Your Curriculum with Your Goals

As you seek to align your curriculum with your school's goals, it is recommended that you follow the three stages below:

### Step 1: Review Stage

Review your current curriculum and evaluate it against the philosophical and scriptural goals of your school's mission statement and vision. Does your current curriculum adequately reinforce your curriculum goals for the relevant subject? Does it meet your standards and expectations? Are students thriving and growing in knowledge as a result? This internal focus reviews the scope and sequence methods that are unique to your school's curriculum offerings.

An *external preview* will examine the material that other similar institutions are using. No curriculum materials with a secular worldview should be considered or adopted for student use unless, after thorough research, there appears to be no biblically based materials of equal or better quality available. When considering external examples, always determine if materials are secular in intent. Only adopt secular materials that uphold broad biblical truths (e.g. a high-quality mathematics text, or high quality, timeless literature). Ultimately, God's Word should be the heart of the curriculum!

## Step 2: Pilot Stage

Piloting has a purpose. Here, you take what was previewed and present it as a potential part of your current materials. Do not eliminate your previous curriculum during this step, as piloting is not overhauling! In essence, you are attempting to increase the beauty of a puzzle, rather than trying to begin with an entirely different one. Be continually aware that changes should be for the sole purpose of enhancing what you currently offer. Curriculum teams have a tendency to want to paint a broad-brush over current materials, mainly because of the longing for fresh material. There is danger with this mindset, as students should not be used as guinea pigs for change, and suffer academically as a result. Pitfalls also arise when schools blindly adopt an unproven "boxed curriculum." There is a maze of curriculum choices available to choose from. Experienced teachers, on the other-hand, come to the table with tried and tested materials from various publishers and authors. Their wisdom and experience should be considered as you move forward.

## Step 3: Polish Stage

Polishing is for the purpose of improving, refining or rendering a finished product. At this point in the review process, you may find it necessary to polish and perfect new curriculum materials that have been added. This is to ensure that they integrate well with current materials being used. Questions to consider: Are these additions ministering to students in their appropriate academic stage? Have the modifications been refined properly to be placed within the skeletal support system of your school?

## Step 4: Publish Stage

At this stage, curriculum changes are completed and ready to be entered into your permanent curriculum. Once these revisions are published, your administration now owns it. Be prepared to defend your curriculum philosophy at lengths, as well as have a legitimate purpose for any changes. While no perfect Christian curriculum exists, be in prayer that the Lord will provide you with one that will effectively communicate the biblical worldview and help you disciple students to Christ.[42]

---

42 Ps 127:1

## Use of Secular Material

*"Be not conformed to this world, but be transformed by the renewing of your mind..."*[43]

If secular materials are considered for student use, the following are necessary:
- Any secular material should be rigorously examined and countered in philosophy with biblical/true perspectives (e.g. presenting the elements of the theory of evolution is desirable, but it must be subjugated in time and emphasis to the elements of the creation account), in keeping with the scope of the course.
- Falsehoods and unbiblical philosophies should always be identified as such.
- Biblical principles within and/or related to the course objectives should also be presented to the students (e.g. while using a secular United States history text, the teacher should identify and emphasize the biblical foundations of our country.)

## Controversial Subjects

With an awareness that controversial subjects will arise, you need to establish a guideline that will help your school respect the convictions of parents and teachers in various academic subject areas, while at the same time maintaining your goal of teaching all subjects in the light of a comprehensive Christian worldview. This should apply to all teaching staff in the course of their teaching duties. It however does not apply to non-teaching staff, or to the teaching staff on their own time.

A controversial subject is a subject which Christian families and churches commonly consider divisive, whether or not the introduction of the topic was planned by the teacher or brought up by a student. If in the course of teaching a class the teacher observes that a subject has come to the surface that could be considered controversial, he must consider whether or not the discussion will help him to achieve the goals set forth in the curriculum guide. If it would indeed be helpful, the teacher should allow class time for the discussion moving cautiously and purposefully while using the following procedures:
- Instruct the class on the responsibility of Christians to be charitable in debate.
- Reiterate the responsibility to honor the teaching they have received from their parents on this subject.
- As appropriate, direct the students' attention to informed sources on each side of the subject concerned. This may be done in a variety of forms, such as a research paper, guest speakers, reading differing authors, etc. Strongly encourage the students to become knowledgeable of the most widely held views on the topic.

---

43  Rom 12:2

- Refrain from pursuing tangents or other unplanned subject matter that will lead to a possible mishandling/poor teaching of controversial subjects.

According to Scripture, teachers are required to be mature, Christian, adult role models to the students. As such, teachers are never to enter into an adversarial debate with students on controversial subjects within a classroom setting. Even though a teacher may hold strong personal convictions regarding a subject, they are to encourage a gracious and scholarly attitude in the students.

## Doctrine Guidelines

For a discussion of the proper role of the teachers, I encourage staff members to review *The Seven Laws of Teaching* by John Milton Gregory. The chapter on the law of the teaching process is especially applicable as it states:

> True teaching, then, is not that which gives knowledge, but that which stimulates pupils to gain it. One might say that he teaches best who teaches least; or that he teaches best whose pupils learn most without being taught directly. But we should bear in mind that in these epigrammatic statements two meanings of the word teaching are involved—one, simply telling, the other creating the conditions of real learning.[44]

In my experience, the following doctrines and topics have been identified as controversial and considered secondary. Discussions of these doctrines are not recommended:
- Old earth vs. young earth creation
- The morality of polygamy
- The existence of celestial beings that the Bible calls "gods," especially in relation to the gods of Greek mythology.
- The accuracy of the Greek concept of Hades
- Differing views on the Sabbath. Is it a Christian obligation?
- Calvinism v. Arminianism
- Man's will v. God's sovereignty
- Predestination
- Premillennialism v. Postmillennialism.
- Is it ever morally acceptable to deceive (e.g. in a war)?
- Can a Christian lose his salvation?
- Satan's authority in the present

---

44  John Milton Gregory, *The Seven Laws of Teaching* (Grand Rapids, Michigan: Baker Book House, 1884), 40.

- Roles of men and women
- Arranged marriages
- Capital punishment
- Does the Old Testament civil law apply today?

   Historical topics
- States' rights: Union v. Confederacy
- The morality of slavery

   Social issues:
- Environmentalism
- Spanking infants
- The "proper" role of government. Social welfare programs, art, heath care, education, etc.

## Selecting Debate Topics

Put guidelines in place that are designed to assist your secondary teachers as they select topics for in-class debates. Teachers working with students in the pert and poetic stages should use debates regularly. The use of guidelines should not lessen the use of class debate when appropriate, rather assist with topics that are in keeping with the secondary doctrine guidelines and meet with the approval of most Christian parents.

Guidelines:

- Teachers may choose to notify parents in your class of a debate topic prior to holding the debate. This will provide parents with the opportunity to express their concerns in a timely manner. It should be the teacher's option to do this.
- When selecting topics, consider the effect that the debate will have among the Christian students in class and in the student body as a whole. Avoid topics that will be divisive among Christians.
- Safe and yet profitable topics such as political decisions and current events should not be neglected.
- Avoid using topics that have recently been local topics of debate, avoiding unnecessary division within the Christian community.
- Use topics that relate to the course content objectives.
- When selecting topics, show grace to concerned parents. If a parent has a concern with a particular topic, try to use an alternative topic if possible, even if the topic is an appropriate one as defined by these guidelines.

## What Is Classical Education?

The word "classical" refers to the structure and form of the education. "Grammar" pertains to the fundamental rules of each subject. "Logic" is the ordered relationship of particulars in each subject and "Rhetoric" is how the grammar and logic of each subject may be clearly expressed. In all levels, programs, and teaching, seek to emphasize grammar, logic, and rhetoric in all subjects.

In the 1940's the British author, Dorothy Sayers, wrote an essay calling for a return to the application of the seven liberal arts of ancient education, the first three being the "Trivium" - grammar, logic, rhetoric.[45] Miss Sayers also combines the three stages of children's development to the Trivium. Specifically, she matches what she calls the "Poll-parrot" stage with grammar, "Pert" with logic, and "Poetic" with rhetoric. Dorothy Sayers' essay "The Lost Tools of Learning," which can be read in its entirety in Appendix G, discusses these stages in detail, giving readers a solid view of classical education. I encourage you to read and explore this methodology, as I have seen great educational strides when it is put into practice.

## Curriculum Recommendations

### Non-Denominational Guidelines

If your school is non-denominational, as discussed as an option in the first chapter, do not allow a particular Christian denominational doctrine or distinctive to be presented as favored within the school, particularly any that extends beyond the foundational statements you have established. Keep in mind that your school is comprised of families from a variety of Christian congregations, each with their own historical heritage regarding issues of liturgy, governance and doctrinal emphasis. The discussion and debate of these historic differences is permissible and encouraged as a part of the rhetorical curriculum, however it should be done with due respect in the spirit of Christian charity, with scripture as the rule.

### Recommended Curriculum Goals by Subject:[46]

## Bible

*Bible Goals for all Grades:*
- Students should be encouraged to seek personal application of the Scriptures. An exclusively academic (i.e. studied but not applied) approach is a distortion of the truth.[47]
- Seek to give the same priority as God did to the themes presented in His Word, e.g. the highest priority being the Gospel.[48]

---
45 Dorothy Sayers. *"The Lost Tools of Learning,"* (Oxford, 1947).
46 Logos School, *Logos Curriculum Guide* (Moscow, Idaho: Canon Press, 2013).
47 Jas 1:22
48 1 Cor 15:3-5

- Reading, understanding, memorizing and applying, as appropriate, the entire written Word of God, in context, will be a high priority in all Bible classes. A subordinate goal will be familiarizing the students with good study helps.[49]

## English

*The Christian Worldview of English*

God has chosen to reveal Himself to man through His Word. "In the beginning was the Word, and the Word was with God, and the Word was God."[50] God has communicated His message of salvation to man through His Son, the living Word of God, and through the Scriptures, His written Word.

Language and the desire and ability to communicate are obvious gifts from our Creator to man. Language reflects the very character and nature of God, as does all His creation. "Every good and perfect gift is from above, coming down from the Father of the heavenly lights, who does not change like shifting shadows."[51]

The function of language is two-fold. By it we are able to understand others, and through it we can express ourselves. Because God has used language to communicate to man, we in turn can use it to glorify and praise Him. If we have a superficial knowledge of English, we will necessarily have shallow capabilities of communication, in understanding both the written and spoken word. But if we have a profound grasp of the language, we will be able to receive far more from all we read and hear and give far more to others in our writing and conversation.

Language is a tool in the Christian's hand. With it great things can be accomplished for the glory of God. When misused, it can cause great damage. What are the uses of the tool?

Believing students can be motivated to study their mother tongue so that they can understand the Scriptures and Christian writing and become more conformed to the image of Christ in their pursuit of holiness. Beautiful language can be employed in hymns, poetry, stories, essays, books, and conversation. Language study also equips them to refute the world's false philosophies with clarity and precision.

If the student is well taught in the basics of English, he will be protected from misunderstanding the Scriptures (as well as from misunderstanding other, less important, works). For example, knowledge of figures of speech is important in the study of Scripture. Knowledge of who is the subject and what is the object of this or that particular sentence is also important. The student will also be protected from doctrinal error through understanding the difference between indicatives and imperatives. A list of many such things could be expanded far beyond the scope of this book.

The application of English to the other disciplines is obvious and far-reaching. What student can approach his field of study without employing language? A ready grasp of sentence

---

49 2 Tm 3:16,17
50 Jn 1:1
51 Jas 1:17

structure and an expansive vocabulary will only make his other studies more delightful to pursue and more rewarding to attain.

Apollos is described in Acts 18:24 as "an eloquent man mighty in the Scriptures." Certainly he must have been a lover of language and the Word. Language is the means by which the Christian student can shine his light before the world in relationships with family, friends, and so forth. Perhaps he will be called to full-time Christian service as a pastor or missionary, where his job will be to communicate the gospel clearly. But a thorough understanding of language can facilitate success in any occupation.

It is easy to point out the uses of language in the English classroom. There are many opportunities in literature study to examine the uses of language and evaluate the worldview of the author by what they say or how they say it. Composition assignments and vocabulary study afford instances where the student can apply new skills and refine old ones. Grammar must be seen as the frame that language is stretched upon like a canvas, giving it form, and enabling us to appreciate its beauty.

Once a student is taught to love language, he can enjoy limitless possibilities in self-instruction through reading, understanding, and appreciating the Scripture and secondarily, through many great literary works. The goal of the teacher is to impart that love!

*English Goals for All Grades*
- Equip every student with the skills necessary for good writing, including correct spelling and grammar, pleasing style, clarity of focus, proof-reading, and self-correcting.
- Put a major emphasis on good writing by requiring the students to write often and correctly in each subject area.
- Encourage clear thinking by requiring clear, focused writing.
- Introduce the students to many styles of writing using the Bible and other high-quality literature.

## Writing

*Writing Expectations for Middle School Students*

Students should receive guidance in finding materials in the library. They should be shown how to look up information on the computers in the public libraries and how to locate books in the library. Outlining skills should be reviewed if students are expected to outline material from texts or develop outlines for written assignments.

Expectations for note-taking during lectures should be low. All logic phase teachers who expect students to use this skill should give students specific guidance on accomplishing this task. During the first semester the teacher should periodically collect notes from the students to check on their success in taking notes. (This need not be graded, although it could be.) Teachers should write key words and phrases on the board. They should avoid writing out complete sentences for the students.

Students need to have experience writing research reports. Specific expectations for research reports should be made clear to the students. Remind your teachers to define plagiarism and emphasize the importance of avoiding this practice.

*Writing Expectations for High School Students*

High school students should be expected to have mastered the junior high school skills and be weaned from using encyclopedias for research reports. Students should write a maximum of four major papers each year. When papers are assigned, class time should be scheduled to work on the papers, and sufficient time be given to complete the entire paper. Teachers should coordinate large research papers with one another in an effort to not overload the students. A sample schedule for assigning major papers and projects is shown below.

*Sample Schedule for Assigning Major Papers/Projects*

Table 1. Sample Paper/Projects Schedule

|  | 1st Quarter | 2nd Quarter | 3rd Quarter | 4th Quarter | Length |
|---|---|---|---|---|---|
| 7th | English | History | Theology | English | 3 pgs. |
| 8th | English | History | Theology | English | 5 pgs. |
| 9th | American Literature | American History | Theology | American Literature | 6-7 pgs. |
| 10th | Classical Literature | World History | Theology | Classical Literature | 8 pgs. |
| 11th | British Literature | Theology | British Literature | Rhetoric | 10 pgs. |
| 12th | Great Books | Apologetics | Great Books | Rhetoric | 10-12 pgs. |

*Note: Other classes should not assign any major papers unless all work is to be done in class.*

## Science

*The Christian Worldview of Science*

What does it mean to think of science "Christianly"? It means to teach science indeed. Science is the systematic study of creation, based on observations. Three fundamental questions that need to be addressed are:

- Where did the creation come from?
- What is it saying?
- Is knowledge of the creation necessary?

In the Bible we are told explicitly that in six days the Lord made heaven, earth, the sea and all that is in them. Clearly the creation or nature is God's handiwork, and the more we study about creation the more we will know about Him. In a similar way, students of Vincent Van Gough do not merely study biographies and critiques written about this famous artist. Instead they should study the handiwork of the artist in order to appreciate who he was. A close investigation of his actual paintings is an essential element of the discipline.

Now that we know where the creation came from, let's turn to the second question. Is nature saying anything in particular? Romans 1:20 states, "For since the creation of the world His invisible attributes, His eternal power and divine nature, have been clearly seen, being understood through what has been made, so that they are without excuse." What is it that is clearly seen, being understood through what has been made? God's invisible attributes, eternal power, and divine nature are seen. This passage says that these things are not only seen but clearly seen through what has been made, through creation. This means the creation is in effect a sermon on the invisible attributes of God, His eternal power and His divine nature. The creation is testifying to these things, and the result of this sermon is that man is without excuse. Need a Christian have any stronger motivation to study creation? When we investigate nature, we are, in a very real sense, examining a sermon on the invisible attributes, the eternal power and the divine nature of our creator—exposition with a microscope.

Another reason that Christians should study science is so that they can fulfill God's mandate for dominion. The first command that God gave to man after his creation was to "be fruitful, and multiply, and fill the earth, and subdue it; and rule over the fish of the sea and over the birds of the sky, and over every living thing that moves on the earth." One tool that aids us in our efforts to obey this command is science and the fruit of science, technology. An obedient study and application of science helps the Christian to fill, subdue, and rule over the earth in an effective manner.

Since the creation is in fact a creation, a masterpiece made by the Lord our God, it is not surprising that Christians throughout history have led the field in science. As we teach our children more about the creation, it is important that we keep in mind that all of this was made by the Creator, that it all is proclaiming His attributes, that knowledge of it helps a servant to exercise subordinate dominion over creation and that all of creation is sustained, presently and graciously, by and for Him.

## History

### *The Christian Worldview of History*

Christianity is a religion of remembering. From creation to present the children of God have been commanded to remember His justice, righteousness, holiness, faithfulness, etc. to his people. History is the record of God's providential dealings with men. From a Christian standpoint, the importance of examining and understanding history is inestimable. As Christians, our faith rests on the historical truth of Christ's advent, life, death, and resurrection during the first century A.D., in the locale of Jerusalem, under the political control of the

Roman Empire.[52] The truth of the record of creation in Genesis also forms the basis for the totality of Christian and biblical thought.[53]

Further, we believe that a Christian worldview of history must begin with a biblical view of man, his nature and destiny. The biblical view allows us to interpret and evaluate his actions according to God's unchangeable commands and principles. Students should come to understand that the actions of man are always under the superintendence and sovereign control of God.[54] Thus, the study of history educates us about God's interactions with our predecessors and thereby provides lessons for us and our descendants.[55] God raises up and brings down nations.[56] He blesses nations and individuals that follow His righteous standards, and those that rebel against Him are cursed.[57] For example, we believe that many of the colonial leaders and, later, the founding fathers of the United States of America sought to bring glory to God through this nation, grounding many of our primary governmental documents on God's Word. Therefore, God uniquely blessed this nation with freedoms and abundance. However, in recent generations, due to our rebellion against His decrees, we have lost many of our former blessings. Certain other principles related to our beliefs about the study of history are:

- History is linear, not cyclical; that is, it is proceeding along the path God directs from creation until Christ's triumphant return.
- Historical sources, both primary and secondary, are to be compared and examined in the light of God's Word and sound scholarly standards.

Finally, we believe that, through the examples in and of His Word, God demonstrates that the careful study of history is a necessary activity for all believers as they seek a better understanding of and obedience to His will.

*History Goals for All Grades*

- The students should understand a Christian (providential) view of history.
- The students need to be able to identify whether or not history has been written from a Christian or a non-Christian perspective.
- The students should be taught how to study history, how to critically evaluate reading material, identify primary and secondary sources, and apply the historical method.
- The students need to know the value of ancient history and the history of western civilization.
- The students should know a general time line of historical events from Biblical times to the present, focusing primarily on western civilizations.

---

52  1 Cor 15:14
53  Col. 1-2
54  Prv 21:1
55  Ps 78, Ps 102:18, Rom 15:4, 1 Cor 10:1-11
56  Ps 2
57  Prv14:34

## Mathematics

### *The Christian Worldview of Mathematics*

Christian schools should have the goal of teaching all subjects as part of an integrated whole with the Scriptures at the center. Included in these subjects is mathematics. In no way should Christians believe the lie that, though history, literature, science, and other subjects can be successfully integrated with the Christian worldview, mathematics is somehow worldview neutral. On the contrary, mathematics is a very theological science, being an expression of the numeric aspect of God's character and of the logic that is in Him. In the preface to his *Almagest*,[58] Ptolemy wrote that the mathematical sciences were the best evidence of divinity because of their consistency and incorruptibility. Mathematics seeks to discover, examine and apply those fundamental laws by which God gives order to his creation.

The foundation of all truth, including the truths of mathematics, is the God of Scripture. The various spheres of mathematics are expressions of His logical character and His creative, sustaining power.

First, God Himself has a numerical nature. He is one God in three Persons: Father, Son, and Holy Spirit. The unity of God is declared in Deuteronomy 6:4, "Hear, O Israel: The Lord our God, the Lord is one!" The plurality of God is declared in passages such as 2 Corinthians 13:14, "The grace of the Lord Jesus Christ, and the love of God, and the communion of the Holy Spirit be with you all. Amen."

Because God has a plural nature, creation reflects that plurality. The ultimate reality is not one, but one and many. Creation is real, and really has distinguishable, countable particulars. As King David said, "O Lord, how manifold are Your works! In wisdom you have made them all".[59]

God created all things such that the creation reflects some of His attributes. Thus, we have a trustworthy basis for mathematical concepts. Briefly, the countable attributes of God provide a foundation for arithmetic. God is present in space,[60] thus there is true measure and a foundation for geometry. The infinity and immensity of God[61] also give us a foundation for the concept of infinity used in calculus.

As we study mathematics, we should, as Christians, expect to see God's handiwork everywhere. We should not be surprised to discover mathematical regularity in physics, astronomy, chemistry, and other sciences. Indeed, we should expect the mathematical formulas we derive to have application to the real world, because God has given mathematics as a tool for extending godly dominion over creation.

---

58  Claudius Ptolemy, *Almagest* (New York: Springer-Verlag, 1984), Preface.
59  Ps 104:24
60  Ps 139:7
61  Ps 90:2; 1 Kgs 8:27

*Mathematics Goals for All Grades*
- Ensure that the students have a thorough mastery of basic mathematical functions and tables.
- Seek to put an emphasis on conceptual, as well as practical, understanding of math through the frequent use of story problems.
- Illustrate God's unchanging character through the timeless, logical, mathematical systems He gave to man through His gift of reason.

## Literature

*The Christian Worldview of Reading*

Parents who want their children to receive a classical education will be reluctant to direct them in a course of sappy books, whether or not the authors are Christians. And parents who want their children to go to heaven when they die will be reluctant to turn them over to a course of reading produced by erudite and eloquent God-haters. The problem is compounded by the fact that, unlike the government schools, private schools excel in teaching their students to read. And once the children learn to read, they roar through all the good books available, and a major problem then presents itself. What do we do now? Our kids are all dressed up with no place to go. But before embarking on the quest for the "perfect book list," it is important to master certain principles first. Otherwise, your students' reading list is more likely to be based on whims and fads and the "latest rage" than upon sturdy biblical principle.

The first thing to realize is that biblical thinking and captivating writing are not antithetical concepts. The fact that the combination is so rare in our contemporary culture is simply a testimony to the retreatist mentality that has afflicted evangelical Christians since the general cultural apostasy of the last century. As believing Christians, our desire should be to do everything we do to the glory of God. This means we should not write, and we should not read, Christian books which are a bunch of nothing. A Christian literature program is not one in which the students read "Christian books." A Christian literature program is one in which the students are taught to read great literature and to think while they read, as Christians. As they do, our children should be taught to appreciate a finely-crafted sentence-to the glory of God. As Christians, we are people of the Word, and consequently, we should be people of words. We should understand words and use them well.

The second principle we should understand is that biblical faith is not moralism. What many mean by Christian books is simply decent books-some kids' story with "Disneyfied" standards. But this sort of thing is rarely Christian; it is simply G-rated paganism. When this principle is understood, many parents are tempted to rate books according to some very simple shibboleth —i.e. "Does it have swear words in it?" The problem, of course, is that some utterly humanistic books meet such standards, and some wonderful Christian books do not. Also related to this is the fact that our modern moralism is detached from biblical moorings, and is consequently determined by the latest rage in contemporary "ethics"—whether political correctness, self-esteem, feminism, or whatnot. This results in the reader being confronted with the spectacle of a King Arthur, say, working through his problems with low self-esteem.

The third principle is that, if your children are being educated to think like Christians to the glory of God, they should be equipped to read and analyze, and to a certain extent, appreciate, the writing of godless writers who were, nevertheless, craftsmen. One can appreciate some of Twain's writing, for example, while understanding his despair and refusing to follow him in it.

The temptation is, once the children have learned to read, to turn them over to the books. But this is abdication and not teaching. Christian teachers should not use books the way many government schoolteachers use video-as a cheap babysitter and no-brainer. Parents, and teachers they hire, are responsible for what is going into their children's minds - it does not matter if the source is television, the neighbors' kids, or the books checked out from the school library. But in order to avoid such abdication, parents and teachers must be diligent readers as well, and they should have a good idea of how books are shaping both their children's worldview, and this includes their understanding, and appreciation of well written literature.

*Reading Goals for All Grades*

- Adequately equip each child with the phonetic skills and practice necessary to read well, that is, smoothly and with good comprehension.

- Carefully monitor and guide the child's growth in reading-related skills, e.g. comprehension and vocabulary development, while he is reading and enjoying worthwhile, time-tested, challenging literature.

- Seek to expose the child to a wide variety of literature styles and forms and not restrict him to one common, dull basal.

- Integrate the love and practice of reading with many other areas of study, e.g. the Bible, history, and science to help the student become a read-to-learn person all his life.

- Teach your students to read carefully and critically with an understanding of the Christian worldview and with the ability to identify opposing worldviews of the authors they encounter.

## Foreign Language

*The Christian Worldview of Foreign Language*

We should begin with the recognition that foreign languages must first be understood as languages. After we have addressed this, we may then proceed to discuss the importance of the study of a language foreign to the student. It is not an accident that Christianity is a religion that has, and perpetuates, a high view of words. The Lord Jesus Christ is Himself described as the Word (*ho logos*). We should therefore understand that our theology of words must be dependent upon our theology of the Word. So we should begin at the beginning. We see in the creation of Adam that language was not a tool developed by man. Rather, it was (and is) a gift from God. It was a design feature in man which enabled him to communicate with God[62], about God,[63] and about the world God made.[64]

As a result of God's great language program at the Tower of Babel, the Bible teaches that there are many languages in the world, and none of them are "without significance."[65] But the Bible does not teach that all languages have equal significance. Indeed, in this passage the apostle Paul is arguing that a misuse of language (divorced from understanding) was a source of confusion in the church. That which was given to man to enable him to communicate becomes, through misuse, a hindrance to communication. This kind of confusion can result because one language speaker does not understand the other language at all (as was happening in Corinth), or it may happen because one speaker or listener has a comparatively poor grasp of the language in question. When this happens, it is correspondingly difficult to communicate about God or about His world. I recall a Korean friend one time enquiring "why Jesus told His disciples not to take a staff with them on a journey—why would they want to take a secretary or administrative assistant?" Anyone who has little children growing up in a home can testify to the interesting confusions that result from an inadequate grasp of language.

But some, poorly educated in language arts, never grow out of imprecise, fuzzy-around-the-edges communication. As they are educated in the language arts according to a Christian worldview, they are enabled more accurately to speak with God, about God, and about God's world—and all to the glory of God. What wonderful tools prepositions are! All these arguments can be applied, and ought to be applied, to one's native language. But how does this understanding apply to the study of a language foreign to the student?

First, modern foreign languages can be studied for obvious pragmatic reasons. Spanish can be studied and then later utilized in evangelism, preaching, etc. in a Spanish-speaking country. Second, the classical language of Greek can be studied, not because anyone speaks it today, but because the student will be better equipped to commune with God and learn about God in the original language of the New Testament.

But why study something like Latin? In the study of Latin, the student is benefited in a number of distinct ways. Some are unique to Latin, while others are the fruit of studying any foreign language. Such study prevents linguistic provincialism. The study of another language (whatever it is) helps a student come to understand not only the nature of the grammar of this new language, and not only the grammar of his native language (although this will occur), but

---

62 Gn 1:28
63 Gn 3:2-3
64 Gn 2:20
65 1 Cor 14:10

it will give him a grasp of grammar itself. This acquisition of knowledge about deep grammar will help even in non-linguistic areas like science, math, etc.

The study of Latin is a roundabout way of studying English. More than any other single language, Latin has supplied English with much of its raw material. Because virtually all of our students will spend the rest of their lives seeking to glorify God in English, the more we help with their abilities in English, the better off they will be. One goal of our Latin instruction is to give the student a working vocabulary in Latin. This accomplishes something in two languages. This obviously equips the student to work in Latin, but it also greatly expands his command of English. Because about 50% of English vocabulary comes from Latin, the more words a student learns in Latin, the more he learns in English. And just as a craftsman wants to choose the right tool for the right job, so someone who is trained in language can choose the right word for the right job. As Christians, our job is to glorify God, which we are better able to do.

An individual with a vocabulary of 150 words is extremely limited in how he can communicate with God and about God, and is equally limited in his ability to communicate with precision about the world God made. There is no way to talk about anything with any degree of accuracy and precision apart from vocabulary acquisition. I recently heard a junior high student talking about something he appreciated. He could have said it was "neat" and we would have understood he was generally pleased. But he said it was "providential", and by so doing, he communicated with far greater precision. Therefore, an important part of the Latin program is to give our students a good grasp of Latin vocabulary and to show and emphasize the etymological connections to English. This is done in three ways.

First, the students are expected to learn the Latin vocabulary contained in their textbook lessons. Second, the students are given ten Latin words a week to learn with the corresponding English derivatives. These English derivatives are not common English words, but rather ones which are comparatively rare. This is to give the student a greater capacity to talk with God, about God, and about God's world with a much greater degree of precision than previously possible.

Second, a Latin program emphasizes a grasp of basic Latin grammar. In Latin, the rules for identifying what a word is doing in a sentence are much more defined than they are in English; the student of Latin can work with a language that is more grammatically refined and precise than English is. This will result in a much more versatile approach to expression in English. And finally, at the end of a Latin program there should be translation work which will include portions from the Scriptures in Latin, as well as theological writing in Latin. Thus, the goal of a Latin program should be to enable students to think and speak with much greater precision—whether they are talking with God, about God, or about what He has done.

# Recommended Courses for Secondary Students

## Junior High School (Grades 7 and 8)

Table 2. Junior High Recommended Courses

| SUBJECT: | SEVENTH GRADE: | EIGHTH GRADE: |
|---|---|---|
| Bible/Classical Languages | Bible/Classical Languages | Bible/Classical Languages |
| English | English 7 | English 8 |
| Math | Algebra ½ | Algebra I |
| Science | Physical Science | Logic |
| History | History 7 | History 8 |
| Electives | (5x/week) | (5x/week) |

## High School (Grades 9-12)

Table 3. Recommended High School Courses

| SUBJECT: | NINTH : | TENTH : | ELEVENTH; | TWELFTH: |
|---|---|---|---|---|
| ENGLISH | American Literature | Classical Literature | British Literature | Great Books |
| BIBLE | Bible Interpretation | Systematic Theology | Historical Theology | Apologetics |
| FOREIGN LANGUAGE | Spanish I | Spanish II | Greek I | Greek II |
| HISTORY | US History | World History | Rhetoric I | Rhetoric II |
| MATH | Geometry | Algebra II | Pre-Calculus | Calculus |
| SCIENCE | Anatomy | Biology | Chemistry | Physics |

*(The above courses are of course subject to change at the discretion of the respective principal.)*

As administrators, we need to encourage every student to develop a love for learning and live up to their academic potential. This goal is impossible to realize unless the teachers have a real love for the subject. If the teacher is not excited about having this knowledge, then why should the student be excited about acquiring it? Necessity may induce the student to learn the material; it will not induce him to love it. If he does not love it, he will content himself with some minimum standard. The origin of this travesty of education is a teacher who also is content with some minimum standard.

If this goal is successfully reached, then the student will spend the rest of his or her life building on the foundation laid during his or her time at school. Not only did they receive the tools of learning, they acquired the desire to use them. And, unlike most tools, they do not wear out with use.

## Advanced Courses and Advanced Placement Program

Advanced courses (A.D.V) in lieu of Advanced Placement courses may be offered. They are weighted on the following scale: A=6, B=5, C=4. Advanced (A.D.V.) courses are taught the same as honor classes with a mandatory additional class period commitment during an elective period, in order to prepare students for the A.P. exam. The students should sit for and pass the A.P. exam with a score of 3, 4, or 5 to receive the (A.D.V.) weighted scale on their transcripts.

Two prerequisites for the classes are:

1. A student <u>should</u> have had an A average in the respective areas starting in the ninth grade.
2. The student should also have scored above the 90$^{th}$ percentile on the Stanford Achievement or Scholastic Aptitude Test the spring of their ninth or tenth grade year.

For example, juniors may take a maximum of two advanced classes while seniors can take a maximum of three. Several recommended advanced/AP class options are listed below. Extra books and materials are required and will be required.

Recommended Classes:
- Calculus (AB)
- U.S. History
- Biology
- Chemistry
- Physics B
- World History
- English Language
- European History
- English Literature
- U.S. Government & Politics

## Promotion Guidelines

### Elementary Grades

Establish a consistent set of guidelines or standards as it applies to determining grade promotions. Elementary students in grades K-6 should meet the following basic criteria for promotion to the next grade level:

- Pass reading, math, and English with at least a 75% average.
- Have no more than one 'F' (or 'U') per quarter in any given subject. It is incumbent upon the appropriate teacher that all due curriculum objectives, grading guidelines, and

teaching requirements be faithfully executed. For example, the requirement that there be at least 10 objective grades per subject area by which the quarterly grade is computed, has a significant bearing on a complete and accurate assessment of a student's success in that area. Too few grades can force the teacher to make a poorly documented and therefore an unobjective judgment call.

- In addition, when considering promotion of students currently enrolled, special emphasis should be given to the appropriate level of mastery of required skills such as:
    o Behavioral maturity
    o Reading readiness/silent and oral
    o Writing ability/neatness and complete sentences
    o Adding and subtracting with 75% mastery
    o Social interaction skills
    o Completion of grade level objectives

## Secondary Students

Secondary students should be required to pass all Math, English, History, Logic and Science course work in order to be promoted to the next successive grade.

## Academic Probation

Secondary students should be required to maintain *at least a 2.0 grade-point average* during any two, consecutive quarters. This guideline is intended to provide additional motivation to students whose academic achievements are not up to their capability. If implementation of this guideline would be counterproductive to this end, you may decide not to place a student on probation. A written record explaining this decision should be signed and placed in the student's file.

Grade point averages for each secondary student should be calculated at the end of each quarter. Elective courses and independent study courses are not included in the G.P.A. calculation.

- If a student's G.P.A. is below 2.0 (i.e. a "C" average), that student should be placed on academic probation during the following quarter, and a parent-teacher conference arranged.
- If at the end of the next quarter the student's G.P.A. (for the quarter) has not risen to at least a 2.0, that student should be expelled.
- Students who are on academic probation are ineligible to participate in extracurricular activities.

## Guidelines for Retention

Guidelines are created to complement and support the school's promotion guidelines and should be used in such a manner. The primary purpose of these guidelines is to increase the communication from the school to the home in the instance of a child possibly needing to repeat a grade. This is to assist the parents, as the final decision-makers regarding their child's education, in making as informed a decision as possible.

Considering and recommending a student for possible retention in a grade is always a very serious matter. Every step of the process should be well documented.

In my experience, a number of similar questions have emerged in my experience that may help in the initial stages of considering whether or not a student may need to repeat a grade. The following is not intended to be an exhaustive list, but includes samples of some pertinent questions the teacher may want to document and go over with the parents:

- How old is the child? (Age plays a tremendous role in a child's ability and maturity to succeed in school. The more mature the student, the easier school tasks become.)

- What is the sex of the child? (Very frequently boys will have a harder time adjusting to school patterns than girls will. Boys often need more time to mature than girls.)

- Did the child attend kindergarten? (Certain school habits and behaviors begin in kindergarten. Depending on where and whether the child attended can reveal some insights to the behavior and aptitude causing the current concern.)

- What is the home life like for the child? (Things to consider include: saved vs. unsaved, single-parent, divorce, remarriage, working parents, etc. Essentially, is the child's home life one that instills security and love, with predictable patterns of living? The importance and influence of the home is without equal in the life of a child.)

- Are reading and the love of books evident in the home? No other single academic factor plays a greater role in the educational success of a child. Do the parents like to read and do/did they read to the child frequently?

- Is the cause for concern here primarily behavioral, academic or a combination of both? The primary cause for concern should be singled out. Behavioral problems may still indicate retention is necessary, but identifying the concern will help determine the best plan for correction.

- Has the child had to repeat a grade before? (If not, this is moot. If so, when and why did the child repeat? Due to the rapid physical growth of a child, I do not recommend a child repeating the same grade more than once. It is also unlikely that repeating two grades would truly address the problem.)

- What are the specific indicators the teacher has identified that give rise to the current consideration? (These should be documented.)

NOTE: The first three (K-2) years are the most critical years for a child to set the patterns and learn the basic skills that will be built upon in later school life. Retention should be a greater possibility in these years, rather than in upper grades, in order to give the child additional time to mature and master the basic skills.

## New Student Placement Guidelines

Consider that all new students meet the following criteria to be accepted into the next successive grade level:

- Provide documentation showing that they successfully completed the previous grade by a demonstrated proficiency of at least 75% or higher in reading, math, and English. They also should have satisfactorily (70% or higher) completed science and "social studies" (history and/or geography) within the previous curriculum.

- Recognize that many public schools (and some home-schools) do not use letter grades (A-F) or percentages to indicate academic proficiency in the elementary grades, a mark of "Satisfactory" in at least 90% of the subjects on the student's transcript/report card will be acceptable. However, if there is any doubt as to the student's abilities or the quality of the curriculum used previously, the student should be tested in the three critical areas (reading, math, and English mechanics) using an in-school screening test and/or the appropriate subtests of the Stanford 9 or Stanford 10 standardized testing and scoring materials.

- If the new student has taken any standardized tests, the student should have earned national scores of at least 50% or higher in reading, math, and language (as appropriate to age level). If he has never taken any standardized tests and there is any doubt as to his abilities, the previous step should be followed.

The results of any in-school testing should be combined with the new student's report card and any previous standardized testing scores, in order to determine the best grade level placement at your school. If the combined results are not satisfactory, the parents should be apprised of this and encouraged to consider having their child retained at the previous grade level.

## Homework Philosophy and Guidelines

The assignment of homework should not be a prerequisite necessary to provide a rigorous education. Fulfilling the goals of a quality Christian education does not necessitate assigning several hours of homework each night. Teachers should have a specific purpose in mind when they assign homework. Students should be encouraged to begin work on assignments during class. Homework then, consists of work that was not completed during class. Remind your teachers that assigning homework may take away time that would otherwise be spent in involvement in family activities. Some guidelines can be as follows:

- Bible, Science and History: completion of assignments not finished during allotted time in class, reviewing information presented during class (such as studying for tests).
- Math: completion of problems not finished during class.
- English: completion of reading or writing assignments not finished during class.
- Foreign Languages: completion of assignments not finished during class, review of vocabulary and grammar.
- Rhetoric\Debate, Logic: preparation for presentations and tests.
- Electives: suggestions for extra voluntary student work. Homework may be assigned as needed.

## Honors and Awards

Consider having a system of formal honors and awards for the following reasons:
- To increase the academic motivation of all the students by demonstrating that good work and good behavior are rewarded.
- To recognize and show appreciation for those students qualified to be listed on the honor rolls.
- To draw public attention to the academic quality and outstanding behavior of the secondary students.

## Honor Rolls

Students who have earned placement on the honor roll for each quarter should be recognized at a year-end awards assembly as either an "A" honor roll or all "A-B" honor roll student. The "All A" honor roll, as well as the "A-B" honor roll, should include elective classes. To be on the "A-B" honor roll a student should have two "B" grades or less, including elective classes.

## Faculty Commendation Award

This high school award is based on three factors: exemplary conduct, academic achievement, and a positive attitude toward school. In order to receive this award, students should be unanimously selected by core curriculum teachers. They personify the attributes exemplified by an ideal Christian school student. If a student is selected for this award in all four quarters, he/she should receive an individual plaque at the end of year awards assembly. In addition to the individual plaques, students' names are placed on a perpetual plaque that remains on permanent display at your school. This is considered to be the highest honor the staff can bestow upon a student.

## Perfect Attendance

This award is presented at a year-end assembly to students who have not missed one day during the school year.

## Valedictorian and Salutatorian

The high school principal and a committee of secondary teachers select the senior class valedictorian and salutatorian. The committee evaluates the students based on the following criteria (in order of priority): spiritual testimony, academic performance, extracurricular activities, and honors received. To be eligible to receive this award, a student should attend your school for more than one year, as well as have a cumulative grade point average of 3.5 or higher. In addition, a student who is suspended during his or her senior year should be ineligible to receive these awards.

## High School Graduation Guidelines

Academic records from grades 9 through 12 should be used as criteria for graduation. Examples of guidelines may be:

- To graduate a student should earn 24 credits.
- Students should earn three credits in Bible, four credits in English, two credits in history, four credits in math, two credits in rhetoric, four credits in science, and three credits in foreign language.
- Students should take the S.A.T. exam during their junior year.
- Students who are transferring from another school or home school should receive credit for previously completed work provided it is of similar nature, i.e., similar course objectives and similar time of study. Make sure there is sufficient documentation of their previous work.

Upon written request of the parents, you may waive or reduce up to four course credits for students who have academic difficulty subject to the following conditions:

- The student is a long time student .
- The parents have demonstrated a clear commitment to their child's education by working with your school and administrators.
- The parents and administrator agree that the work required is too difficult for the child in question.

# Credits Required for Graduation

Table 4. Recommended Credits for Graduation

| Subject: | Courses: | Credits: |
|---|---|---|
| Bible | Bible Interpretation 9, Systematic Theology 10, Historical Theology 11, Apologetics 12 | 3 |
| English | American Literature, Classical Literature British Literature, Great Books | 4 |
| Foreign Language | Spanish I, Spanish II, Greek I, Greek II | 3 |
| History | United States History, World History | 2 |
| Math | Algebra I, Geometry, Advanced Algebra Pre-Calculus, Calculus, Trigonometry | 4 |
| Rhetoric | Rhetoric I, Rhetoric II | 2 |
| Science | Anatomy, Biology, Chemistry, Physics | 4 |
| P.E./Athletics | | 2 |
| **TOTAL:** | | 24 |

# Conclusion

By taking every opportunity to integrate biblical principles and Christian philosophy within your schools curriculum, you are molding the lives of students entrusted to you. Any one of these goals taken in isolation would be an inadequate basis for education. Taken together, I believe they establish a remarkably firm foundation. We as administrators should look forward to seeing the minds of many young people educated in a way that, tragically, is very rarely seen today. As God blesses, we hope to see that change.

# Chapter 4

# Student Discipline and Behavior Guidelines

*"The Lord disciplines those He loves, as a father the son he delights in." Proverbs 3:12*

One of the most difficult matters for any Christian school is *effective* biblical discipline. Effective discipline is the result of prayerful decision making, empowered by the Word of God. The discipline decisions you make are a direct result of the philosophy that you hold and live out before your students. The Bible provides a firm philosophical basis and clear guidelines for those in authority. In a Christian school where God-fearing teachers require biblical values and standards, education can reach its highest level.

## Effective Biblical Discipline

Effective discipline, as described by Dr. Dennis Mills, means "the classroom is relatively free from confusion, disorder, and anti-social behavior. Each student and the group as a whole operates freely within a structured framework which they understand, accept, and incorporate into their behavior without constant reminders and punishment."[66] When students are aware that they are in a protected and orderly classroom environment, they know that the standards will be used fairly. They are confident that students who refuse to adhere to those standards will be disciplined or removed from the classroom thereby allowing their learning to be uninhibited.

As we seek to discipline students, our desire must be to reach their heart and help them align their behaviors with God's standards. We must seek to disciple and redirect the student so that his future choices will honor God and obey His commands. As a Christian school, we are not only equipping students academically—we are equipping them with "everything good for doing His will"[67] so that their future fruit may be pleasing to God. We must remind students that although discipline may not be pleasant for the moment, it will "produce a harvest of righteousness and peace for those who have been trained up in it."[68] Your school should be training and expecting students to submit to authority while reminding them that in doing this, they are strengthening their relationship with God and His power in their life.

In a Christian school, our goal of discipline is to produce self-discipline along with biblical patterns of behavior. In the 1871 Address, the Commissioner of Education in Washington, D.C. stated, "The present is an age of insubordination, and can we doubt that this has resulted from

---

66 Dennis W. Mills, Ph.D, "*Classroom Discipline: A Management Guide for Christian School Teachers,*" http://www.csrnet.org/csrnet/articles/classroom-discipline.html. (accessed October 1, 2006).
67 Heb 13:21
68 Heb 12:11

the loss of authority in the family and school!"[69] We, as Christian administrators, must strive to be examples of godly authority for our staff and our students. We do this by first maintaining the same standards that we expect from those under our authority; we practice what we preach knowing that "more is caught, than taught." In Luke 6:40, we are clearly reminded that a "student will be like his teacher." A powerful cue that your staff and students will internalize your values, beliefs, and goals.

## Consistency: Its Crucial Role

As in any environment, whether in the home, an institution, or church, the number one goal for discipline must be *consistency*. Historically, the majority of discipline problems in schools will occur for one or two reasons: either the discipline program is inadequate and unclear, or the implementation of the standards is ineffective. You should train your staff to clearly define the expected standards and consistently follow through with discipline! Although the methods might vary, the standards must not be neglected. Throughout the discipline process there should be:

- *Flexibility:* There should be a reasonable balance in firmness tendered with flexibility and very consistent consequences for broken rules.
- *Set Rules & Expectations:* Clear and concise expectations should be set in the very beginning. Have few rules and be 100% consistent!
- *Consistency:* Students should be able to count on their teachers to be the same in regard to discipline every day.
- *Perseverance:* Decide on the boundaries and stand firm. If students are allowed to push or move the boundaries, they will continue to test them.

## Basic School Rules

*A successful chant we use in our Christian school is,*
*"Obey right away, all the way, every day in a cheerful way!"*

Students should maintain a courteous, grateful, respectful, obedient and cooperative attitude, exercise restraint, and forgive freely. As Christians, expect them to share, take turns, love and serve one another, refrain from teasing, name-calling, bad language, pushing, pulling, and fighting while at school. Students should be expected to show consideration for their teacher and their classmates by complying with the following examples of standards:

- There should be no talking back or arguing with teachers or staff. Prompt and cheerful obedience is expected. Requests from a teacher should not have to be repeated.
- Students should not talk while the teacher is talking, or interrupt other students during class discussion.

---

[69] Mills, 109

- Students should not bring laser pointers, radios, MP3 players, I-pods, or personal CD players to school.
- Students should be held responsible for damage done to school property, including textbooks. Book covers should be required to protect your curriculum materials.
- Be punctual and regular in attendance. Be seated when the bell rings.
- Dress in compliance with the uniform policy. If found to be in violation, accept correction and consequences graciously and respectfully.
- Remain at home due to illness and until temperature has returned to normal for a period of twenty-four hours.
- Work responsibly and independently in the classroom without distracting others unnecessarily.
- Public displays of affection should not be permitted at school or during school activities.
- For obvious reasons: do not allow students to pass notes, throw things, climb or horse around in the classroom, or vandalize school property (desks, chairs).
- Students should not chew gum at school.
- Students should not write on the whiteboards or touch the teachers' desk and materials without the permission.
- Guns or knives are prohibited on the school grounds.

## Additional Recommendations for Teachers

Teachers should pray for love, wisdom, patience, and guidance on a daily basis. When possible, your staff should diffuse student confrontations with humor or a gentle word, not escalating the situation. However, if a confrontation develops, it is important that the students understand that they are under the teacher's authority.

- A teacher should never begin speaking to the entire class until they have the attention of all the students. They should never "talk over" conversations that the students may be having.
- If a large number of students are misbehaving during a discussion or review game, the teacher should end the discussion and finish the lesson with written work.
- *Late Assignments*: If an assignment is turned in one day late, the grade should be reduced by ten percent. If the assignment is turned in two days late, the grade is reduced by twenty percent. Assignments turned in more than two days late (unless due to an unplanned absence or a planned absence of three days or more) receive a zero.
- *No book/pencil/paper, etc*: Students should not be allowed to leave class to retrieve a forgotten item. However, they should be allowed to borrow a necessary item from a fellow student. Students need accountability, as well as consequences for their actions.

- *Dismissal*: Teachers should not dismiss their class early as it will disrupt other classes. They should always have some productive way to fill a few minutes.
- *Eating/Drinking*: Students should not be allowed to eat during class (with the exception of parties).
- *Paper Formatting Guidelines*: Enforce the requirements for manuscript form on all relevant written assignments.
- *Bathroom Requests*: Generally, students should be allowed to use the bathroom as requested. If one student or a class begins to abuse this, a new rule should be made.
- *Room Cleanliness*: Last period teachers should see that some students pick up and straighten the classroom each day before they leave.

## Controlling Student Talking

It is not surprising that all schools have problems with uncontrolled student talking. As a Christian institution, we should seek to train students to think critically from a biblical worldview, as well as give them the tools that they need to express themselves logically and eloquently. However, it can become a problem and may need to be addressed. Following are a few helpful hints for your teachers:

- Plan lessons that develop student interest. By doing this, they may eliminate uncontrolled talking in class.
- Develop and use a seating chart in order to help control classroom discussion. However, this has limited effectiveness. Suggest a periodic change in seat assignments as necessary in order to control talking.
- The lecture method is the most difficult style of teaching. If using this method, they should be prepared to control student responses.
- Require that students raise their hand, stand, and be recognized by the teacher before speaking. This also promotes the practice of respect.
- Be consistent in enforcing rules and discipline for all forms of talking without permission.
- Students should be praised when their behavior meets the classroom standards.

## Discipline as a Result of Student Talking

The sin of disruptive student behavior in class is *selfishness*. Disrupting the lesson demonstrates a lack of consideration for other students who want to learn. The following are guidelines for handling such disruptions, as well as minimizing their future effectiveness:

- *First Offense:* Rebuke the student publicly. Gain eye contact with the student, identify the inappropriate behavior, and let them know that you do not want them to do that again. If the offense was committed in public, i.e., in view of other students, it is appropriate to rebuke the student in public. The teacher may choose to move the student to another desk at this time or record their name on the board.

- *Repeated Offense*: This is the second offense during the same period. The first discipline effort has been ineffective. Teachers may choose to not allow the student to participate in class discussion. If the student rejoins the discussion and misbehaves again, they should be sent to the office for rebellion.

## Posture - Position Recommendations

You many also choose to adopt a posture and positions rule for students. The following is one that I have successfully adopted in our K-12 school.

- *Position 1:* Feet on floor. Chair is close to desk. Good posture. Hands folded on desk with eyes on teacher
- *Position 2:* Chair pushed back slightly with feet remaining on floor. Ready to stand-up with straight posture
- *Position 3*: Standing straight and tall. Arms and hands to the side.
- *Position 4*: Sitting in regular work position. A more slightly relaxed position than position #1. Students are in this position most of the day for their seatwork.

## Uniforms and Dress Code

The purpose of school uniforms is to foster a sense of unity among the students, to provide a consistently attractive and neat appearance, and to avoid peer pressure in matters of dress. Below are additional reasons to adopt a uniform code.

- The neat appearance created by a uniform code enhances a ready-to-learn atmosphere.
- A uniform code instills school spirit and a sense of belonging, while providing enough choice to allow for individual expression. The student is part of a group identity that strives for excellence and the code establishes a tradition.
- A uniform code saves time, since most uniform items, including accessories, can be purchased at the same source. This may save parents energy as well. In addition, time may be saved each morning as the "what to wear" issue is eliminated.
- Having a uniform code saves money by de-emphasizing the social impact of dress while helping focus the students on character and academic issues.
- Uniform codes also address security. On field trips, students in uniform may aid the teachers in keeping track of everyone. On the playground or in the school, teachers and staff can clearly identify students from outsiders.

Parents and students alike should be required to read your uniform policy. They need to agree, in writing, to uphold it. Your student parent handbook should list specific appearance guidelines and compliance expectations such as:

- *Dress neatly* - All shirts tucked in, shoes tied, no holes/tears in clothes, clothing appropriately sized for the wearer.
- *Be clean* - Recently washed/bathed and hair kept.
- *Be modest* - Skirts and shorts should be reasonable and modest lengths. Outlandish or distracting clothing or appearance will not be allowed.
- *Hats* - Unless granted permission for special days or events, students should not wear hats while in the school building. Students who do so should have their hats confiscated and not returned until the last day of school.

All students should wear the designated school uniform unless otherwise specified by the administrator. New enrollees should wear "dress code attire" until uniforms can be obtained. Teachers and staff members should check the students regularly to ensure that each student is in compliance with the uniform code.

## Enforcement

The school administration should determine if there is a violation of the dress code, either in fact or in attitude. Students not complying with the code should be required to rectify their appearance as quickly as possible. Cheerful, consistent compliance should always be expected. Grumbling and challenging attitudes need to be subject to disciplinary action.

When a student is found to be in violation of the uniform guidelines, a verbal warning should be given. Subsequent violations should be recorded on a violation notice form that is mailed to the parent. (See Appendix C for sample violation.) If a student continues to violate the uniform guidelines, he/she should be sent to the school office where the parents are called to bring the proper uniform attire for their child. This will assist in holding the parents and students accountable to their agreement.

## Office Visits

When is it appropriate to send a student to the office? You, as an administrator, should help teachers understand that they are the students' immediate authority and need to maintain control of the discipline among the students in their class. Accordingly, their judgment and handling of problems, within the constraints of biblical principles (e.g. restitution, apologies [public and private], swift/painful punishment, restoration of fellowship, and no lingering attitudes), are to be accepted and supported by students, parents, and administration. However, when situations arise where the student's behavior is flagrant, frequent, or fails to elicit a response of repentance, the offending student should be sent to the office for more serious discipline. This level of discipline will require communication with the parents and needs to be documented in the student's permanent file.

As in all other areas of the education at your school, love and forgiveness need to be an integral part of the discipline of a student. It is, however, vital for all concerned to realize that maintaining an orderly atmosphere in the school and the classroom is critical to the learning process. The following are some basic behaviors that should automatically necessitate discipline from the respective principal or administrator (versus the teacher). Those behaviors include:

- *Disrespect* shown to any staff member. The staff member will be the judge of whether or not disrespect has been shown.
- *Dishonesty* in any situation while at school, including lying, cheating, and stealing.
- *Rebellion*: I.e., outright disobedience in response to instructions.
- *Fighting*: I.e., striking in anger with the intention to harm another student.
- *Obscene language*: including taking the name of the Lord in vain.

During the office visit, the respective principal or administrator should determine the nature of the discipline. He may require restitution, janitorial work, parental attendance during the school day with their child, formal attire to be worn by the student to school, corporal punishment, or other appropriate measures consistent with biblical guidelines.

If for any reason a student receives discipline from the principal or administrator, the following methods should be observed:

- The first two times a student is sent to the office for discipline, the student's parents should be contacted and given the details of the visit. The principal or administrator should make a note of each occasion that the parents are contacted after an office visit, and enter that record in the student's file. The parents' assistance and support in averting further problems should be sought.
- The third office visit should also be documented and parent contact made.
- Should the student require a fourth office visit, a two-day suspension should be imposed on the student. A meeting with the student's parents and administrator should be required for the student's re-admittance.
- If a fifth office visit is required, the student should be expelled from the school.

## Expulsion and Suspension

As a Christian administrator, you should realize that expelling a student from your school is a very serious matter and should always be carefully dealt with on a case-by-case basis.

Forgiveness and restitution are fundamental to total discipline. However, should a student and his parents not be able to eliminate behavioral problems before a fifth office visit, the student should be expelled. Serious acts may result in bypassing the office visit process and an expulsion imposed immediately. Examples of such serious misconduct could include acts endangering the lives of other students or staff members, gross violence, vandalism to the school facilities, violations of civil law, or any act in clear contradiction of scriptural commands. Students need to be made aware that they are subject to school discipline for serious misconduct, even if it occurs after school hours.

## Re-Admission

It is your sole discretion to re-admit a student that had previously been removed from school. This should be determined based on the student's attitude and circumstances at the time of re-application. The student should remain on continual probation, as well as be aware that they can be refused reenrollment for the following school year.

## Conclusion

As we consider the area of discipline, administrators and their staff should realize that learning cannot take place without it. We should remember that the word "disciple" comes from the Latin root meaning "one who learns." If your goal as an administrator is to provide an excellent education, you must be able to provide an atmosphere that is conducive to that goal.

# Chapter 5

# Personnel Guidelines

As administrators, we must aim to cultivate Christian qualities in our staff, desiring them to be professional and diligent in their work, gifted in teaching, loving their students, as well as their subjects. They should clearly understand Christian education, how it will function in their classroom, as well as how their work fits into the whole; that they possess a lifelong hunger to learn and grow; and that they have opportunity to be refreshed and renewed. The goal is to see them coach and nurture new staff, while serving as academic mentors to students. We should strive to see our staff continually mature in Christ, growing in the knowledge of God, as well as their own children walking with the Lord.

## Teachers – The Key Element

The teacher is the leader of the classroom and will prayerfully use the time delegated by parents wisely, as well as model an exemplary Christian life to the students entrusted to your school. The teacher plans, implements, and oversees all instruction within the classroom. The teacher should have a heartfelt desire to develop the students into mature, able and responsible Christians. Having the spiritual maturity, academic ability, and personal leadership qualities to "train up a child in the way he should go," the teacher maintains a servant heart and an attitude to do all things to the glory of God.

Teachers should:

- Recognize the role of parents as primarily responsible before God for the education of their children and be prepared to assist them in that task.
- Demonstrate the character traits of enthusiasm, courtesy, flexibility, integrity, gratitude, kindness, self-control, perseverance, and punctuality.
- Meet everyday stress with emotional stability, objectivity, and optimism.
- Maintain a personal appearance that is consistent with that of a Christian in cleanliness, modesty, good taste and always in accordance with the school's guidelines.
- Use acceptable English in both written and oral communication.
- Demonstrate respectful submission and loyalty to authority.

Require a teaching applicant to be a mature, born-again Christian, a college graduate or mentored teacher, and certified or certifiable where appropriate. Foremost, they should have a desire and a calling from God to teach in a Christian school.

## Hiring and Managing Staff

As the administrator, you are responsible for not allowing conditions that are unfair, unsafe, unbiblical, undignified, or unlawful. Accordingly, pertaining to paid staff, the administrator *should not*:

- Discriminate on the basis of race, national origin, age, handicap, gender, or military status
- Operate without written personnel policies, which clarify personnel rules for staff, provide for effective handling of grievances, and protect against wrongful conditions
- Discriminate against any staff member for expressing an ethical dissent
- Prevent staff from grieving to the board when internal grievance procedures have been exhausted or the employee alleges that board policy has been violated to his/her detriment.
- Fail to acquaint staff with this policy.
- Fail to employ teachers that meet the approved qualifications. Accordingly, all teachers and administrative personnel must:
    o Profess a personal faith in Jesus Christ as Savior and Lord and maintain a positive Christian testimony.
    o Be an active participant in a church of Christian faith. There can be no deviation in the belief system of the applicant from the Statement of Faith.

## Staff Church Attendance

It is always a challenge to make sure the staff members at your school are being held accountable and under a local congregation. Church pastors are a valuable resource for accountability. During your career as an administrator, you will inevitably call upon a local pastor regarding a staff member, for problems with: marriage, children, bitterness, disrespect, unprofessional behavior, promptness issues, appropriate dress, general behavior and more. Churches are a necessary link to the health of a Christian school. The school cannot develop godly character within individuals on its own. Local churches ensure that individuals follow the same principles and tenants of Christian behavior by holding to a scriptural standard.

Evangelical Christian fellowship is defined as any church in substantive agreement with your school's Statement of Faith. All staff and faculty members should be required to regularly attend any local protestant evangelical Christian fellowship. You should be prepared to answer any questions about which churches meet this criterion. If there is still a question, it should be referred to the school board. It is important to remember that your school is only as healthy as the local body of churches it represents.[70]

---

[70] 1 Cor 1:10

## Staff and Student Relations

In order to facilitate proper, professional relationships and inhibit potential sinful, destructive behaviors between staff and students, the following guidelines should be understood as representative of the practices and philosophies of the school.

- Staff members are to remember that they serve as professional, adult role models before the students.[71] Relationships between staff members and between staff members and students are to be friendly and courteous, not familial or intimate.

- Staff members are to be careful that any physical contacts and verbal interchanges with each other and with students avoid even the appearance of impropriety.[72]

- Flirtation, sexual innuendos, casual disrespect toward authority, excessive familiarity, etc., are examples of the kind of unprofessional and inappropriate behavior that will not be tolerated. Necessary and cautionary measures required to limit these kinds of behaviors should be corporately and individually taken.

- If it is necessary for a male staff member to spend time alone with a female student or staff member, it should be arranged that they are easily visible to the public (e.g. an open door, windowed room, etc.)

- Staff members should not travel alone in a car with one student of the opposite sex.

- On any school-sponsored trips lasting overnight and involving students of both sexes, the spouses of chaperones should accompany their spouses. Single staff members may be included on such trips only with the prior approval of the school administrator.

## Dress Code for Staff Members

All staff members, teachers, administrators, office personnel, and maintenance staff alike, serve as models of adult Christians to the students. They should always portray attributes of cleanliness, modesty, and be well groomed. Therefore, the appearance and dress of staff members is always to be given serious attention. Maturity and modesty in dress, appearance, and overall behavior should be required. For example:

- Jeans of any color, dirty or torn clothing, tennis shoes, and similar casual apparel should not be worn unless required for a field trip of a nature that would damage good clothing.

- Women should be encouraged to wear dresses as frequently as possible. Make-up should be used sparingly.

- Men should also be encouraged to wear sport or dress slacks and ties. Hair, including facial, should be neat and clean.

---

71  Ti 2:7,8
72  1 Pt 2:12

## Guidelines for Staff/Teacher Evaluation

Evaluations of teachers are mandatory for any educational institution that purports to be accountable to its patrons. Constructive criticism, as well as positive feedback, are valuable tools for the growth of your staff. Teaching performance should be evaluated to determine effectiveness and ways of improving. It is in the best interest of everyone connected with your school, especially teachers and students, that regular, formal evaluations be conducted. Simply put, evaluations are done to help your teachers teach better.

- All teachers, full or part time, should be observed twice the first semester.
- New teachers should be formally observed once each quarter.
- All evaluations are confidential between the administrator and the teacher. At appropriate times, the board may be privy to evaluations.

Prior to visiting a teacher's class for a formal observation, meet with the teacher to set a mutually agreed-upon time. During this meeting you can determine the lesson to be observed and what particulars, if any, your focus will be on. At this point, you can review the teacher's job description and address any questions on how they will be evaluated. (See Appendix D for sample forms.)

A post-evaluation conference should be arranged within three days of the observation. The completed observation form, including your comments and recommendations, should be given to the teacher. Questions and comments regarding the evaluation are addressed at this time. If the teacher has a concern regarding the evaluation and desires another evaluation to be done, before it becomes part of their personnel file, you should comply with this request. Both the administrator and teacher sign the year-end evaluation form. The original form should be placed in the teacher's personnel file, a copy made for your keeping, as well as one given to the teacher.

## Morale - Keeping a Healthy Balance

Staff morale can be affected in a variety of ways. Remember, negative attitudes are contagious. Remove any individuals who do not meet the school expectations and requirements of your administration. The bible tells us, "When the scoffer is punished, the simple is made wise; but when the wise is instructed, he receives knowledge."[73] However, refrain from disciplining the entire staff for the mistakes of a few individuals. Be sure to give one positive comment for every negative one—balance is vital in this area.

It is also essential to keep your staff growing, challenged, and content. You can motivate your employees by rewarding those who have met a standard or an expectation set by your administration. Lift up these individuals in front of their peers with recognition such as: "Teacher of the Year" or "Feature Teacher of the Month" awards at staff meetings. As an

---

73 Prv 21:11

administrator, you will inevitably be pulled in dozens of directions, however make yourself available to your teachers and staff. Write them notes of praise and encouragement, as well as make time to dialogue.

## Training & Certification

You may consider paying for continuing education, training, or certifications for your staff members. This should be determined on a case-by-case basis. Two major considerations for approval should be the individual's longevity potential with your school, as well as monies available within the budget. Ensure that all requests for approval and or financing are submitted to your office.

Encourage your staff to obtain any necessary certifications or training needed to benefit their job efficiency. It is important to recognize and reward these individuals with awards such as a pay raise, plaque or gift, school blazer and/or corporate body recognition for attaining any required certification(s).

## Compensation Guidelines

As administrator, you will determine base pay levels and salary schedules for teaching and office staff. When considering personnel positions and salaries for your school, you should consider several things. What would the cost be to replace a specific grade teacher? What is the market value of that position? For example, the principal's position is more challenging to replace. The responsibilities that this position entails place it on a more knowledgeable and strenuous level. Daily interactions with students, teachers, parents, corporation members, grandparents, and individuals within your community require him to be well rounded and well versed. As a result, the market value of this position is greater as well as the salary.

Salary scale principles apply to teachers throughout the various grade levels. I have found it beneficial to tier teacher salaries within grade levels, taking into consideration responsibility, qualifications, and the market value of staff replacement. It is easier to replace a K-2 teacher, as their market value is significantly less. At this level, the base salary should remain the same. As we move up to grade levels 3-5, teaching will require more content knowledge and as a result the base salary will be slightly higher. As the grades progress to middle school, teachers should master deeper and broader subject knowledge, as well as build upon what the students have learned in the previous grades. Again, with grade progression, the salary ladder increases.

Along with grade progression, student mental capacity increases, they grow larger physically, socialization and interaction also increase, while their ability to think, socialize and interact, demand more energy from your staff. High school students in grades 9-12 are more dynamic now, as they have been taught logic and grammar. They require a higher skill set and knowledge level from teachers. As these needed qualifications increase, it will become more difficult to find and replace a secondary teacher. They need to have a great deal of information at their disposal in regards to rhetoric, debate, as well as in the areas of physics, chemistry, calculus, apologetics and more. This educational stage is the apex of the information pyramid. Secondary teachers should encompass expertise in many subject areas and therefore are the highest paid teachers on staff.

I have been asked, "How do you look at that in regards to the total cost?" One thing I always remind my K-2 and 3-5 teachers of is the *cost per classroom*. The cost per classroom in grades K-5 is often equivalent or surpasses the cost of what the high school teachers are being paid. Phonics and grammar school teachers often have an assistant, requiring a teacher salary in addition to a salary for the assistant. If you add those up, they are often equivalent to or even more than a high school teacher's salary. Average these costs out for your school, as they will enable you to justify a salary scale. By doing this, I am able to fairly justify paying the upper level teachers a higher salary.

Positions Defined:
- Full-time staff: teachers who teach at least 4.4 to 6 periods daily
- Part-time staff: teachers who teach less than 4.4 periods daily
- Administrative staff: staff whose main responsibilities are administration
- Other employees: janitor, building maintenance, bookkeeper, etc

Other factors that should be taken into consideration include: longevity with the school, workload, and other components such as increases related to degree attainment or certifications. Part-time teaching pay should be based on the portion of a six-period day the teacher teaches. You also establish the salaries for other principals, the Development Officer, Athletic Director etc., as well as set the hourly wage. The board, on the other hand, should annually set the salary of the head administrator.

## Employee Leave of Absence Guidelines

As head administrator, you solely authorize staff leave requests, as well as make any necessary salary decisions according to the employee's time off from work.
- *Staff/Staff Member:* all employees with a written ministry/job offer.
- *Personal Leave:* unplanned, non-emergency time taken from what would otherwise be a staff member's normal working hours/days.
- *Sick Leave:* available in the event of employee's, spouse's, or child's illness or minor injury.
- *Emergency Leave:* unplanned, but necessary time off due to serious circumstances such as illness (personal or family not covered under sick leave above), death in the family, serious injury, etc.

- Any leave taken above and beyond what is authorized should be designated as leave without pay
- Leave days should not be accumulated from year to year
- You may choose not to recognize any form of maternity leave, with the explicit biblical desire for the mother to be with and raise her young child. If a female staff member becomes pregnant while under a work agreement with the school, under the direction of her husband and doctor, she may work as long as considered wise. If she needs to leave before the final working date stated on the work agreement, a replacement should be obtained to fill the entire remaining period.

## Family and Medical Leave Act (FMLA):

As an educational institution, your school is considered a covered employer for the purposes of the Family and Medical Leave Act (FMLA) and should comply with the requirements of this act. To be eligible for FMLA leave, an employee must have worked for at least 12 months and at least 1,250 hours (approximately 31.5 weeks for full time staff) prior to the leave time. The employee is responsible for making the request for this leave 'as soon as is practicable' and may be required to provide additional information for consideration.

## Personal Leave Guidelines

- A staff member may request up to three days of personal leave without forfeiture of pay each academic year. A day is calculated as three increments of the normal working time. For example, if a teacher has only two classes per day, the leave available is equal to missing each of those classes three times.
- Requests for personal leave should be submitted in writing at least one week prior to the planned leave. Granting leave on shorter notice may be at your discretion.
- A staff member, taking personal leave, should be solely responsible for arranging a substitute. Administration should be made aware of these arrangements prior to the leave.

## Sick Leave Guidelines

- Full-time employees may take five sick days per year. Part-time employees may receive an amount of sick leave calculated and allocated based on the percent of time or periods worked per week. This should be stated on their individual employment contract.
- Staff members needing to take time off work for typical illnesses (flu, colds, etc.) should immediately contact their appropriate supervisor to explain the circumstances and potential loss of time related to their problem.

## Emergency Leave Guidelines:

Staff members should be granted up to five consecutive days emergency leave without any loss of pay should emergency circumstances of following occur:
- Extended recovery from injury or illness, but not requiring hospitalization.
- Loss of immediate family member and resulting funeral attendance.
- Illness or injury of immediate family member (necessitating staff member's presence).
- Circumstances resulting from wife giving birth.

You, as administrator, are authorized, to grant a staff member additional days if deemed appropriate or necessary. These days may be granted with or without pay due to circumstances in which:
- Loss of pay would greatly aggravate the staff member's current crisis.
- In all probability, the staff member will be able to return to work no later than the end of the consecutive ten days.
- The staff member has consistently demonstrated, through time and practice, a high degree of reliability and punctuality.
- The unique circumstances of the current emergency make it highly unlikely that another such situation will occur within the foreseeable future (at least the current school year).

If a staff member's emergency situation requires a prolonged (more than ten days) absence from work, the staff member should review the school's disability insurance policy. If eligible, the employee should submit a disability claim to the insurance company.

## Employment Separation/Termination Guidelines

If the separation of employees or termination becomes a necessity, the following guidelines may be helpful:
- *Voluntary Separation*: employees may choose to voluntarily resign at the culmination of a standard work agreement period.
- *Unforeseen Circumstances:* due to events such as death, disability, school closure, etc., the employee may not be able to continue his work.
- *Non-Renewal of Work Agreement:* at the normally scheduled time for re-signing the annual work agreements, the employee may not be offered a new work agreement.
- *Dismissal*: immediate dismissal of an employee is always an option that the administrator may exercise for discipline. This is to cover unforeseen circumstances of gross misconduct on the part of an employee.

Promptly address and meet with the staff member and discuss your concerns. After listening carefully, thank them for meeting with you and state that you will "consider what was discussed." Be in prayer and take enough time, even several days if necessary, to consider the situation and take action. Many administrators get themselves into trouble within this area, as they want to respond and remedy the situation immediately. Proverbs 14:29 reminds us, "He who is slow to wrath has great understanding, but he who is impulsive exalts folly."

Reasons for dismissal should result from the following:
- Two or more very low evaluations without notable improvement
- Immorality
- Mistreatment of or harshness with students
- Blatant disrespect toward parents, staff or students
- Disrespect to or blatant disobedience to you, a principal or others in school authority

## Do's & Don'ts of Employee Dismissal

Avoid legal traps by following a well laid out dismissal procedure. Proper, clear communication and documentation is crucial! administrators should always remain humble and subdued in a conflict meeting. *Never* rise to or meet the level of anxiety of a disgruntled employee remembering, "A quick tempered man acts foolishly."[74]

*Important Steps to follow*:
- Present a written warning(s) to the staff member. Remember to keep a copy in the employee's permanent file. Document everything!
- Arrange a conference with the staff member's immediate supervisor, specifying the time allotted for correction (if restitution is offered)
- A follow-up evaluation conference should be held at the end of the specified time of correction.
- If adequate improvement is not apparent, immediate dismissal is in order.

To eliminate uncertainty or any legal questioning of your dismissal process, be more precise than simply stating, "Dismissal will occur in the event of gross conduct." List *specific* instances in your staff handbook and employee contract that will result in immediate termination such as:
- Disrespect and/or disobedience for authority
- Acts of immoral conduct
- Un-Christ like behavior
- Three poor evaluations without improvement

---

[74] Prv 14:17

For additional legal protection, have each staff member sign a form at the beginning of the school year, stating that they "have read and agree to abide by the school guidelines." By signing this, your staff is bound to uphold your school's Christian rules and expectations. Be sure to file these completed forms in the unfortunate event you have a resentful employee. Keep in mind that in legal matters, a short response is always the best response. Avoid lawsuits claiming a wrongful or discriminatory discharge by:

- Documenting each instance. Keep a good paper trail!
- Meeting with the employee and refer directly back to the staff handbook. Identify the area(s) of disobedience by re-reading the staff expectations together verbatim.
- A witness or third party is an additional source of protection. For clarification purposes, as well as to eliminate any incorrect or accusatory recollections of an employee conflict meeting, have your administrative assistant take notes on what is discussed.
- Suspending an employee with pay, in order to protect the morale and health of the school.

Remember, disgruntled or disobedient staff members are a cancer within an otherwise healthy organization. Remove them quickly and quietly, divulging no personal information toward staff and parent inquires. Be familiar with your legal statutes regarding "employment at will," and "term contracts" for independent schools. If you find yourself in a difficult personnel situation, call on another experienced administrator for counsel and feedback. There is wisdom in a multitude of counsel. Proverbs 15:22 instructs us, "Plans fail for lack of counsel, but with many advisers they succeed."

# Chapter 6

# Athletics

## Athletic Philosophy

Sports can illustrate powerful principles and metaphors of biblical truths. Virtues such as discipline, trust, perspective, stamina and faith develop strong athletes with strong Christian character. God has gifted students with abilities in many areas such as athletics, drama, music, and more. Your school should provide opportunities for students to develop and use their God given abilities in these areas. Athletic programs enhance the morale of your school by allowing students and parents to express school spirit, as well as show your programs to the broader community. More importantly, when done biblically, participation in a Christian athletic program encourages a student in their walk with the Lord. They learn that diligent teamwork, a strive for excellence, as well as Christian integrity, reveal their commitment to Jesus Christ.

Christ-like character and behavior should be encouraged from all athletes, fans and coaches. Whether home or away, ahead or behind, our words and actions during athletic competitions should glorify the Lord! Regardless of opponent conduct during sporting events, words should be uplifting, encouraging, and positive.[75]

## General Objectives and Guidelines

### Participation

Participation levels include middle school, junior varsity and varsity. Each athletic level has specific purposes to clearly exhibit the schools' primary goals and objectives. The following guidelines have been successful in the middle and high school departments of a Christian school.

- *Middle School:* The objectives of the middle school program are improvement through participation and the development of basic skills. Coaches teach basic rules and principles of the game. Middle school athletics need to give each student the opportunity to participate and grow in Christian sportsmanship character. Each athlete should be allowed to reasonably participate in every game/match contingent on his or her attitude and participation in practice. Playing time should vary according to the level of competition and the level of readiness for competition. Play time for games should remain contingent upon the athlete's attitude and participation during practice. All "cutting" decisions should be approved by the athletic director, in advance of announcing cuts to parents or participants.

---

[75] Eph 4:29-32

- *Junior Varsity (JV):* The objectives of junior varsity athletics are to reinforce basic skills, to start to develop advanced athletic skill and Christian character at an increased competitive level. At this level, each athlete should play and have the opportunity to experience a more intense, organized level of play. Each athlete should be allowed playing time, although not necessarily in every game. The amount should be determined by the players' skill, age, and attitude as viewed by the coach.
- *Varsity:* The objective of the varsity level is to exhibit impeccable sportsmanship and advanced excellence. Varsity athletics are highly competitive. At this level, the athlete will be scrutinized more thoroughly in his character, ability, attitudes and skills. The most qualified athletes should be allowed on the varsity team. Playing time should be at the discretion of the coach.
- A maximum of twenty athletes should be carried on the combined roster for JV and Varsity volleyball and basketball teams. If more athletes turn out, coaches may make cuts. The varsity coach should make all cuts within the first week of practice. Prior to announcing cuts or final rosters, the coach should meet with the athletic director. They are to ensure that cuts made in compliance with school guidelines, and are in the best long-term interests of the athletic program.
- *Seniors participating in athletics:* If sufficient numbers of athletes turn out for the junior-varsity and varsity teams, seniors should be placed on the varsity roster. Most of the playing time at the junior varsity level is reserved for younger players. Early in the season, coaches are encouraged to meet individually with seniors who will receive limited playing time. Coaches should ask the athletes to consider whether they are willing to cheerfully accept limited playing time, as well as make a positive contribution to the team.

## Rules and Regulations

All applicable athletic association rules, school policies, and or guidelines established by your school's administration should apply to students participating in extracurricular programs. The administrator, athletic director, and all coaches, should be familiar with the rules and regulations. The athletic director should be responsible for ensuring that all players meet participation requirements, as well as notify coaches of any ineligible players. Coaches and directors should submit a list of participants at the beginning of the season, in order to facilitate this review.

Require that students have written parental permission to participate in athletic programs. This permission requirement should also include a signed medical authorization form completed by a parent or guardian. (See Appendix E for school release and medical authorization forms). A student who is absent from school more than one-half day, should not participate in extracurricular activities, either in practice or games unless the administrator gives specific approval.

## Classification and District

Classification of your school within an athletic association is determined by student enrollment in grades nine through twelve.

## Sportsmanship Ideals

The following ideals are listed within the NCISAA (North Carolina Independent Schools Athletic Association) handbook for athletic competitions:[76]

*Players should:*
- Play within the rules of the game
- Win with humility and lose without excuses
- Respect officials and accept their decisions
- Never play with intent to injure an opponent
- Never forget that they represent their schools, their coaches, and their families as well as themselves
- Respect the property and facilities of their opponents

*Coaches should:*
- Inspire in their players a love for the game and the desire to win
- Teach that it is better to lose fairly than to win unfairly
- Show restraint and respect when dealing with officials
- Serve as positive role models for their players
- Hold their players accountable for unsportsmanlike behavior

*Participating Schools should:*
- Have a responsibility to treat officials, opposing teams, and their spectators as guests
- Have a responsibility to educate their supporters to cheer the strengths and victories of their own teams and never to denigrate the performance of opponents or officials
- Not tolerate any spectator, either adult or student, whose behavior is disrespectful toward players, officials, coaches, or other spectators
- Not permit any type of spectator behavior that detracts from the proper conduct of the game

---

[76] North Carolina Independent Schools Athletic Association, "North Carolina Independent Schools Athletic Association Athletic Handbook." *available from http://www.ncisaa.org/rules.htm,* (accessed November 1, 2006).

## Try-outs

Try-outs, and the team cutting process, should be conducted during the first days of practice. Attendance is mandatory from the first day of try-outs. Generally, any student allowed to try-out late should have a valid emergency reason for doing so. They should be required to participate in at least five practices before game participation.

- If fewer try-out for a sport from a given grade than the designated total number permitted for that grade in that sport, the number allowed for other grades may be adjusted by the athletic director.
- Prior to making the final roster and cuts, the coach should meet with athletic director. The coach and athletic director are to insure that cuts are made within these guidelines in the long-term interest of the athletic program.
- Dual sport prospects should be subject to the same cutting criteria as all other athletes.

Attempt to include players who have been cut from the team by offering them opportunities of being a team manager, scorekeepers, statisticians, etc. Coaches may also choose to extend the opportunity for students to continue to practice with the team as an added incentive for participating as a manager.

## Academic Eligibility

Students participating in extra curricular activities should maintain an overall grade point average (GPA) of 2.5 or above at the end of the quarter (grading period) preceding the start of a sport season. This requirement should be maintained throughout the entire season.

## Sunday or Non-School Day Practices

Mandatory Sunday practices or optional practices should be prohibited. No organized practices—even optional attendance—should be held on Sundays. "Remember the Sabbath day by keeping it holy."[77] Except as approved by the athletic director, all non-school day practices should be optional.

## Games and Practices Over School Breaks

Be sure to notify families well in advance if their child's team must compete over a school break. Reiterate that your athletic program has considered the long-term success and ramifications of this requirement. Failure to participate in a required game over the break should require a consequence of non-play of a regular season game. This policy will enable you to be consistently competitive and remain in good standing with other athletic affiliates. An athlete's inability to attend optional practices should not result in negative consequences.

---

[77] Ex 20:8

## Single Season Dual Sport Participation

If academically eligible, a student may participate in two sports during a single sports season. The following conditions should apply to dual sport participation:

- The student should designate one sport as their priority sport. Participation in that designated sport would take precedence in the event of a conflict preventing participation in both on a single day.
- Although coaches should be obliged to allow dual participation, coaches may consider the impact of a dual participant in "cutting" and playing time decisions. Coaches should be allowed to decipher if a dual participant athlete is less able to make a positive team contribution, as opposed to a comparably skilled single sport athlete.

Dual sport participants need to attend as many practices, competitions, and games as possible in both sports. Thus, a volleyball player with a "day off" should attend tennis practice rather than going home to rest. Participation in both teams' practices should be encouraged when possible. Athletes are expected to maintain regular communication with coaches of both their primary and secondary sport teams.

## Practice and Event Guidelines

Coaches, players and parents of your school represent the name of Christ during public events. Therefore, compliance with the following guidelines should be expected:

- Comments by coaches, directors, participants, and spectators should be uplifting, positive, encouraging statements. Ephesians 4:29-32 instructs us, "Let no corrupt word proceed out of your mouth, but what is good for necessary edification, that it may impart grace to the hearers. And do not grieve the Holy Spirit of God, by whom you were sealed for the day of redemption. Let all bitterness, wrath, anger, clamor, and evil speaking be put away from you, with all malice. And be kind to one another, tenderhearted, forgiving one another, even as God in Christ forgave you."
- Verbal abuse and/or un-Christlike language or tones of speech toward athletes or referees is strictly forbidden. The athletic director should determine whether or not such abuse has occurred.
- Actions of coaches, directors, and athletes should set a positive, encouraging example of Christian conversation and behavior for spectators.
- Coaches should demonstrate Christ-like decision-making during a game where there is large lead. They should consider how the margin of victory will reflect on your school, as well as the impact it might have to the players, fans, and coaches of the opposing team. Coaches should be expected to take proper measures to avoid the humiliation of lop-sided scores, including

but not limited to, removing starters, playing players out of position, limiting who can score, even playing with fewer than the number of allowed competitors (if done discreetly).

- Conduct judged to be improper by the coach, administrator, or athletic director should result in immediate withdrawal from the activity, as well as further disciplinary action. All sportsmanship-related technical fouls, yellow cards, ejections, etc. should result in a game suspension for a first offense. Additional offenses should result in game suspensions.

- Coaches should be required to report any occasions where they themselves, or a team member, are officially rebuked for sportsmanship violations (technicals, yellow cards, ejections, etc.). Coaches and team members should be subject to suspension or removal for inappropriate behavior, even if an "official" rebuke is not given. Any ejection from a game or match by an official should result in a minimum of a two game suspension from athletic events.

- Coaches should limit "complaints" and "arguing" with officials to matters of rule interpretation and rarely, if ever, argue judgment calls. Philippians 2:14-16 tells us, "Do everything without complaining or arguing, so that you may be blameless and pure children of God, without fault in a crooked and depraved generation, in which you shine like stars in the universe as you hold out the word of life."

The preeminent goal of the athletics program should be to train young ladies and gentlemen to put their talents to work skillfully and graciously in order to extol and enjoy the excellencies of the Creator. In light of that fact, gracious and respectful behavior should be expected at all times toward coaches, players, officials and fans.

## Personnel and Volunteer Policies

### Coaches and Volunteers

The head coach is responsible for the proper training of an assistant coach or volunteer. These individuals should be required to agree to and adhere to all policies in your sports handbook. Coaches are to remember that they do not function above parental authority, but rather with delegated authority from the parents. Final acceptance for coaches or volunteers is the responsibility of the athletic director.

### Head Coach Job Description

The head coach reports directly to the athletic director. Within the framework of the entire athletic program, the head coach is to provide leadership in the ongoing development and improvement of his coaching area through coordination, planning, evaluation, and implementation of programs. His responsibility should be to assist in the coordination of all (6-12) programs within the following:

*During the season:*
- Implement "Athletic Standards" as outlined in your handbook.
- Provide information for transportation, officials and game management.
- Assume responsibility for constant care of equipment and facilities used.
- Assume supervisory control over all phases of teams in this program.
- Organize and schedule practice sessions on a regular basis with the idea of developing the athlete's greatest potential.
- Apply discipline in a firm and positive manner as outlined in the Athletic Handbook.
- See that building regulations are understood and enforced.
- Emphasize safety precautions and be aware of best training and injury procedures.
- Conduct himself and his teams in an ethical manner during practice and contests.
- Report a summary of all contests and provide any publicity information that would aid this program and his athletes.
- Instruct his players concerning rules and rule changes, new knowledge, and innovative ideas and techniques.
- Communicate to parents (in writing) all travel plans: game times, locations, directions, departure and return times.

*End of Season:*
- Arrange for the systematic return of all school equipment and hold the athlete responsible for all equipment not returned.
- Arrange for the issuance of letters and special awards.
- Arrange for cleaning, sorting, and inventory of all equipment.
- Be concerned with the care and maintenance of this facility by making recommendations concerning additions and improvements.
- Recommend any concerns about equipment that needs to be purchased or repaired.
- Maintain records of team and individual accomplishments.

*Contracts and Evaluations for Coaches*
- Coaches should sign a one-season contract with no guarantee of yearly renewal. Team performance should have no bearing on renewal or non-renewal of contracts.
- Coaches should be evaluated at the end of the sports season by the Athletic Director. This evaluation should include performance observations taken during practices and games, as well as input from athletes and their parents.
- In the event of a necessary dismissal, use termination guidelines as explained in Chapter 5.

## Team Managers and Assistants

Additionally, managers may attend away games with the team and enter at no charge. Coaches are responsible for acquiring needed managers, scorebook keepers, clock operators, ball boys, and linesmen. High school student managers may "Letter" after two years of service.

## Code of Conduct at Athletic Events

The greater purpose of your athletic program should be to move athletes toward Christ-likeness, by demonstrating the fruit of those who have His spirit within themselves. "When the Spirit controls our lives he will produce this kind of fruit in us: love, joy, peace, patience, kindness, goodness, faithfulness, gentleness, and self-control."[78] The following are some behaviors you should expect from all families that attend your athletic events:

- Be mindful of our witness to unbelievers. Colossians 4:5 reminds us to "conduct yourselves wisely toward outsiders…"

- Be mindful of our witness to our children. Our behavior gives our children an implied permission to behave the same way. "Let no unwholesome word proceed from your mouth, but only such a word as is good for edification…that it may give grace to those who hear."[79]

Coaches, students and parents alike are not to "boo," grumble, complain, chant derogatory remarks, cheer unkind or inflammatory cheers, taunt, ridicule, cheer unkindly or shout in anger, ridicule or criticize officials, referees, nor approach them in anger before, during, or after a game or match.

## Athletic Expectations and Etiquette

- Be appropriately dressed and outfitted for athletic competitions.
- Pre-game warm-up time is no time for horseplay. Drills should be done with a serious attitude, preparing for the upcoming competition.
- There should be no socializing with fans or family during warm-up time, half time, or any time until the game is over and post game activities are complete.
- Athletes should not talk to friends or family in the stands during the game.
- Game Day Apparel: It is a common tradition is for all athletes to wear full dress uniforms to school on game days.
- Players should never argue with or complain to or about game officials. They should *never* speak unkind or derogatory comments toward opposing players.

---

[78] Gal 5:22
[79] Eph 4:29

- If an injury should occur to a teammate or opponent, athletes should be expected to respectfully "take a knee" on the field or court and bow in prayer.
- Players should not respond to questionable referee decisions with any kind of verbal or body language indicating displeasure, shock, anger or negative emotion.
- A decision by an official is to be adhered to by coaches, parents, athletes, and the school administration without further discussion.
- After a game, players should line up single file to greet the opposing team with a handshake, congratulate them, and offer encouraging words.
- Athletes should keep all changing rooms, locker rooms, bench areas, fields, or dugouts, clean and removed of any debris.

All policies for student behavior adopted by your school Board should apply to athletic events. The following policies include: academic probation and discipline. The same consequences for disobeying the discipline standard of the school should apply toward misbehavior during extra curricular activities. When discipline is necessary, the coach may administer any of the following options:
- Suspension from part or all of practice(s)
- Suspension from one or more events
- Suspension from the team, with approval of the activities director

Parents should be notified beforehand of all major disciplinary actions. The coach is responsible to notify the athletic director of any discipline, who in turn should notify the parents. In the event a player is suspended from a team, participation fees should not be refunded.

All discipline should be administered in the light of the individual student's problem and attitude, and based on biblical principles, e.g. restitution, apologies (public and private), punishment restoration of fellowship, no lingering attitudes, etc. In order to maintain consistency, coaches should meet regularly with the athletic director.

**Practice Attendance Policy**

Consistent practice or attendance at scheduled practices should be required for athletic participation. In general, students should only be excused from practices for sickness, injury, doctor appointments, or family emergencies. Students should make a vigorous effort to notify coaches of their need to be absent for any of these circumstances.

Any athlete, who does not attend practice, fails to appear for a game, fails to make scheduled team or individual meeting, or fails to attend school on game day or practice days, should not be allowed to suit up for any game or games for a period of time to be determined by the coach and athletic director. Excessive absence from team practices, games or meetings may be cause for removal from the team.

It is expected that athletes commit to their school team above and before "outside" activities. For example, if a practice or game conflicts with a city league game, it should not be considered an excused absence. Coaches should use their discretion in allowing practice to be missed for other situations. It is important to require students to make up missed conditioning prior to participation in the following game. Absences should be treated as unexcused and the athlete should not be allowed to play for one-half of the next game or match (at least one half game benching per absence). Exceptions to the policy should require approval of the athletic director or administrator. Players who join the team after the season begins, should practice at least five days before participating in a game or match.

### Missed Academic Time for Athletics

Your school's policy for pre-arranged absences should apply to athletics as well. Athletes should discuss early game dismissals in advance with their teachers. They must be mindful that all academic assignments must be completed on time. Athletics should not take precedence over academic excellence.

## Awards Eligibility and Presentations

High school athletes may receive cloth letters for meeting the requirements outlined below.

- An athlete receives a letter for participation in his or her first varsity sport, along with the pin for that sport. All future varsity participation results in a pin only.
- Athletes not eligible for letters (i.e. junior-varsity athletes and those not meeting the specified requirements) should receive a certificate of participation.
- Students enrolling late in the season should participate in at least 50% of the season in order to be eligible for a letter.
- To be eligible for a letter, a student must not have been suspended or subject to any serious school or team disciplinary action.
- Students who manage a varsity team for two seasons may be awarded a letter.

Coaches may, at their discretion, recommend lettering for students who have not met the specific requirements but have shown dependability, determination and effort in all practices and games. The athletic director should give final approval for this exception.

Athletes should attend practices and matches faithfully, as well as work hard with a good attitude during games and practices, in order to achieve a letter or a pin. A coach may recommend to the athletic director that a student who has not met these criteria receive a certificate of participation. Such students should be notified, well in advance of the season end, if they have fallen short of these criteria. Parents as well should be notified of the problem in a timely manner.

## Award Schedule

These high school athletic awards may be given as follows: A letter and pin may be awarded to a student manager who fulfills their responsibilities for two *entire* seasons. Team captains should be recognized in each sport. Team captains receive a pin as well. Other awards that can be given are: Leadership Award, Most Improved Player, Best Defensive Player etc.

## Presentation of Awards and Certificates

Award programs should be scheduled at the end of each sports season. Middle school participants should receive a certificate of participation. These certificates should list special attributes of the athlete that the coach wishes to acknowledge. Coaches should not address negative or embarrassing qualities and/or characteristics of an individual instead commend them and present them with their certificate.

Managers sacrifice a great deal of time for the benefit of the team. Their service should be appropriately recognized as well. Do not forget to thank them publicly for their service. Parents who have assisted with the program (drivers, stats keepers, etc.) should also be recognized.

# Safety in Athletics

## Safety and Risk Management

During both practices and competition, coaches are responsible for continually evaluating facilities and coaching methodologies (drills, conditioning, etc.) for safety risks. This includes, but is not limited to, damaged or altered facilities (hole in the ground, wet gym surface, etc.) and equipment (cracked helmet or bat, etc.).

Coaches need to monitor any inherent danger of student athlete participation in their respective sports. What is the worst-case scenario? Coaches should always err on the side of safety and require students to have an annual physical before beginning a sport.

## Injury Related Unconsciousness

Any athlete, who becomes unconscious or blacks out for any length of time during a game or practice, is ineligible to continue practice or re-enter the game for the remainder of that practice or event. Parents should be contacted immediately.

## Insurance

It is recommended that you have each family check with their insurance provider for adequate medical coverage during sports activities. This could be critical for collision sports. Most insurance companies provide supplemental coverage for athletics.

## Scheduling Updates and Notifications

Questions pertaining to practice and game scheduling (times, locations, departures, returns, etc.) should be directed to the team coach and not the athletic department. Last minute changes can be posted on an athletic hotline that your school can create. This will insure clear communication on an hourly basis and can post detailed changes in schedules as they occur.

Another convenient way for coaches and parents to access scheduling information, cancellations and scores, is through a school website. Here, coaches and parents can sign up to receive automatic e-mail notification of schedule changes from the website. The website may also be used as a back-up source for parents to access your school's athletic handbook and other necessary forms.

## Additional Guidelines

### Inclement Weather Guidelines

Coaches and Athletic Directors should follow National Federation guidelines[80] on inclement weather disturbances. Assign staff to monitor local weather conditions before and during events.

- Lightning: Adhere to the following criteria for suspension and resumption of play.
    a. A thirty-second or less flash-to-bang count calls for removal of the athletes from the field to an appropriate shelter. That is, if you see a flash, however distant it appears and can count to less than thirty before the sound of thunder, leave the field promptly.
    b. Thirty-minute rule: Once play has been suspended, wait at least thirty minutes after the last flash of lightning is witnessed or thunder is heard prior to resuming play.
    c. No more than two thirty-minute delays will be allowed before either considering the game/practice cancelled/postponed. (Maximum of one-hour total delay time.)
- Develop an evacuation plan, including identification of appropriate nearby shelters. Indoors is best, an open but covered shelter next best, and cars are an acceptable third option.

All games postponed or cancelled due to inclement weather should be rescheduled at the earliest and most convenient date for both schools. Conference games should take precedence over non-conference games.

- *Soccer/Football/Lacrosse:* A game is considered complete if one half or more has been completed. If less than a full hour weather delay has occurred, every effort will be made to play as much of a full game as possible considering deadlines and safety rules.

---

80  National Federation of State High School Associations, *National Federation of State High School Association 2006-2007 Handbook*. *available at* http://www.nfhs.org/web/2004/01/nfhs_sports_publications.aspx (accessed October 1, 2006.

- *Baseball/Softball:* The game is considered complete after the completion of five innings.
- *Tennis:* Five matches should be finished to be considered complete (a minimum of three wins by either team is a complete match).
- *Cross Country/Track:* Generally is "complete" only when all events are complete.
- *Heat and Humidity:* Coaches should closely monitor athletes when temperatures are 90 degrees or above, especially on high humidity days. Allow frequent breaks for water, rest, and shade when the heat index is high.

## Athletic Fees

There should be a predetermined fee for both middle school and high school athletes. This fee should be paid before initial participation in any game or match.

## Uniforms and Game Apparel

Recommended uniform guidelines:
- Coaches should not distribute game uniforms until all fees and forms have been collected and approval has been given from the athletic department. Uniforms will be dispersed to the students at school before their first game. Athletic uniforms should be worn for games only; not for practices. The goal of the uniform is unity. With that in mind, expect athletes to dress in such a way as to promote unity over individuality.
- Uniforms should be returned by students on the day that team pictures are made at the conclusion of the season, or after the last game of the season.
- Uniform washing instructions should be adhered to, and tears or holes repaired as needed.
- Game shoes should be in recommended colors or combinations of those colors only.
- Game socks for each team should be uniform in color, style, and length, and issued with the uniform.
- For safety purposes, jewelry should not permitted in any form during game events.
- It is strongly recommend that male athletes purchase groin protection for sports.
- Uniforms should be worn in the most modest fashion possible.

## Transportation

Your athletic director should be responsible for arranging transportation to all away games. He should determine what time the students will need to be released from class and make sure it is properly communicated. Early release should not be determined by the coaches.
- All parents should be required to sign a permission form allowing their child to be transported by the school (see a sample in the Appendix I).
- At least one coach should ride with the students to all away games.

- Coaches should always travel with a copy of each student's emergency medical form. The athletic director should provide the coaches with these forms.

All drivers transporting students should fill out a driver application form, (see Appendix I for sample form) as well as receive school approval before driving well in advance of the planned trip. Every driver should be approved by the school before driving students. Do not allow students to ride in a poorly maintained vehicle, or one without adequate seatbelt restraints.

## Equipment

Each coach should receive a copy of an inventory sheet at the beginning of each season. They should check the inventory sheet for accuracy when it is received. Coaches should be expected to return all equipment to the athletic director.

## Public Relations

All high school coaches and directors should make appropriate contact with the local newspaper. Coaches are expected to contact the newspapers after every contest outside the local circulation area, as well as after a local win. Encourage your coaches to make additional weekly contact with school and conference websites.

# Chapter 7

# Finances

When considering finances, the most important principal to remember is that all things have been given to us by God for *His* purposes, that He may manifest His glory in all our efforts. This includes, but is not limited to, those gifts that have been given to us by God in the way of monies, resources, facilities, and people. In Luke 12:48, God reminds us that "To whom much is given, much will be required." Whether we realize it or not, we demonstrate our faith and our beliefs by how we utilize these many gifts. Our testimony, which is being observed by all, is *evidenced* by our actions. Therefore, we must be above reproach and recognize the necessity for proper financial management.

As a Christian school, it is critical to operate within the financial means God has provided, regardless of needs and desires. We know, of course, that God will supply all of our needs.[81] We must be aware that others in the surrounding communities are closely observing our financial decisions as a Christian institution, as well as God's blessings of prosperity.

Financial management requires *competence* and *devotion* in equal parts; competence to make the best use of the resources available, and devotion to the educational ideals of your school. Every effort should be made to achieve these ideals *within* the resources available to the school. Assuming that the devotion has been sought and secured, though this may be no easy task, this chapter will concentrate on various aspects of financial competence and the practices that can frequently be improved.

## The Role of the Board

In the financial area, as in all others, policies at the board level are an essential point of departure. One of the board's main responsibilities is to develop clear and concise financial policies and to confirm answers to the following questions:

- To what extent should our school meet its operating expenses through tuition; to what extent should we rely on gifts?
- Who shall be responsible for budgeting?
- Who will control the financial performance of our school?
- How much money do we need to allocate to an emergency to ensure that money will be available for replacements—a central part of an institution.
- Should reserves for this emergency fund be subsidized by tuition or by development?

---

81 Phil 4:19

Questions such as these may seem basic, but it is surprising how many Christian schools are unprepared to answer them, or to *act* on them. Without clear answers, the administrator must operate in the dark—a very dangerous place to be. His decisions are bound to be haphazard since they have no frame of reference in which to relate. He is defeated before he can even get underway.

This is why the board, who oversees the administrator, should set clear parameters in regards to *expenditures* and *reserves*. This will allow him to work freely within the given parameters. If in desperation the administrator tries to set his own financial policies, he is not only usurping what should be a main responsibility of the board, but he is running a grave risk that *his policies will not sufficiently support the overall objectives of the school*. As an example, the administrator may be able to see that certain parents are not fulfilling their financial responsibility to the school, yet he may *not* be able to grasp how this impacts public relations and other aspects of the school's operation.

As the board oversees the financial responsibility of a school, it is also their job to protect the institution as a business by being good stewards with all monies, paying staff appropriately and on time, and upholding all financial contracts. The board should also be required and prepared to deliberate credit and collections even if all parties involved are Christian. In my experience, I have seen how necessary it is for a school to have clear financial contracts with all parties, including but not limited to, the parents that are hiring them to educate their child(ren). At times the board may be required to hold parents to their financial obligation as outlined in their original contract. This contract should have clearly communicated all obligations and expected consequences of defaulting on their financial commitments. At times it may even be necessary to remind them of their responsibility before God (to pay in full and on time), holding true to their Christian word. Details for being *released* from their financial obligation should have been clearly stated in their contract in order to avoid any confusion, and also as a protection for the school.

I have personally been aware of situations where parents have attempted to sue a school for expecting funds they had obligated to pay, even when the family had the financial resources available. (Yes, even when the family professed to be Christian). Clear, concise contracts are a must for the benefit and protection of all concerned (see Appendix C and F for a sample contracts).

## The Role of the Administrator and Business Manager

### Administrator: Chief Budget Officer

One of the main points in discussing finances is clearly defining the responsibility for budget preparation and control. Since a budget is an "educational plan", it is inescapably your responsibility as an administrator to serve as the *Chief Budget Officer*. Your role is to assist and uphold the development of the school budget, its goals, and the long range objectives for the school. Other financial responsibilities should include:

- Developing the budget in its entirety
- Seeing it is reviewed and approved by the board
- Controlling performance within the budget
- Reporting actual vs. budget results to the board on a regular basis

Given these responsibilities, leadership is key in setting and achieving the school's long-range objectives and goals. Since the annual operating budget is a financial expression of the schools current activities, you should make sure the current annual budget is consistent with your planned long range objectives as they are understood by the board. You may choose to decentralize particular budget preparation responsibilities while maintaining close scrutiny and control via periodic reports. This will encourage initiative and secures much more willing cooperation on the part of all individuals who are spending the school's money. In this process, the role of the Business Manager is to assist you with necessary adjustments, as well as, help you prepare the final budget for the board.

If circumstances deem it necessary, you would be the one responsible for making decisions regarding transfers of monies from one line item to another. While monitoring finances, you may find it necessary to make large adjustments by relocating expenses being mindful to stay within the bottom line, especially if there is a large one-time needed expense. Although large budget adjustments should be rare, in wisdom you should consult the board for their approval and alert them of the unexpected changes. The school's budget history should be *studied* before the next budget preparation is underway. If there are historical trends that have required budgetary changes, they should be taken into account as you plan for the upcoming year.

Although it may be common practice for most administrators to make expenditure changes in the budget throughout the year, it is desirable and helpful for them to be provided with a contingency fund. This fund, will provide the needed resources when unforeseen circumstances arise. The amount of the fund should be determined by studying past year budgets and be a percentage of the budgets bottom line as opposed to a specific amount.

## Proposing Policies

As an administrator, it will be your duty to draw up tentative, but sound policies in which to operate. These policies should be submitted to the board for discussion, review and approval. Your school's policy governance manual should include guidelines for setting yearly parameters for reserved expenditures and monies. These financial policies should cover at least some of the following:
- The proper and most desirable balance among the various sources of income. (Tuition, fees, gifts, and incomes from development)

- A policy with the fee structure in regarding the payment and collection of fees. Tuition for example should not rise more than 1½ to 2% each year (a good policy)
- Responsibility for financial management and to the extent they are to be delegated in the policy governance manual.
    - o How the budget is to be planned and controlled.
    - o Provides budget updates (monthly and quarterly)
    - o Guidelines for preparation and operating of capital budgets
    - o How much money should we have in reserves?
    - o How much for capital improvements in regards to replacing a roof or parking lot?
    - o Policy governing items that need to be replaced or items that are going to impact school and resources for example a practice field, or purchasing land down the road for a high school (a policy for long term vision.)

The above areas should assist you in discerning which additional financial policies may be needed, or which policies require modification. Both you and the board should assume responsibility for formulating the *"need to submit policies"* that will help guide all concerned. Remember, *"boards set policies, administrators administer policies."* Both entities must work in tandem to insure that all school goals and objectives are being met.

## Budgets

### Two Types of Budgets

As you seek to develop a plan, it is imperative to think of a budget as a *planning tool*. There are generally two types of budgets:
- Operating budget: used for continual activities
- Capital budget: used for one-time expenditures

The *operating* budget is defined as the "school's financial plan," procuring all its current activities. This budget is crucial for the current and future financial health of your school. It describes in details the financial terms of how your school will achieve its educational and financial objectives. A six-year combined budget is also recommended as it will compare the previous five years to the projections of the upcoming year.

The *capital budget* serves a similar, but long-range purpose with regard to expansion of the facilities or as a one-time replacement cost. Both budgets are necessary and equally important. Competently practiced, the budget is not simply a once a year occurrence, but rather a continual process. It represents one of the most effective ways a school can achieve economical operation and success. It is a blueprint for future action, and should be drawn up as early as eighteen months or two years before the actual expenditures are made.

Keep in mind that the operating budget is an instrument of the school and not of its master. It is a *guideline,* not a precise chart to be followed ritually regardless of unexpected circumstances. Budgets are designed to "give you a plan," not to "*direct* the plan." If needs arise or plans require change, the budget should be designed in such a way as to allow you to work within the financial parameters and goals of the school while making the necessary modifications. Category parameters are meant to be tracking devices, not handcuffs. The ultimate "financial goal" for your institution should be the ability to pay your bills at the end of each month and year. To do this, you must have the flexibility in the line items with a strong intent to stay within the bottom line.

With an effective budget system, you can determine what is required in terms of personnel, supplies, materials, equipment, services, and facilities. You should be familiar with internal operational needs and be able to make decisions that will insure your school's programs and objectives are being met. For this to happen, you must oversee each requisition turned in for monies spent. It would be foolish to have one person overseeing the budget while never seeing the expenditures. In my opinion, you should see every check that is written and have a clear understanding where money is being spent, remembering that you are ultimately accountable and responsible to God, and other constituents, as you make sure that expenses are being well managed.

## Developing an Effective Budget

All schools have some version of a budget; however few have an *effective* one. One of the most common faults of school budgeting is developing a financial forecast based on what was spent the previous year. In lack of wisdom and wise counsel,[82] administrators assume that each year they will need at least as much as last year's figure with a little extra room for stretch. When budget estimates are made in this haphazard way, expenditures will automatically increase. With the absence of a precise plan or reasoning as to how the school's available monies should be spent, *financial trouble is inevitable.*

Another frequently encountered *weakness* in larger private schools occurs when the administrator develops the budget alone without any participation from other principals or athletic directors. This may appear in the short-term to save time, but it is crucial that the individuals who are *making expenditures* understand the parameters of the budget. Otherwise, they will have no particular conviction to abide by budgeting limits.

I have over time witnessed some schools that were so late with budget preparation, that they had actually started the next school year before the budget was even approved. This is very reckless and does not allow the budget to be used as a *control device* for keeping expenditures within planned boundaries. This more often than not, happens as a result of not providing periodicals, actual vs. budget expenditures, to the principals allowing expenditures to be

---

82  Prov 15:22

monitored. The end result: expenses begin getting out of control. If actions are not taken to correct the situation, serious financial consequences will follow.

Many private Christian schools are at fault when they treat "line item control" as a *minor* responsibility. It is a tremendous oversight and does not allow for *all* essential areas of the school to be properly provided for and enhanced; including, but not limited to, personnel, facilities, long-term planning, and vision. Attention to this detail is critical and should be one of the primary responsibilities of the board. At the same time, your school's goals and objectives must be clearly understood by all administrators/principals so that *they* are prepared to make educated decisions on a day to day basis.

## Establishing Good Budgetary Standards

As an administrator, you should consider the following standards and questions. How much will it cost per square foot to keep your school building clean? What will be the incurred cost of books per student? Below you will find recommended indicators you can use to determine cost and anticipated expenses.

- Student/teacher ratio
- Supplies per student
- Total cost per student
- Necessary athletic supplies and expenses per student
- Total administrator cost as a percent of operational procedures
- Operation cost as a percentage of total value of the facilities and the percent of total budget
- The total operating expenses per student

Ask yourself, "What is your bottom line?" Begin with discerning how much it will cost to educate and facilitate education within your facility. This will be the driving cost of your tuition. Line item costs are not only useful in developing your budget, but are necessary for analyzing specific deviations from it. For example, a budget should have a standard for school supplies on a per capita basis determined by the number of students. Reports showing significant deviations from this standard should be accompanied by an explanation of why additional monies were needed. The previous allocated amounts can be reevaluated and accommodated when the need is verified. This does not however take away from the importance of budget. The original budgetary goals are *necessary* and will allow a board and the administrator to develop a more accurate budget for the following year. It is recommended that your budget include each of the following line items. They should be broken out individually and categorized. I will give you examples of these line items in Appendix H along with examples of a monthly budget, a year-end budget, and a six year long-range budget.

Typical divisions of expenses should include:

- Administrative expenses include expenditures necessary for the operation of all the administrative offices. It can incorporate the director of development, the business manager, the athletic director and his assistant. It may include all that is needed to organize and run a school.

- General expenses may include taxes, printing costs, legal fees, auditor fees, and office supplies.

- Instructional expenses will cover salaries for teachers, social security costs, insurance, any pension plans, assistance, materials, books and anything that deals with the instruction of the school.

- Operation/maintenance expenses of the facility should include purchase of fuel, upkeep of vehicles, building and grounds cost, contracts with cleaning crews, lawn care, projects including playground equipment, and facility operations.

## Developing Long-Range Plans

More and more Christian schools are realizing the value of long-range planning. If they are to grow and survive, they must think more than one year ahead. Accordingly, many of them are beginning to develop long-range fiscal plans that project and anticipate expenses three to five years into the future. Such a plan, updated yearly, is useful to the board for evaluating such matters as: enrollment to be sought, necessary staffing and the size structure that will be needed to realize these goals.

If your school's goal is to increase substantially in size and yet maintain quality, it will be imperative that you have a *strong* staff. Your long range plans need to take into consideration the possibilities for locating and hiring the standard of staff required, keeping in mind that *an excellent product is directly related to excellent staff.* Such a plan will assist the board as they consider the effects of economic changes or the financial impact various policy decisions might make. Capital and operating requirements should be budgeted well in advance. With assistance from your business manager, it is your responsibility to prepare such a plan. The basic procedure is similar to that of the general operating budget, although less detail should be needed.

A three to five year plan should include revenue projected three to five years out with tuition and any possible fee increases. Projections for expenditures, salaries, supplies, personnel, and construction (the cost that larger enrollment would bring) should be included as well. Operation costs of your facility will likely rise with additional classrooms providing more rooms to maintain, more fields, parking, etc. There will also be additional items such as capital outlay due to the increase of expenses for a growing facility. A three to five plan, similar to an operating plan, should be divided into the following sections:

- Revenue
- Expenditures (broken down for administration, construction, operations, main & facility upkeep)
- Capital long range outlay

One of the benefits of creating long-range plans is the product of positive action it will demand of a board. In advance, they will need to discuss and discern the overall goals of the school. It is therefore critical for the administrator to know what the board envisions for the future of the school. Questions to consider might include: "What size should our institution seek to grow? What sources of funds need to be sought to encourage growth?" These, and similar questions, should produce at least tentative answers on which to base projections of future operating income and expenses knowing that they can be modified if necessary.

## Managing Deficits

If a deficit is imminent, you should fully understand the reasons for this financial decision and communicate it clearly to the board. This can only occur if you are fully aware of *all* the ongoing factors which affect the monies required to run the school verses the monies being spent. Equipped with this information, you can then discern whether monies should be pulled from other areas, such as development, in order to accommodate unexpected needs.

Communication therefore is key in making sound financial decisions, in addition to insuring the financial health of the school's future. *Over communication* is a must in areas susceptible to overspending. Prudence therefore should be demonstrated in creating a plan to meet those deficits. Schools *are not* beset with financial problem because the administrator or the board is not making plans. These problems occur due to actions not being taken to put the *plan to work*. As an administrator, you should be proactive and remember that the budget is used as a planning instrument. The school should have a systematic method of administering its finances on the basis of its goals as a whole. It can then direct its available resources of money and people to the matters of highest priority in areas of greatest importance.

Is a deficit really required? Often, many schools operate in such a way that the "squeaky wheel gets the oil," allowing individuals who ask persistently to receive the funds. You as an administrator should never give into these requests outside of considering the budget as a whole. You need to also clearly communicate school priorities to the individual making the request. This will allow you to govern in a way that demonstrates a steadfast commitment to the school's educational objectives. An example of this might be not allowing the art department to have twice as much money allocated to it than the English department. If you are aware of what is being spent and what the priorities are in relation to the objectives, you can discern what expenditures need to take place, and which ones may jeopardize the financial support for more critical needs. This will require you to "hold the line" in regards to expenses and to say "no" when approached with a request that is not in the best interest of the school.

## FFNA: Assisting Families with Financial Hardships

As you prepare a draft budget, one of the needs you will want to address is scholarships. One area of the budget that needs to be taken into consideration is the funds you will use to assist families who are struggling with financial hardships. A neutral company such as FFNA (Family Financial Needs Assessment) can assist you in this process. They facilitate by reviewing submitted applications and discerning which families should receive tuition deductions. You can begin this process by determining the amount of funds to allocate for this line item. The funds to assist these families will usually be a percent (somewhere between 4-6%) of the total budget. Provide the families requiring assistance with an application obtained directly from FFNA's website: http://www.ffna1.com/. Have the parents sign the packets out leaving their contact information while reminding them of the deadline to submit the completed request. This will assist you in following up with them before final decisions needs to be made. Families should not receive an allocation of over 50% tuition. Your responsibility in this process will be to take recommendations from FFNA and determine what is best for the school. Here is an example of allocated funds: If you have a two million dollar budget and within that budget 5% has been allocated to assist families in need, a company such as FFNA will make recommendation based on the amount of funds allocated for this purpose. You will however, have the final say where the funds are divided.

## Setting Up a Budget Calendar

There is no universal template of a budget calendar that will function for all schools. Schools that are fortunate enough to have all the initial work completed before the close of spring term, and who have a full enrollment with waiting lists by May or June, can approve their budgets for the upcoming year well before the end of the current fiscal year. I highly recommend you begin this process in January. Initial re-enrollment for current students will reveal the amount of open seats available. You can advertise in the community and continue family interviews as you receive new applications.

In May you should begin collecting tuition for the following school year. Our school draws a tuition draft the second week in May for the following school year. This allows us to see the number of families that have drafted their account therefore ensuring a secure number on which to project your budget on.

*December: Draft next years faculty budget, staff schedules, and elective offerings*

Begin developing a *faculty budget* for the following school year in December. This should take into account: salary increments, probable placements, and additions to the faculty/staff.

As you determine the amount of students moving up, you can begin preparing your staff schedule. If there is growth, you will need to determine how many teachers will be required for each grade and how many new teachers you will need to hire. Put together a *master staff schedule* and *elective offerings* based on the predicted number of teachers and students. If there are points during the year where it appears there will be less or more than the current enrollment, then you can make adjustments for staff. For example: if in December you realize you need to add another fourth grade section and will need an additional teacher, you would confirm the need based on re-enrollment in January. This will help you to prepare a draft budget. If you then loose students for fourth grade in April, you can drop the section and need for another teacher. This is why flexibility within the budget line items is crucial.

*January/February: operating budget, re-enrollment begins*

Preparations for the *operating budget* should begin as the number of students re-enrolled is confirmed. Make sure you communicate with your administrative team the general financial climate of the school for the next budget year as determined by the number of re-enrolled students. A faculty budget should be presented to the board in January.

*April/May: Tuition Drafts*

At this time, any adjustments in the expense totals should be submitted to the board. Once the board has received the preliminary budget in the spring, they should study and vote on its approval. The board will have time for a final view of the budget if the following has taken place: a time schedule has been followed, enrollment has been completed, and income is certain. This will allow the board to have a final viewing well in advance of the fiscal year. Some schools may choose to divert final approval until September when exact income figures, as well as, all expenses items are known. Historically, this has not proven to be a wise plan. Unknown factors such as enrollment dropping could force the need to let personnel go or result in the school not having adequate funds to purchase necessary supplies.

*June: Budget lockdown after May draft*

Be prepared to lock down your budget in June after your May draft. I am aware of many schools, including good ones, where prospective students are not allowed to apply until late spring or even summer. This makes it impossible for the administrator to know what the next year's tuition income will be. No matter what the circumstances, it is important to have a plan and develop a budget in logical stages.

## Presenting the Budget to the Board

As you prepare your budget for the board, you should be prepared to keep it short; not long or excessively detailed. Otherwise the approval process will become tedious and difficult.

Tabulations or figures should be accompanied by brief written comments from the business manager explaining the most important features. It should include estimates based on the following:
- Historical income and expenditures from recent years
- Number of projected students
- FFNA results
- Personnel needs
- Financial projections

As mentioned before, a sample monthly budget report has been provided in Appendix H. It is clear, short, and contains brief details of any needed information that is not in the numbers. Your report should show the following:
- Status of the funds
- Realization of the tuition
- Profit and loss statement
- All balance sheets

A budget report should be rendered to the board every month in an effort to keep them well informed of the current financial health of your school. This will also allow them to identify any red flags and address any issues that need attention before they become problems. These reports are especially helpful if the board is unable to meet for any given reason.

## Billing

### Sensible Billing Strategies

Billing in any school, but especially a Christian school, is a sensitive area. In addition to the lack of general policies covering this subject, some schools have adopted the ineffective practice of sending out continual bills with separate charges for individual fees. This is costly, irritating, and time-consuming for all concerned. If some schools do not receive funds immediately, they will go on to waste resources by sending multiple reminders. And yet other schools will send too few. As a result, the institution looses money and appears very unprofessional. Tuition and fees should be *streamlined* and grouped into a single fee. All tuition cost should be clearly communicated upfront with no hidden fees appearing on later bills.

### Collections

Collecting payment can often be as sensitive as billing families for the tuition they have agreed to pay. There is almost an assumption that if you are a Christian organization and someone is delinquent on payments, you should not pursue it. The connotation here is that it is ungodly or un-Christian to hold people accountable to their word or contract. However, Scripture clearly states that as believers, we are to be "wise as serpents; harmless as doves."[83] Both require discernment and a desire to accomplish God's will. When these situations arise, they must be handled gingerly. The board should be made aware of the circumstances and each case considered carefully. If you become aware of a family who is unable to pay their child's tuition due to financial hardship, you should encourage the parents to come to you in confidence. If they are doing all they can to honor their part of the contract, you should allow them to continue to send their child(ren) to the school as you trust God to make a way to compensate for the tuition. It is vital as a Christian school that we bend over backwards to assist families knowing we are a part of a ministry. We must seek to do all that we can to provide consistency and continuity during adversity, especially for the sake of the children.

On the other hand, if parents refuse to operate in or under biblical principles or there is prideful bitterness, I believe the school should reveal their rebellion against God and His Word. Prayerfully, through such discipline, we as administrators can help individuals who refuse to honor their commitment, as we follow direction from Matthew Chapter 18.

The steps in disciplining for this offense would include the following:

- Call the responsible individuals in for a private conference.
- If repentance and restoration of the commitment is not evident, you should communicate with and/or bring in their pastor or elder as laid out in Matthew 18: 15-17.
- If after all these attempts, the individuals refuse to fulfill their commitment, then an outside party such as a collection agency may be needed.

In twenty-one years of administration, I am thankful to say I have witnessed only a small percentage of people in which the school had to go to such extremes. In each of those cases, I can assure you that love and grace was extended beyond measure. Sadly, due to the accountability and follow through of consequences, individuals at times, may still be convinced that the school is "out to get them," I have also witnessed other individuals, who after being approached, have simply removed themselves from the school and/or not supported the school. Thankfully, there are also individuals who have responded repentantly with soft hearts, with the result being full restoration.

As an administrator, you should be prepared to consistently seek wisdom and blessings in these situations, being above reproach and remembering where all things come from. There are over two thousand references to money in the Word of God. If we, being examples, practice good biblical principles with our money, it will demonstrate where our heart is. Unfortunately, sometimes, it demonstrates where our heart is not.

---

83 Mt 10:16

## Other Areas of Finance to Consider

### Accounting: Defining its Function

"Accounting" can be defined as the *record keeping* required to provide necessary information as to the cost of major programs. A *net deficit* or *surplus* of the budget, as well as accurate records, should clearly show how much has been spent year-to-date in comparison with the allotted budget.

In the actual design of your schools accounting system, every effort should be made to keep it simple and organized. Expenses should be collected and reported providing charts for all accounts. Bookkeeping software such as *Quickbooks* is designed to aid in the process. It provides a format where the data can be used without a need for recopying, similar to a database. It will also allow record keeping of all employee earnings, written checks, and payroll distribution in one package. An *effective software* package is crucial for larger schools as it will expedite the workload for your business manager making their time far more efficient.

## Conclusion

As we close on this subject of finances, I want to exhort you as an administrator to take into account the current and future financial health of your school as it relates to God's promises to those who seek to do His will.[84] With a desire to give Him all the glory, you must purpose to seek His wisdom as you prepare and carefully plan for the specific needs of your school. You should be continually mindful that He that giveth can take it away at any time. God has entrusted you with this ministry, and this service. He expects you to be a wise steward with all He has provided. You must not forget that your testimony is being evidenced by your actions. Be above reproach, trust in the Lord always, lean not on your own understanding or wisdom, but in all your ways acknowledging Him, and He *will* make your path straight.[85]

---

84 Mt 6:33
85 Prv 3:5-6

# Chapter 8

# The Function Of The Board

## Purpose and Role of a School Board

The purpose of your school board should be to exercise spiritual leadership and ensure that your school achieves appropriate results, for appropriate persons, at an appropriate cost, *while avoiding* unacceptable actions and situations. They should begin with prayer and a correct understanding of their own responsibilities. These responsibilities should be written down and reviewed periodically by the board secretary. If a board fails to understand their responsibilities, the result will be confusion, poor decision making, and lack of successful planning for a school's future.

In the forward of *Serving God on the Christian School Board*, Derek Keenan writes:

> If a Christian school board is to serve the school effectively, its members must have a clear understanding of what it means to be a part of an organization that works for the Kingdom by educating children. The dedicated volunteers who serve as school board members often come to that position with a strong commitment to the school but with little background in education and with limited knowledge of the functions of a policy-making body.[86]

With this in mind, my goal in this chapter is to provide insight and guidelines that will aid board members in understanding the functions of the board and those of the administrator.

## Appointments and Qualifications for Board Members

A board of directors should consist of seven elected individuals serving for a period of three consecutive years. It is important to stagger appointments to the board so that only two or three members' terms expire at the same time. Nominations to the board should be made by a nominating committee that is appointed by the board. The nominating committee should consist of approximately three members, with one being on the current board. Qualifications for nomination should include the following:

- Knows Christ
- Be spiritually discerning
- Knows the Scriptures
- Have a positive testimony in community
- Be competent in fervent prayer

---

86 Jr. Roy W. Lowrie and R. Leon Lowrie, *Serving God on the Christian School Board* (: Association Christian Schools International, [Rev. ed.] edition (1998)).

- Not a recent convert
- Be committed to the educational philosophy outlined in your by-laws
- Be a member or regular attendee in good standing of a local church
- Demonstrate a loving concern for children

If unexpected vacancies on the board occur during a term they should be filled by election at your school's corporation meeting. A majority of the board may appoint an interim person to temporarily fill the vacancy until elections can take place. Any such interim appointee should meet all the qualifications for an elected board member.

## A Boards Charge

As a board begins to prayerfully write its own job description, it must fully understand its role in the big picture. In a Christian school, a board's role for any Christian school will likely include: exercising spiritual leadership and guidance, establishing biblical policies and procedures, hiring a capable godly administrator and managing his role, maintaining fiscal stability and growth, providing adequate facilities, and praying diligently over God's vision for the school. Below is a culmination of the duties a board should seek to fulfill as they seek God's will at every point.

A board should:

- Govern with an emphasis on (a) biblically-based integrity and truthfulness in all methods and practices; (b) outward vision rather than an internal preoccupation, (c) strategic leadership more than administrative detail, (d) clear distinction of board and administrator roles, (e) collective rather than individual decisions, (f) future rather than past or present, and (g) proactivity rather than reactivity

- Be responsible for determining and demanding appropriate organizational performance

- Accomplish its responsibilities with a governance style consistent with its policies, and should follow an annual agenda that (a) completes a re-exploration policies and (b) continually improves board performance through education and enriched input and deliberation

- Commit itself and its members to biblical, ethical, businesslike, and lawful conduct, including proper use of authority and appropriate decorum when acting as board members

- Commit itself to the individual and collective participation of its members to insure leadership success

- Establish procedures for identifying and solving problems before they become critical

## Governing Policies

A board should be responsible for determining and demanding appropriate organizational performance. They should produce written governing policies that, at the broadest levels, address each category of organizational decision:

- *Ends* - Organizational products, effects, benefits, outcomes, recipients, and their relative worth (what good for which recipients at what cost).
- *Executive Limitations* - Constraints on executive authority, which establish the boundaries within which all executive activity and decisions should take place.
- *Governance Process* - Specification of how the board conceives carries out and monitors its own task.
- *Board/staff Linkage* - How power is delegated and its proper use monitored; the administrator role, authority, and accountability.
- *Document Revisions* - Revisions to these written governing policies should be approved by the board. Notice of revisions should be communicated to the board and the Administration, with receipt acknowledge required.

A board should produce assurance of administrator performance and from time to time, be involved in the raising of funds.

## Board Member Code of Conduct

A board should commit itself and its members to biblical, ethical, professional, and lawful conduct, including proper use of authority and appropriate decorum when acting as board members. They should represent loyalty without conflict to the interests of the ownership. This accountability should supersede any conflicting loyalty such as that to advocacy or interest groups and membership on other boards or staffs. It also should supersede the personal interest of any board member acting as a consumer of the organization's services.

Board members should always seek to avoid conflict of interest with respect to their fiduciary responsibility. There should be no self-dealing or any conduct of private business or personal services between any board member and the organization except as procedurally controlled to assure openness, competitive opportunity, and equal access to inside information. When the board is to decide upon an issue about which a member has an unavoidable conflict of interest, that member should absent himself without comment from not only the vote but also from the deliberation.

Board members should never use their positions to obtain employment for themselves, family members or close associates. Should they or their spouse desire employment (excluding supplemental staff such as substitute teachers, bus drivers and outside coaches) within the organization, he or she should first resign. Accordingly, they should never attempt to exercise individual authority over the organization except as explicitly set forth in board policies. Their interaction with the administrator or with staff should recognize the lack of authority vested in individuals except when explicitly board authorized.

In regards to the board's interaction with the public, press or other entities, they should recognize the limitation and the inability of any board member to speak for the board except to repeat explicitly stated board decisions. In regards to the administrator or staff performance, board members should never give consequence or voice to individual judgments. They should always respect the confidentiality appropriate to issues of a sensitive nature and should give unconditional acceptance to your Statement of Faith.

## Individual Board Member Responsibilities

A board should commit itself to the individual and collective participation of its members to insure leadership success. Therefore, each board member should be expected to participate in the following ways:

- *Attendance* - As board contemplation, deliberation and decision-making are processes that require wholeness, collaboration and participation; attendance at board meetings should be required of all board members. Members should not be absent from more than four of the board's regularly scheduled meetings in any fiscal year. Any absence, which exceeds this allotment, should be interpreted as that member's resignation from the board.

- *Preparation and Participation* - board members should prepare for board and committee meetings, and should participate productively in discussions, always within the boundaries of the established disciplines. Each member should be expected to contribute his own knowledge, skills and expertise to the board's efforts to fulfill its responsibilities.

- *Members as Individuals* - the administrator is accountable only to the board as an organization, and not to individual board members. Accordingly, the relationship between the administrator and individual members of the board, including the board president, is collegial, not hierarchical.

- *Volunteerism* - As the functioning and success of the organization depend largely on the involvement and dedication of volunteers, all board members should be expected to contribute a minimum amount of hours (inclusive of board meeting time) annually to the school. In view of the administrator's responsibility for operational activities and results, members of the board acting as operational volunteers should subject to the direct supervision of the administrator or responsible staff person.

- *Contributions* - Each board member should be expected to contribute generously within their individual means to make an annual financial contribution to your school. The demonstration of support, rather than the amount of the contribution, is of principal importance; members are expected to contribute only within their individual means.

- *Prayer* - Members should commit to regularly pray for the school.

## Cost of Governance

It is highly recommended that a board invest in its governance. Board skills, methods, and supports should be sufficient to assure governing with excellence. Training and retraining should be used for the purpose of preparing new members and candidates for board membership. This is also helpful in maintaining and increasing existing member skills and understandings. Monitoring assistance should be arranged so that the board can exercise confident control over organizational performance. This should include a fiscal audit.

In regards to training cost, monies should be allocated for training including attendance of conferences, workshops, retreats and monthly meetings. You should also allocate funds for surveys, focus groups and opinion analyses. Although these expenditures are considered necessary, they should never endanger development and maintenance of superior capability.

## Board Meeting Recommendations

- It is recommended that your board meet at least once a month. These meetings should include a time that members of your corporation can attend, allowing them to address any questions or concerns.
- A closed executive session can follow where non-member attendees are not present.
- You should require a quorum of at least four board members.
- If emergency or unexpected meetings are needed, the president of the board or a majority of its members can call the meeting with at least three days notice.
- Reports of the subject matter to be discussed should be provided to all board members in advance.
- No formal business should be transacted at this meeting except the intended subject.

## Two of the Board's Greatest Responsibilities

A successful, effective, well-run board has two *critical* functions:
- To be the visionaries of the school
- To hire the right administrator

As the board communicates the vision, the administrator instructs the workers in what needs to be done. He is the facilitator between the leaders and the workers, as well as under the supervision and directives of the board. He balances both the long and short term goals, all while paying attention to the resources needed and effectiveness of the methods begin used. Strong communication and leadership is crucial to successfully carry out these tasks.

The administrator is responsible for managing your school's overall day to day operation. He is solely responsible for training and motivating the staff, all while ensuring that they have the tools necessary for a successful mission.

There are several mistakes a board can make that affect the course and progress of their school. In my twenty-on years of experience, I have come across several instances where the board has made decisions that were detrimental to the overall school's overall success. For example, a board may meet and decide to go in a particular direction, communicating this ideal or vision to their administrator. From this point forward, the administrator meets with all the appropriate individuals, such as the development officer, business manager, the staff, the bank, etc. He will spend hours directing and driving the operations of the school to reach the board's intended goal. To his dismay, they announce at a future board meeting that they have changed their minds and want to proceed in a different direction. Hours of resources, time, effort, and money have been spent on the original plan. Though the board has ultimate authority, this can be extremely frustrating for the administration, and may result in loss of confidence in the board.

Another large error boards make is not fully understanding their own role, or the role of the administrator, before they hire him. As a result of this, many good schools have failed and ceased to exist. It is crucial that the board fully understand roles and prepare job descriptions that will communicate these expectations. They should understand that it is not their role to micro-manage the day to day operations of the school, but to look ahead towards the intended vision. Getting involved in daily operations can become a distraction of their mission to protect your institution.

### Hiring an Administrator: What Makes a Good Administrator?

The hiring of an administrator is perhaps the most important decision they will ever make, thus they must fully understand the qualifications necessary for this vital role.

The most important role of an administrator is problem solving. It is not possible for a board to communicate daily task an administrator will need to complete, therefore finding someone with the right qualifications is crucial. I have listed some qualifications that will guide you in selecting a capable administrator.

I recommend that a potential administrator candidate have a Masters degree in Educational Leadership, Educational Administration, or Church Leadership. Past experience as a teacher will enable them to lead successfully, as they are ultimately the "teacher of all teachers." An ideal candidate would preferably have both educational certification and a high level of experience. A qualified candidate should:

Love God
- Able to ask for forgiveness when he offends another
- Seeks biblical principles in all instances
- Is true to his word everyday[87]
- Is submissive in cheerful obedience to the board

---

[87] Mt 18

Be Disciplined (have high self control)
- First one to arrive and the last one to leave (normal school day)
- Should spend time in God's Word each day (individual sanctification)
- Keep himself in good shape: mentally, socially, spiritually and physically
- Details, details, details

Have High Accountability Standards and Standards of Order
- Staff meetings
- Evaluations
- Classroom management consistency
- Teacher/parent conferences
- Budgets/salary
- Class schedules
- Scope & sequence
- Curriculum
- Interviews: family, staff, board

Accountability to Confront the Issues
- Must be willing to confront students
- Must be willing to confront parents
- Must be willing to confront teachers

Efficiency (puts a lot in a little)
- Communication
- Meetings/meet & eat

Have a System of Curriculum (a playbook/plan)
- Teach others (should know it first themselves)
- Train teachers (book club/reading)

Be a People Person and not a People Pleaser
- An administrator must be willing to do what is right regardless of "power or popularity"

It is important to remember that every administrator will bring his own gifts, talents, and abilities that God has equipped him with, however the responsibilities of the position from school to school, should be quite similar. Periodically, the board should review the administrator's duties realizing that revisions may be necessary as the school continues to grow.

## Guiding Principles for an Administrator

Below are some principles intended to assist administrators in areas that are not likely covered in a classroom. They are, however, vital to his role in leadership. I call them the "Vowels of Administrative Success".

- **A** – Accountability: (to parents, students, teachers, board)
    - Must know what to hold everyone accountable for
    - Convey accountability through staff, student/parent, and coaches handbooks
    - Finances, school objectives, behavior of staff, students and parents, evaluations, expelling students, academic probation, 1st quarter trial period, non-renewal of families, teacher observations, memos/communication, and parents.
    - Be Confident! execute, execute, execute

- **E** – Efficiency: (make the most of your time)
    - Arrive early to do all paperwork
    - Have your assistant type all material, keep your schedule, and answer all calls
    - Be available when people are there
    - Get to the point! (Avoid lengthy conversations by asking, "How can I help you, what do you need?")

- **I** – Investing: teacher training, get to know the students, book club, birthday celebrations, peer evaluations, observations, curriculum teams, conferences with parents.

- **O** – Order/Organization: scheduling, budgets, start & end times, car pool procedures, grading, discipline, scope and sequence, uniforms, transcripts, athletics and activities, practice schedules, assemblies, lunch times, special classes, electives etc.

- **U** – Understand before trying to be understood.
    - Daily staff meetings
    - Be a good listener: two ears-one mouth, listen twice as much as you talk
    - Monthly and quarterly informational newsletters
    - Monday folders for parental communication

*And sometimes…*

- **Y** – Yourself (self improvement: reading and studying)
    - Have an advisory team – other experienced administrators to help guide you in times of trials.
    - Heart, soul, strength and mind (read, exercise, pray, and laugh)
    - Go home everyday at 5:30 p.m./when home don't answer phone
    - Protect your weekends!

# Policy Governance Manual

## Managing Your Administrator

In all my experience, I can tell you that the most effective method a board can use to manage an administrator, is through the use of a *Policy Governance Manual*. This manual or document's purpose should be to define the responsibility of the board and the delegation of responsibility from the board to the administrator. There should be no policies in this document that supercede any of the by-laws of your school. Below is an outline of topics you can follow in writing your own governance manual.

**Mission of Organization**

Your mission statement should sum up your organization's reason for being; explaining its intent, priorities, and values. It is helpful to include:

Governance Processes
- Governance Commitment
- Governing Style and Values
- Board Job Description
- Agenda Planning
- President's Role
- Board Members' Code of Conduct
- Individual Board Member Responsibilities
- Board Committee Principles
- Board Committee Structure
- Cost of Governance
- Corporate Meetings

Board/Staff Linkage
- Governance-Management Connection
- Unity of Control and Communication
- Authority and Accountability of the School Administrator
- Delegation to the School Administrator
- Monitoring School Administrator Performance

Executive Limitations
- General Executive Constraint
- Treating of Consumers
- Hiring and Treatment of Staff
- Financial Planning/Budgeting
- Financial Condition & Activities
- Asset Protection
- Emergency Administrator Succession
- Compensation and Benefits
- Communication and Support To the Board
- Programs/Services

## Authority and Accountability

The administrator should be the board's only link to the operational achievement and conduct of the school. Therefore, as far as the board is concerned, all staff and operations of the school are directly under his supervision.
Accordingly:
- The board should never give instructions to persons who report directly or indirectly to the administrator.
- The board should refrain from evaluating, either formally or informally, any staff other than the administrator.
- The board should view administrator performance as identical to organizational performance, so that organizational accomplishment of board-stated ends within board-proscribed executive limitations should be viewed as successful administrator performance.
- Only decisions of the board acting as a body, by majority vote, are binding on the administrator.

## Delegation to an Administrator

The board should always seek to instruct the administrator through written policies, what needs to be achieved, and describe organizational situations and actions to be avoided, allowing the administrator to use any reasonable interpretation of these policies.
Accordingly:
- The board should develop policies instructing the administrator to achieve certain results, for certain recipients at a specified cost. These policies should be developed systematically from the broadest, most general level to more defined levels.

- The board should develop policies, which limit the latitude the administrator should exercise in choosing the organizational means.

- As long as the administrator uses any reasonable interpretation of the board's policies, he should be authorized to establish all further policies, make all decisions, take all actions, establish all practices and develop all activities.

- The board should be able to change its policies, thereby shifting the boundary between board and administrator domains. By doing so, the board changes the latitude of choice given to the administrator. However, as long as any particular delegation is in place, the board should respect and support the administrator's choices.

- Should the administrator violate a board policy, he should promptly inform the board to guarantee no violation is intended to be intentionally kept from the board, not to request approval. board response, either approving or disapproving, should not exempt the administrator from subsequent board judgment of the action nor should it curtail any executive decision.

### Monitoring Administrator Performance

Systematic and rigorous monitoring of the administrator's job performance should be done by the board and solely based on the expected administrator job duties including organizational accomplishment of board policies and organizational operation within the established boundaries.

Accordingly:

- Monitoring should be for the purpose of determining the degree to which board policies are being met. Data that does not do this should not be considered to be monitoring data.

- The board should acquire monitoring data by one or more of three methods: (a) by internal report, in which the administrator discloses compliance information to the board, (b) by external report, in which an external, disinterested third party selected by the board assesses compliance with board policies, and (c) by direct board inspection, in which a designated member or members of the board assess compliance with the appropriate policy criteria.

- In every case, the standard for compliance to the policy being monitored should be any reasonable interpretation by the administrator.

- All policies, which instruct the administrator, should be monitored at a frequency and by a method chosen by the board. The board should be able to monitor any policy at any time by any method, but should ordinarily depend on a routine schedule.

## Communication and Support

The administrator should continually inform and support the board in its work. Accordingly, the administrator should not:

- Fail to submit monitoring data required by the board in a timely, accurate and understandable fashion, directly addressing provisions of board policies being monitored.
- Allow the board to be unaware of relevant trends, anticipated adverse media coverage, material external and internal changes, and particularly changes in the assumptions upon which any board policy has been previously established.
- Fail to advise the board if, in his opinion, the board is not in compliance with its own policies; particularly in the case of board behavior that is detrimental to all working relationships.
- Fail to marshal for the board as many staff and external points of view, issues and options as needed for fully informed board choices.
- Present information in unnecessarily complex or lengthy form or in a form that fails to differentiate among information of three types: monitoring, decision preparation, and incidental.
- Fail to provide a mechanism for official board, officer or committee communications.
- Fail to deal with the board as a whole except when (a) fulfilling individual requests for information or (b) responding to officers or committees duly charged by the board.
- Fail to report in a timely manner an actual or anticipated noncompliance with any policy of the board.
- Fail to supply for the consent agenda all items delegated to the administrator yet required by law or contract to be board-approved, along with the monitoring assurance pertaining thereto.

## Administrator's Board Reports

Monthly reports should be provided by the administrator and submitted to the board. They should contain detailed information on the ongoing progress of the school. Specific status of each school section (i.e. Grammar School, Logic School, and Secondary School) should be written by the appropriate principal and submitted to the administrator for review before submission to the board. A general format of a board report should include, but not be limited to, the following:

Students

- Current enrollment numbers
- New or withdrawn students
- Discipline recordings: incident, punishment, restitution status

- Problem students facing expulsion due to academics or behavior
- Parent concerns and meetings
- Academic achievements (i.e. SAT scores)

Staff
- New staff member introductions
- Teacher performance observations
- Personnel problems or concerns with staff members
- Staff sickness and/or leave updates

Curriculum
- Detail of book orders, costs and/or additional materials needed
- Curriculum review committee updates

Activities
- Monthly detail of special events
- Sports activities/competitions

Other
- Building/construction status
- Budget updates

## Executive Limitations

The administrator should not cause *nor* allow any practice, activity, decision, or organizational circumstance that is either unlawful, imprudent, or in violation of commonly accepted business and professional ethics.

- With respect to interactions with consumers or potential consumers, the administrator should not cause or allow conditions, procedures, or decisions which are unsafe, undignified, unnecessarily intrusive, unbiblical, or that fail to provide appropriate confidentiality or privacy.
- With respect to the hiring and treatment of paid staff and/or volunteers, the administrator should not cause or allow conditions that are unfair, unsafe, unbiblical, undignified, or unlawful.
- Financial planning for any fiscal year or the remaining part of any fiscal year should not deviate materially from the board's priorities, risk fiscal jeopardy, or fail to be derived from a multi-year plan.

- With respect to the actual, ongoing financial condition and activities, the administrator should not cause or allow the development of fiscal jeopardy or a material deviation of actual expenditures from board priorities established in the policies.
- The administrator should not allow the assets to be unprotected, inadequately maintained or unnecessarily risked.
- With respect to employment, compensation, and benefits to employees, consultants, contract workers and volunteers, the administrator should never cause or allow jeopardy to fiscal integrity or Christian testimony.
- With respect to the programs produced or services provided by the organization, the administrator should not fail to ensure that these programs and services meet or exceed industry standards for excellence in program quality and safety.

## Compensation and Benefits

With respect to employment, compensation, and benefits to employees, consultants, contract workers and volunteers, the administrator should not cause or allow jeopardy to fiscal integrity or Christian testimony.
Accordingly, the administrator should not:
- Modify or edit his own compensation and benefits
- Promise or imply permanent or guaranteed employment
- Create compensation obligations over a longer term than revenues can be safely projected, in no event longer than one year and in all events subject to losses in revenue
- Establish or change compensation or benefits so as to cause unpredictable or inequitable situations
- Fail to use a formula-based compensation plan for faculty
- Budget more than one percent of salary for bonuses

## Treatment of Consumers

With respect to interactions with consumers or potential consumers, the administrator should not cause or allow conditions, procedures, or decisions which are unsafe, undignified, unnecessarily intrusive, unbiblical, or which fail to provide appropriate confidentiality or privacy.
Accordingly, the administrator should not:
- Use application forms that elicit information for which there is no clear necessity.
- Use methods of collecting, reviewing, transmitting, or storing consumer information that fails to protect against improper access to the material elicited.
- Maintain facilities that fail to provide a reasonable level of privacy, both visual and aural.
- Operate without clear written policies on matters of general interest to students and

parents in order to establish with them a clear understanding of what may be expected and what may not be expected from the service offered.

- Fail to inform consumers of this written policy or to provide a grievance process to those who believe they have not been accorded a reasonable interpretation of their rights under this policy.

- Enroll students who individually and in their home environments are not supportive of the school's biblical orientation. Parent(s)/guardian(s) should be united in their desire to have their child taught from a Christian perspective reflective of your Statement of Faith. It is recommended that at least one parent/guardian have a clear testimony of personal faith in Jesus Christ as Savior.

- Allow school-wide information to be communicated orally or in written form by individual staff or teachers rather than school wide communiqué.

## Emergency Administrator Succession

In order to protect the board and the school from sudden loss of administrator services, the administrator should not fail to designate and inform the board of several individuals who should be familiar with board and school administrative issues and processes.

## Recommended Yearly Agenda for a Board

The following are recommended agenda items for review:

June
- No meeting - Fourth quarter financial report: monitoring report

July
- Social "meeting" with spouses

August
- Process review at end
- Time for the board to evaluate how it did following Policy Governance Manual

September
- Treatment of staff
- Compensation and benefits
- First quarter financial report

October
- Ownership input and education
- Treatment of consumers
- Financial conditions and activities
- Programs/services
- Financial audit summary

November
- End of year review and projections for next academic year

December
- Second quarter financial report

January
- Board review of administrator remuneration
- Financial planning/budgeting

February
- Review registration numbers

March
- Asset protection
- Emergency school administrator succession
- Communication and support of the board
- Third quarter financial report

April
- Ownership input and education
- The board's annual performance review of itself
- Board approval of nominating committee's recommendation

May
- Select nominating committee

## Conclusion

It is important to remember that as a member of a Christian school board, your role and responsibilities are appointed by God for the equipping of the saints, both present and future. Although you may not receive financial compensation for your service, the rewards for serving in this capacity will be plentiful. Your blessings for being in Christian service, seeking to do and fulfill God's plans, will afford you the opportunity to see Him spiritually develop your school, including staff, students and families. You will see first hand God's faithfulness in providing both spiritually and financially for your ministry. You will have the opportunity to make decisions that will not only influence the children and parents of this generation, but God willing, the many generations to follow. You will have the blessing of working along side other Christians who have responded to the call of Christ, experiencing together the joy of seeing students grow in their knowledge of the Savior because of your hard work; the joy of watching students walk across your stage prepared and equipped to serve a mighty God in growing His Kingdom. My personal charge to board members and administrators alike is to remember, that as you serve your school with the many gift God has equipped you with, you are serving Christ. Serve, not just willingly, but enthusiastically, seeking His glory, His will, and His blessings on the work of your hands.

# Chapter 9

# Organizational Calendar

Academic School Year: August–May
*"Let all things be done ... in order." – I Corinthians 14:40*

In addition to the daily administrator responsibilities of staff management, student discipline, counseling, as well as emergency response, it is pertinent to have a well laid out administrative agenda. Over the years as administrator, I have recorded my responsibilities, along with timeframes of these procedures, in a monthly planner. This eliminates any guesswork and will keep you prepared as to what needs to be done. Strive to be organized and prepared for the many tasks at hand over the school year. An academic administrative calendar, such as the example below, will enable you to meet such school needs and deadlines.

## Academic Administrator Calendar

Weekly
- Administrative meeting on Monday mornings with all administrative staff: business manager, development director and administrative assistants
- Morning staff meetings with teachers: book club, new staff

Monthly
- Fire drill and/or tornado drill practices
- K-5 grade individual class assemblies
- Administrative newsletters, that highlight monthly school news, are sent home with students
- Prepare, review and submit your board report to the board of directors
- All staff meeting: brief staff on school events, staff birthdays, feature teacher etc.
- Event planning meeting with your PTA president
- Curriculum review committee meetings
- Student birthdays: prayer and/or present a small gift certificate to each student
- Payroll
- Tax filings (quarterly)
- Monthly board meeting

July
- Review staff manual and make needed revisions in preparation for teacher orientation
- Determine and purchase any additional classroom materials (student desks and chairs)
- Mail informational packets to school families for the start of the school year. Include: final class rosters, an updated school calendar, student elective schedules, supply lists, a "welcome back" letter from your administration listing school policies, as well as a brief introduction of any new staff members
- Mail teacher orientation schedule and welcome back letter to all staff.
- Prepare for teacher orientation meetings and/or assembly
- Prepare for back to school night
- Senior Service Practicum—S.S.P (see "student service" F.A.Q for description)
- Fall sports informational meeting for parents and athletes before the season begins

August
- Teacher orientation with staff breakfast
- Back to school night
- First day of school
- Individual yearbook picture day (scheduled in advance with photographer)
- Student Government Association: Review students constitution and make changes, officer sign ups, student campaigns, speeches, vote and election assembly
- Begin first round of teacher observations

September
- Prepare corporation meeting speech/presentation (includes: school mission, awards, academic progress etc.)
- SSP assembly: seniors give their testimony and a visual presentation of their mission trip to classmates
- 1st quarter midterms sent home
- PSAT preparation
- National Merit Scholarship application
- Meet with seniors for college planning and to review transcripts

October
- 1st quarter ends/report cards sent home
- Fall break
- 11th grade PSAT
- First quarter parent/teacher report card conferences—all staff workday

- Winter sports informational meeting for parents and athletes before the season begins.
- 2nd quarter begins
- Fall sports pictures (scheduled in advance with photographer)
- "F" day for first quarter: parents contacted
- 1st quarter Principal's Newsletter mailed
- School audit
- Plan ahead and reserve facilities and/or rental equipment needed for graduation and protocol (dance)

November
- 2nd quarter midterms sent home
- Meet with juniors to begin college planning for next year
- Begin preliminary budget for next school year
- School wide calendar revisions for upcoming year
- Student/parent handbook revisions: discuss with your administration
- Preliminary staffing schedules for next year

December
- Continue budget development and staff schedules for next school year
- "F" day for second quarter: parents to be contacted
- Semester exams
- 2nd quarter ends
- Christmas and drama programs
- Prepare staff Christmas bonuses
- Staff Christmas party
- Christmas Break/early release
- Revise and prepare re-enrollment packages for next month

January
- 2nd quarter report cards sent home
- 3rd quarter begins
- Re-enrollment packets are sent home with current students
- Open house/open enrollment
- 2nd quarter Principal's Newsletter mailed

February
- 3rd quarter midterms go home
- Meet with senior parents: graduation, protocol, reception
- Spring sports informational meeting for parents and athletes before the season begins
- Winter sports team photos (scheduled in advance with photographer)
- Accreditation visit
- Taxes

March
- Order AP Exams
- 3rd quarter ends/early release
- Spring Break
- 3rd quarter parent conferences-all staff workday
- 4th quarter begins

April
- Stanford Achievement Tests
- 4th quarter midterms go home
- Spring sports photos (scheduled in advance with photographer)
- 3rd quarter Principal's Newsletter mailed
- Meet with senior parents: graduation ceremony, protocol, progressive dinner etc.
- Order PSAT exams for next school year
- Continued preparation for graduation: speakers, catering, decoration, luncheon & dinners etc.

May
- Board campus visitation
- Semester and AP exams
- Senior finals
- Meetings with parents of failing students
- Class roster lottery for upcoming school year
- Elective sheet selections go home
- Spring concerts and/or drama production
- Year end awards assemblies
- Senior assembly
- High school protocol (see FAQ's for description)

- Graduation
- Last day of school/report cards sent home
- Next year's rosters go home
- Year-end teacher evaluations
- Staff contract renewals or non-renewals
- Continue to finalize budget for next school year
- Campus fire inspection

June
- Finalize school budget
- Update student transcripts/final senior transcripts sent to colleges
- 4th quarter Principals Newsletter mailed
- Order all supplies for next year
- Maintenance: strip and re-wax school floors
- Order desk and lockers for next school year
- Hire final staffing needs
- Attend national conference (if applicable)

## Events, Programs and Holidays

The following list of events, holidays, and programs is not meant to be entirely comprehensive. New ideas may be introduced at any time. These guidelines are presented to illustrate what is intended to be a consistent approach to the school involvement or non-involvement in certain events and holidays.

*"Examine everything; hold fast to that which is good." - I Thessalonians 5:21*

Table 5. Events, Programs, and Holidays

| PROGRAM/EVENT/HOLIDAY | DATE(S) | SCHOOL INVOLVEMENT |
|---|---|---|
| STAFF ORIENTATION | First week of August | 1-2 days of staff training |
| BACK TO SCHOOL DAY (OPEN HOUSE) | First week of August | Parents/students meet the teacher |
| LABOR DAY | September | School closed |
| HALLOWEEN | October 31 | No celebrations for this event |

| PROGRAM/EVENT/ HOLIDAY | DATE(S) | SCHOOL INVOLVEMENT |
|---|---|---|
| REFORMATION DAY | October 31 | Events emphasizing the Protestant Reformation |
| VETERANS' DAY | Mid November | No time off; teachers free to emphasize the meaning of the day |
| THANKSGIVING | Mid/Late November | Normally three days off |
| CHRISTMAS | December 25 | Normally two weeks off with major emphasis on Christ's birth and mission celebrations. |
| REENROLLMENT | January | Re-register all current students and siblings |
| OPEN HOUSE | Last week of January | New students/families visit the school |
| OPEN REGISTRATION | First week of February | Kindergarten and all other grades |
| PRESIDENTS' DAY | Mid February | Encourage knowledge of Washington/Lincoln |
| VALENTINES' DAY | February 14 | No time off. Half hour class parties allowed |
| NATIONAL LATIN EXAM | Usually $1^{st}$ or $2^{nd}$ week in March | $5^{th}$ grade Latin students only |
| SAT TESTING | Mid April | Stanford Achievement Test ($1^{st} - 10^{th}$ grades) |
| GRANDPARENTS' DAY/ SPRING CONCERT | First Friday in May | Special program/day for grandparents to visit the school |
| MEMORIAL DAY | Late May | Monday off. Some education as to the reason for the holiday. |
| FIELD DAY | Last week of May | Events to be determined |
| AWARDS ASSEMBLY | Last week of May | Year-end awards |

# Chapter 10

# Frequently Asked Questions

*FAQs and comments that a Christian administrator should expect:*

## I survived public school, so why wouldn't my children survive it as well?

As Christians, one should ask themselves, "Is the final goal for my child simply to survive school, or to be transformed and molded by it? Is my child's "survival" the goal, or is honoring God the goal? In 2 Corinthians 5:9, Scripture exhorts us to "make it our goal to please Him", not merely survive. As Christians, we must remember, even as it applies to deciding where our child should attend school that Christ came so that we might "live life more abundantly."[88] Often, parents and educators believe the myth that education is in itself neutral. They believe a student's mind can be trained without having it effect their actions, attitudes, and spiritual beliefs. On the contrary, they are delicately intertwined, thus creating an open window into the souls of our children. Largely quoted humanist figurehead John Dunphy stated the following in his article *A Religion for a New Age*.

> I am convinced that the battle for humankind's future must be waged and won in the public school classroom by teachers who correctly perceive their role as proselytizers of a new faith; a religion of humanity that recognizes and respects the spark of what theologians call divinity in every human being.

> These teachers must embody the same selfless dedication as the most rabid fundamentalist preachers, for they will be ministers of another sort, utilizing a classroom instead of a pulpit to convey humanist values in whatever subject they teach, regardless of the educational level—preschool day care or large state university. The classroom must and will become an area of conflict between the old and the new—the rotting corpse of Christianity, together with all its adjacent evils and misery and the new faith of Humanism, resplendent in its promise of a world in which the never-realized Christian idea of 'Love thy Neighbor' will finally be achieved.[89]

Clearly, there is an agenda that wages war against the mind and soul of our Christian students if given to the training in government schools. The apostle Paul adamantly addresses this in Romans 12:2 when he urges us to not "conform any longer to the patterns of this world,

---

88 Jn 10:10
89 Bruce N. Shortt, *The Harsh Truth About Public Schools* (Vallecito, California: Chalcedon Foundation, 2004), 374.

but to be transformed by the renewing of our mind." The human mind is renewed by the reading of God's Word and through education of the mind. In Doug Wilson's book, *Excused Absences*, he states, "For over one hundred years, Americans have been running a gigantic experiment in government schools, trying to find out what a society looks like without God. Now we know."[90] A neutral education, according to God's Word, is impossible. Either you are "for Christ" or "against Christ." You cannot remain lukewarm without the consequences promised in Revelation 3:16.

Hearing the phrase, "I survived…" does not necessarily substantiate that it was what was best. Often times when we look back on and consider our life's struggles and largest challenges, we too easily assume that since we survived it, it is by design counted as a meritable accomplishment. It is human nature to reflect back on our lives and recall only that which was positive. We by nature, cope with life by protecting our minds from the memory of negative consequences.

So parents must ask themselves, "What is *best* for my child?" It is also important to note that public schools of this generation are very different than the generations we grew up in. Many of us experienced governmental schools when Godly influences shaped our education, as well as the values of most families. Today, anything *except* God is allowed to shape our views. Christian values have been turned upside down and shunned.

Twenty one years ago, when I was a public school administrator, I began each school day with Christian prayer reading from the book of Proverbs. Just eleven years later I would have been terminated immediately for praying the same prayer and for reading the same scriptures. This is a profound example of how of nation currently views Christianity. Although our public schools today will acknowledge the importance of good morals and character, they *will not* acknowledge Christianity or that these values came from God Himself. They will exhort the students to "treat others as you would want to be treated", but will teach them that these are the morals and standards of democracy, not that of Jesus Christ. Bruce Shortt, in his book, *The Harsh Truth About Public Schools*, states, "Government schools have effectively become parochial schools for secular humanism and many varieties of New Age spirituality. Moreover, for decades the unacknowledged moral code of government schools has been moral relativism."[91]

In considering whether to send your child to a public or Christian school, you must consider that if Christ is Lord, *He must be Lord over all*. He must be Lord over *all* influences that shape our children including their home, church, relationships, and education. He is, afterall, *the* author of all truth, and commends parents in Deuteronomy 6 to fear Him and serve Him *only*; *and* to impress *His truth* on the hearts of our children as it relates to every area of their life.

---

90  Douglas Wilson, *Excused Absence: Should Christian Kids Leave Public Schools?* (Mission Viejo, CA: Crux Press, Inc, 2001), 115.
91  Bruce N. Shortt, *The Harsh Truth About Public Schools*, 13.

## If my child does not go to public school, can they still get an athletic scholarship?

In error, many parents believe that if a school is small, it will hinder their child's opportunity to receive athletic scholarships from a prestigious, Division 1 college or university. Your response should lead this questioning toward the sovereignty of our Heavenly Father. For if God who blesses students with athletic abilities and talents, desires them to take these abilities to the next level, He, in His sovereignty, will provide what is necessary to fulfill this purpose.

It is true that Christian schools are generally smaller by enrollment standards than their public schools counterparts. So can students from Christian schools get scholarships? Yes, they can! Even if the school is small and not very competitive? Absolutely! We must remember where all good things come from. As a father gives good gifts to his children, so THE Father gives good gifts to His. God says in Matthew, "If you then, though you are evil, know how to give good gifts to your children, how much more will your Father in heaven give good gifts to those who ask him!"[92] Christian students, who have received scholarships in the past, along with those who will receive them in the future, must ask themselves, "Who created this scholarship? Who paved the way for me to receive it? Who gave me the abilities to attain it? GOD DID!" So the response to your question is, "Have faith, God is in control!"

If parents send the message to their child that the reason they are six-foot-eleven inches, or the reason they are playing baseball, is to gain an athletic scholarship at a prestigious university, they are missing the target God intended. Even as it relates to athletics, we must urge them to "seek first the kingdom of God and His righteousness"[93] and all things will be given to them as God wills it. We must encourage them to take "every thought captive to the obedience of Christ"[94] and to determine how they can best serve God with the gifts and abilities He has given them. Then we trust God for the results. This is training and educating with a biblical worldview.

## Why teach Bible in math and science classes?

God is the creator of math and science. Genesis 1:1 tells us that God created everything, "In the beginning God created the heavens and the earth." The very word "Genesis" means "beginning." The beginning of "us", creation, and all subjects under God. So you ask, "How is this relevant to math and science?" or "How is integrating scripture going to prepare students for the AP test and college entrance exams? Didn't the state institutions write the curriculums for AP math and science? Logically, God created those institutions and enabled them to create such tests and curriculums. In 1 Corinthians God says, "I will destroy the wisdom of the wise; the intelligence of the intelligent I will frustrate."[95] When we as humans seek to rise above God

---

92  Mt 7:11
93  Mt 6:33
94  2 Cor 2:5
95  1 Cor 1:19

and proceed to think ourselves to be intelligent, God reminds us how foolish we truly are. As Christians, we believe not only that God created everything in existence, but that He created it in His order and in His timing, and that He did it perfectly! When schools seek to remove God from their curriculum, be it math or science, they are removing the very author of its order.

Schools who profess to be Christian must be charged to always elevate Christ's name above all names, including in math and science.[96] Together, all Christians must hold one another accountable to following God's premises and commandments in regards to educating our children; to give Him all the respect He deserves in ALL curriculum areas. We do this with excellence by preparing students for life, with the highest levels of math and science. It is important to remember that God's way differs radically from mans. Isaiah reminds us in the 55th chapter that God's "thoughts are not [our] thoughts, nor are your ways, His ways… for My ways are higher than yours." In Proverbs, God says: "Trust in Me with all your heart, and lean not on your own understanding; in ALL your ways acknowledge Me and I will direct your path."[97] With such an exhortation from the creator, how can we deem it reasonable to leave Him out of what He created? By doing so, it forces the masses to march along in the time-worn tracks of history, re-living the Old Testament age when "everyone did what was right in [their] own eyes."[98]

## AP Exams in math and science

In order for math students to be prepared for the AP exam, it will require that they prepare and study the material required. It is important to note however, that schools can provide specific electives to assist students with more direct preparation for such exams, but God's Word should be fully explored and taught as it relates to the subject matter at hand. In oneschool where I administrated, we had an optional elective offered for this exact purpose. Due to it being scheduled at the end of the day, students may opt to go home, leave for community service, or go to a job/internship. They may also choose to participate in other electives such as: orchestra, band, drama, mock trial, or debate. They may attend an AP science class where students who aspire to take such exams for biology, chemistry or physics, can meet with other interested students for the purpose of further study. During the class, students may need to cover material that is not "of God", however may be required for the exam. The teacher should bookmark this material and tell the students, "This is material which the state has said is important, but in many ways it contradicts the Word of God. But for the state, if you are pursuing this credit from them, you need to prepare for these types of questions and know the following information."

At my Christian school, electives are preceded by a disclaimer stating that "we do not feel that all the information in the AP curriculum or on the AP exams should be completely embraced by

---

96 Ps 138:2
97 Prv 3:5
98 Jgs 21:25

a Christian school." Advanced placement elective classes have been very successful in preparing our students for the intended exams. The current national average is typically below twenty percent, yet our students have been scoring at or above 50%. To God be the glory!

## Must we be Christians to attend your school?

During an Open House is not uncommon to be approached by many non-Christian families with an interest to enroll their children at your school. During this event, you are essentially inviting families from the general public to come and visit your school. Each year I am approached by families, whether they are Buddhist, Hindu, Mormon, or Islamic, regarding their interest in our school. They will say, "We have heard great things about your school. We love the uniform policy, as well as your high academic standards and scores. We agree with everything except the Christian beliefs. Do we have to be Christian to enroll our child at your school?" Emphatically, the answer is always YES! Families desiring to come to your school primarily due to it being a great academic institution or a better alternative than public school are not the ones you want walking the hallways. These are certainly not the families that should be influencing our students. In my opinion, the goal is to have a Christian school that is, well…Christian. This should not only be portrayed by your school's sign and banners, but in the hallways and classrooms as well. Your school should have a Christian aroma that permeates every area of the school. It should be apparent to any observer. If you compromise this position, and allow pagan influences to enter and pervade your school, it will be to the detriment to all those God has called to serve in it. In my opinion, at least one parent (prayerfully both parents as well as the student) should be Christian in order to enroll in your school.

## How is secondary doctrine taught in a school if it is non-denominational?

This topic is certainly an issue that Christian schools face. By in large, Christian schools, as well as Christian churches, do not come apart from the outside—they come apart from the inside as a result of internal warfare! Distinctions between doctrines can cause ugly divisions if grace, mercy, and love are not present. To avoid this conflict, your school's by-laws should have an explanation of the primary doctrine and your statement of faith. The primary statement of faith is absolute truth and there should be no compromise. These beliefs are not up for argument! Every family and every student at your school should be expected to agree to and uphold them as outlined in your parent/student contract. In the event an issue arises, families should be instructed to bring their concerns to your administration. If the doctrinal issue cannot be resolved, or the parents are not willing to abide by your school's statement of faith, prayerfully consider asking them to leave. Again, Christian beliefs are not negotiable, as your school should be firmly established upon biblical premises and precepts.

## What about student service projects and taking care of the "poor and the widows?" It's a Christian school isn't it?

Should our children be serving the less fortunate? Absolutely! This refers us back to serving as Christ served, putting others before ourselves. The Bible reminds us in Philippians 2:3, "Let nothing be done through selfish ambition or conceit, but in lowliness of mind let each esteem others better than himself." I strongly believe that Christian schools should have an active role in serving others by equipping students to integrate Christian faith, academic excellence, and service. Service projects offer a valuable way to teach the importance of caring for God's people. Christian service can be exercised as an individual, a classroom, or as a school.

Service can express itself when a student provides for a peer who has no lunch, or meeting a need of a student unable to afford necessary uniforms. These are opportunities of training, discerning, and meeting the needs of others. "For I was hungry and you gave me something to eat, I was thirsty and you gave me something to drink, I was a stranger and you invited me in, I needed clothes and you clothed me, I was sick and you looked after me, I was in prison and you came to visit me. …I tell you the truth, whatever you did for one of the least of these brothers of mine, you did for me."[99]

As a classroom, students can serve the needy through service projects such as collecting food or other items in response to a need that has been brought to their attention. Classes can visit nursing homes, make and send encouraging cards to the grieving or sick, or pray for individuals with certain needs. Serving and sacrificing as a class, often allows students to experience and develop a bond that otherwise would not be gained.

As a school, we should seek to do the same, assisting needy families within our student body as if serving Christ himself; providing for them in any way we can as an institution. Additionally, we can choose to develop, review, and approve service projects that will also support instructional and biblical objectives. It is important to remember that the unconditional love Christ calls us to have for others, is naturally better "caught" than "taught," so our modeling service as an institution is a part of equipping our students to serve the kingdom of God.

Schools should also keep in mind that they are not a church but an educational facility, and need to be sensitive not to attempt to supplant the efforts of the church or family. In an organization such as a school filled with a great deal of families, needs will become apparent. This does not, however, automatically conclude that the school as a whole should become involved. Use discernment in deciding whether these needs should be met by your school, the church or by particular individuals.

At our Christian school, we have developed what we call our "Senior Service Practicum." During a senior's last year, we provide them with the opportunity to apply the abilities they

---

[99] Mt 25:35

have gained in their Christian education by sending them on a mission trip. Knowing we have thoroughly equipped them with the aptitude to think and speak, the ability to discern with good reason, and the biblical principles and skills necessary for Christian service, we send them to serve the school, the poor or the widows. In doing so, we are helping them to realize the potential of using their skills to serve Christ. This trip has always served to bond students together, uniting them in the work of Christ. They learn the blessing that it is "better to give than to receive"[100] and have the opportunity to give back to the cause of Christ. They always return from a week of giving with such humble hearts, and are welcomed back by an assembly of students where they proceed to articulate all that which they have learned in their week of service. They testify as to how it has given them a new purpose and vision; how it has caused them to turn from their goal being that of self, degrees, and gaining money, to that of serving their fellow man. They learn during that week the true meaning of love, the true value of love, for each other and those God puts in their path. They are often awakened and shaken by the realization of the many needs that exist.

We choose to send them on this journey at the beginning of their senior year hoping to focus their goals on the meaning of life and to bring to their minds the importance of education; for it *is* the equipping of the saints allowing them to go forth and do the work of God. We have found this to be one of the greatest experiences of their young lives as it provides them with the motivation, momentum and encouragement in realizing the fullness of God's grace and the work of the Spirit in their own lives.

## Shouldn't boys and girls be educated separately? And what about dating?

It is surprising how many times I have been addressed with these questions. Historically, boys were educated separately from girls, whereas today it is the norm for boys and girls to be educated together. Throughout Scripture there are examples of times when boys and girls were separated, as well as times where women were to be "silent in the church,"[101] thus we do believe that there is premise for when to divide boys and girls. There are certainly times while teaching that necessitate frankness and situations can become awkward. As an educational institution, we feel the daughters enrolled in our school are in submission to their teachers who are an extension of the parents, not to other young men. Boys alike are to submit to their teachers and have no authority over any female student; period! With such parameters and such delineations, at times it is best to separate the genders.

Keep in mind that an educational institution is not a social institution in any way shape or form. A Christian school should not support dating, coupling or public displays of affection. As administrators, we are to make it clear that students are here for direction and instruction, not to find a social mate. During my interview process with families of older students, I am

---

100 Acts 20:35
101 1 Cor 14:34

very clear that these displays of affection will not be tolerated. This expectation should be defined in your secondary student/parent handbook as well.

It is also not the role of a Christian school to educate students in social graces as well as in the way they should treat one another. To aid this however, our school offers events where we teach young men and woman, separately, on how they should view each other. We train them on proper manners, etiquettes and protocol in social situations. Those events and opportunities are optional. Parents should have the final authority as to allow or not to allow their child to participate in them. One such event is called the Protocol.

## Does your school have a prom or school dance?

In lieu of a prom, where students pair up and individuals are left out, a "protocol" is a wonderful Christian alternative. The objective of a school protocol is to train older students in grades 9-12 how to interact with one another in a social environment. The setting is formal. The emphasis is on respect, and the goal is that all attendees will enjoy the evening.

The protocol takes place in a spacious facility that is able to accommodate Scottish folk-type dancing. Dance partners are scripted by lottery so that *everyone* participates and no coupling occurs. This will eliminate any anxieties regarding inappropriate behavior. The gentlemen should be given dance cards at the beginning of the night that indicates their partners for the evening. The dances are traditional group mixers, and individual selections that are pre-rehearsed before the ball. For example: Grand March, Virginia Reel, Patty-Cake Polka, Gay Gordon, Westchester Box Waltz, Post's Jig, and Fairfield Fancy. Dance practices are helpful and allow the students to enjoy themselves at the Protocol. Attendees can be charged a slight fee for this event, in order to cover the costs of refreshments or a facility rental.

As we seek to dance like Christians who honor God, we have a lot to learn and a lot to unlearn. The following are a few simple rules and guidelines that encourage a Christian approach to dancing and inculcate a proper and healthy atmosphere of thankfulness and celebration for this gift of God.

*Student Instruction for a Protocol:*
- *Gentlemen*: This dance requires semi-formal to formal attire. That means, at minimum, dress shoes, dress slacks (no denim), collared shirt, and tie. It is your responsibility to see that all the ladies have any opportunity to dance. Please follow your dance card in its entirety.
- *Ladies*: Modesty is required. Your best church dress will usually suffice. Dresses should have modest necklines (no strapless or spaghetti straps), well fitting bodices (not too tight), and mid-calf or longer hemlines. A full skirt is helpful, as the dances are very lively. You will need shoes that you can almost jog in. Ballet type slippers or flat shoes that won't slip off work well. Dresses should allow your arms to move freely and modestly in all directions. Your fathers should be consulted about your dress.

## What version of the Bible do you use and why?

It is very important to use a version of scripture that K-5 that students can easily read and understand. An understandable version aids students in the use of vocabulary, making it easier to memorize and recall the Scriptures. At my current Christian school, we use the New International Version for grades K-5. In grades 6-12, we have preferred using the New King James Version, where the king's English is still beautiful indeed, and has a flow that makes reading and memorization quicker.

## What about winning and losing athletic events?

Championships, trophies, titles and the recognition they bring should be attained properly. The main goal of athletic competition is to gain more points than the opposing team—but in what manner? Humiliating, disrespecting or playing outside the parameters of a game are not what a Christian school should be teaching as part of its principles. As stated in II Timothy 2:5, "If anyone competes in athletics, he is not crowned unless he competes according to the rules." There is nothing wrong with healthy competition, as long as it is truly viewed as competition. Oddly enough, one of the hardest things about athletic events is getting the *parents* to understand these parameters, not the children.

Done within the rules, the following examples are acceptable:
- Intentionally fouling the opponent in order to stop the clock within the confines of sportsmanship
- A basketball player reaching in and slapping an opponent on the arm, as long as it's not done in a way to hurt the opponent, and is viewed by the officials as not intentionally harmful
- Hitting an opponent really hard, taking him down to make a great tackle even though the opponent might of gotten hurt—as long as it was not done maliciously but in a manner of fair play

Any of the above actions done with intention to injure or hurt an opponent are unacceptable. Unsportsmanlike conduct should not be tolerated, as well as result in disciplinary action.

## Should boys and girls play on the same sports team?

Due to the simple nature of high school level athletics, whether it's blocking out in basketball, checking in lacrosse, or a slide tackle in soccer, there is rough physical touch and contact. It is not biblical, or healthy, to teach our young men to have aggression towards young women in a sense of competition, or conversely the young women toward the young men. Biblical examples portray men as protectors and providers of women and young women ought to see them in these respectful roles. By sharing an athletic field, it compromises these biblical ideals and compels them to challenge one another, an unacceptable practice at our Christian school.

## Do you feel corporal punishment should be used in a Christian school? If so, how do you implement it?

God's word is very clear as it instructs on how to discipline and train children. In Proverbs, God exhorts us, giving us the strength to carry out discipline with the rod knowing that it will bear the fruit of righteousness: "He who spares the rod hates his son, but he who loves him is careful to discipline him."[102] Proverbs 22:15 reads, "Foolishness is bound up in the heart of a child; the rod of correction will drive it far from him." At our Christian school, we believe strongly in corporal punishment as outlined in the word of God; however we feel it should be used for male students only. Outside of detention measures and other suitable punishment, it is best to leave any corporal punishment of girls to their parents if they choose to do so.

Our goal in disciplining students is to bring about the fruit of righteousness, driving out the foolishness and restoring that child back to a right relationship with God and others. Yes, discipline and corporal punishment inflict pain, but recall Hebrews 12:11, "no chastening seems to be joyful for the present, but painful; nevertheless, afterward it yields the peaceable fruit of righteousness to those who have been trained by it." Is that not our goal—to yield peaceable fruit in the lives of our students?

Recognizing that this is a difficult subject for some parents, your school's parent contract should clearly outline any discipline policies. Parents should be required to give, in writing, permission for or against corporal punishment. In the event that corporal punishment is allowed and may occur, parents should always be contacted before any discipline is carried out.

---

[102] Prv 13:24

# APPENDIX A

# CURRICULUM CHARTS

## Scope and Sequences for Grades K-12

| PHONICS SCHOOL (K-2) | | | |
|---|---|---|---|
| Subject | K | 1 | 2 |
| Art | 1x/wk Flash cards | 1x/wk Flash cards | 1x/wk Flash cards |
| Music | 1x/wk (listening) | 1x/wk (listening) | 1x/wk (listening) |
| Bible | Old Testament: Attributes of God, Books In Motion | New Testament: Life of Christ, Rainbow | Old Testament: Genesis, Exodus, and Psalms |
| Language Arts/ Reading/ Literature | Beginning to Read, Write and Listen, McGraw Hill, Sing, Spell, Read & Write songs, Journals | Raceway, SSR & W, 2nd ed., Words I Use When I Write, Saxon Phonics I Literature: Keep the Lights Burning Abbie, The 18 Penny Goose, Frog and Toad Together, Johhny Appleseed, Amelia Bedelia, The Bears on Hemlock Mountain, Sam the Minuteman, Reading for Christian Schools 1-1, 1-2 as needed | With Wings as Eagles, Stories from Grandma's Attic, A New Coat for Anna, "Little House" series, Miss Nelson is Missing, Blaze and the Lost Quarry, A Chair for My Mother, Ox Cart Man, Box Car Children series, The Emperor's New Clothes, Curious George, The Magic Fish, and more |
| Spelling | Beginning to Read, Write and Listen | Saxon Phonics I | Spelling 2 |
| Penmanship | Manuscript/Traditional (modified) | Manuscript/ D'Nealian | Manuscript/ Cursive D'Nealian |
| Grammar/Writing | | Shurley English 1, 2nd ed. | Shurley English 2, 2nd ed. |
| Social Studies/ History/ Geography | Units: Family, Patriotism, Community Leaders, Pilgrims, NC Geography | Units: County, Colonial America, Pilgrims, Beautiful Feet and D'Aulaire Titles | North Carolina History, Geography, Agriculture, State Facts |
| Latin | N/A | N/A | N/A |
| Math | Box It, Bag It, Math Their Way | Saxon 1, 2nd ed. Box It, Bag It | Classical Math, B.J. Jordan |
| Science | Units: Seasons, Senses, Bugs, NC Animal Habitats | Units: Solar System, Polar Region, Penguins, Plants, Frogs | Units: Deserts, Skeletal System, Mammals & Reptiles, Animal Report |
| P.E. | 1x/week | 1x/week | 1x/week |

# Scope and Sequence for Grades 3-5

## GRAMMAR SCHOOL (3-5)

| Subject | 3 | 4 | 5 |
|---|---|---|---|
| Art | 1x/wk Flash cards | 1x/wk Flash cards | 1x/wk Flash cards |
| Music | Recorder - all students<br>1-2x/wk (*listening*) | Chorus 2x/wk - or -<br>Beginning Band 2x/wk (*listening*) | Chorus 2x/wk - or -<br>Continuing Band 2x/wk (*listening*) |
| Bible | Walk through the Bible, John 3 | Sermon on the Mount | Philippians |
| Language Arts/ Reading/ Literature | *The Long Winter, Stuart Little, Misty of Chincoteague, The Courage of Sarah Nobel, Crown & Jewel, By the Shores of Silver Lake, Charlotte's Web, The Great Brain, Homer Price, The Hundred Dresses, The Minstrel in the Tower, Sarah, Plain and Tall, Squanto, Friend of the Pilgrim*, Reader's theatre, Read-aloud plays, Revolutionary plays | *The Wheel on the School, From the Mixed Up Files of Mrs. Basil E. Frankweiler, Caddie Woodlawn, Stonewall, The Lion, the Witch, & the Wardrobe, Prince Caspian, Mrs. Frisby and the Rats of NIMH, The Indian in the Cupboard, Thomas Edison: the Great American Inventor* | *Cricket in Times Square, The Secret Garden, The Witch of Blackbird Pond, Roll of Thunder, Hear My Cry, Rascal, Tuck Everlasting, Where the Red Fern Grows, My Side of the Mountain, Summer of the Monkeys, Escape from Warsaw, Snow Treasure, Pushcart War, Sounder* |
| Spelling | Spelling 3 | Spelling 4 | Spelling 5 |
| Penmanship | Manuscript/ Cursive D'Nealian | Cursive D'Nealian | Cursive |
| Grammar/ Writing | *Shurley English 3, 2nd ed.*<br>*Excellence in Writing* | *Shurley English 4, 2nd ed.*<br>*Excellence in Writing* | *Shurley English 6, 2nd ed.*<br>Research Paper<br>*Excellence in Writing* |
| Social Studies/ History/ Geography | States and Capitals, U.S. Presidents, The First America, Making 13 Colonies, Explorers, U.S. State Facts, Events leading up to the Revolutionary War and the Revolutionary War,<br>*The American Revolution*<br>*Meet Thomas Jefferson, Phoebe the Spy, Give Me Liberty,*<br>*Meet George Washington* | 1800-1900, Civil War,<br>Pony Express, Inventors, Westward Expansion, Immigration, *History of US*, Hakim, Oxford Press Vol. 6,<br>*War, Terrible War, Heritage Studies 4, 2nd ed.* (*supplemental*), Grandparent biography Reading/report of one independent famous American biography | *History Of US 1918-1945*, Hakim, Oxford Press Vol. 9<br>*Heritage Studies 5, 2nd ed.*<br>BJUP<br>*History Of US 1880-1917*, Hakim, Oxford Press Vol. 8 |
| Latin | Latin Primer I | Latin Primer II | Latin Primer III |
| Math | *Saxon 3, 2nd ed.* | *Saxon 54, 2nd ed.* | *Saxon 65, 2nd ed.* |
| Science | <u>Science 3</u>, *BJUP, 2nd. ed.*<br>Units: Rain Forest,<br>Five Senses, Birds, Fish,<br>Rocks and Minerals,<br><u>Birds</u>, <u>Fishes</u> | *Science 4, BJUP, CSI;*<br>Units: Space Exploration,<br>Moon & Planets, Constellations, Simple Machines, Electricity, Energy, Human Circulatory, Skeletal, Respiratory systems, Insects and Insect Collection | *Science 5, BJUP*<br>Units: CSI; Aims, Oceans, Seashells, Periodic Table, Weather, Natural disasters, Matter, Nervous system |
| P.E. | 2x/week | 2x/week | 2x/week |

# Scope and Sequence for Grades 6-8

## LOGIC SCHOOL (6-8)

| Subject | 6 | 7 | 8 |
|---|---|---|---|
| Bible | Logos Objectives<br>Classical Roots A<br>Colossians | Classical Studies<br>Classical Roots B/C<br>Old Testament Theology | Classical Studies<br>Classical Roots D/E<br>New Testament Theology |
| English/Literature<br><br>(Although the curriculum is listed here, Grammar is a separate subject for 6th grade.) | *A Wrinkle in Time,*<br>*The Call of the Wild,*<br>*The Hobbit,*<br>*Watership Down,*<br>*A Christmas Carol, Diary of Anne Frank, 100 Best Loved Poems, Father Brown Stories, Ten Tales of Shakespeare, Up From Slavery,* and various *Henty* novels<br>*Warriner's Composition & Grammar, 2nd course*<br>*Research Paper*<br>*Excellence in Writing* | *Across Five Aprils,*<br>*The Story of a Bad Boy, Treasure Island,*<br>*Johnny Tremain,*<br>*20,000 Leagues Under the Sea,*<br>*Out of the Silent Planet,*<br>*The Prince and the Pauper,*<br>*Hamlet,*<br>*Warriner's 3rd course, Excellence in Writing* | *Great Expectations,*<br>*Wuthering Heights,*<br>*Pride and Prejudice,*<br>*Julius Caesar,*<br>*The Pilgrim's Progress,*<br>*Romeo and Juliet,*<br>*Silas Marner,*<br>*Perelandra,*<br>*Our Mother Tongue,*<br>*Excellence in Writing* |
| Social Studies/History/Geography | History of US 1945-2001, Hakim, Oxford Press Vol. 10 | U.S. History: Early Explorers to American Revolution, <u>New</u> World In View, Gary DeMar, "Reformation to Colonization," Gary DeMar, U.S. History, Garraty, Supplemental Primary Sources | American Revolution to the Civil War<br>Primary Sources<br>U.S. History, Garraty |
| Foreign Language | Vocabulary from Classical Roots A | Vocabulary from Classical Roots B/C<br>Introduction to biblical languages | Vocabulary from Classical Roots D/E<br>Introduction to biblical languages |
| Math | *Saxon 76, 3rd ed.* | *Saxon Algebra ½, 3rd ed.* | *Saxon Algebra I, 3rd ed.* |
| Logic | N/A | N/A | Logic (J.N.)<br>Semester 1 Introduction<br>Semester 2 Intermediate |
| Science | *Life Science for Christian Schools, 2nd ed., BJUP,* Aims, CSI, Units: Trees, Ecosystems,<br>Leaves, Biomes, Food webbs and chains, Digestive system, Integumentary system, Cells, D.N.A., Genetics | Physical Science, *BJUP*<br>*The Physical World: An Introduction to Physical Science for Christian Schools, 2000* | N/A |
| Electives* | Last period | Last Period | Last Period |

# Scope and Sequence for Grades 9-12

## RHETORIC SCHOOL (9-12)

| Subject | 9 | 10 | 11 | 12 |
|---|---|---|---|---|
| Bible | Hermeneutics (Biblical Interpretation) | Systematic Theology | Historical Theology | Apologetics |
| English/Literature (Although the curriculum is listed here, Grammar is a separate subject for 6th grade.) | American Literature, *BJUP*, *The Old Man and the Sea*, *A Connecticut Yankee in King Arthur's Court*, *Bridge of San Luis Rey*, *The Red Badge of Courage*, *The Last of the Mohicans*, *The Scarlet Letter*, *Poems of Anne Bradstreet*, *Beyond Stateliest Marble: The Passionate Femininity of Anne Bradstreet*, *The Great Gatsby*, *The Jungle*, *Inherit The Wind* | Classical Literature; *Iliad*, *Odyssey*, *Classics in Translation*, Vols. 1 & 2 Greek Tragedies: *Prometheus Bound*, *Agamemnon*, *Oedipus Rex* *Antigone*, *Hippolytus Trial and Death of Socrates*, *Poetics*, *Meno*, *Plato*, *Birth of Tragedy*, *Plutarch - Makers of Rome*, *Aeneid*, *Metamorphoses of Ovid* - Classical Translation | Advanced British Literature, *BJUP* text *Beowulf*, *Canterbury Tales*, *Macbeth*, *A Midsummer Night's Dream*, *Henry V*, *Abolition of Man*, *That Hideous Strength*, *David Copperfield*, *Ivanhoe*, *Jane Eyre*, *Code of the Woosters*, *'Till We Have Faces*, *Sir Gawain and the Green Knight*, *Fairie Queen* | Advanced: The Great Books Luther and Calvin: *On Secular Authority*, *The Prince*, *2nd Treatise of Government*, *Leviathan*, *Social Contract*, *Pragmatism*, *Origin of Species*, *Introduction to the Philosophy of History*, *Revolt of the Masses*, *Discourse on Method*, *Count of Monte Cristo*, *Brothers Karamazov*, *Faust*, *Phantastes*, *Lilith* |
| Social Studies/ History/Geography | Civil War to WWI U.S. History, *BJUP*; Primary Sources, *Garraty* *Then Darkness Fled* *The Liberating Wisdom of Booker T. Washington*, *Leaders in Action* | World History (1910-Present), AP *History for Christian Schools*, *BJUP*, *The Killer Angels* (Civil War Series) | Rhetoric I Aristotle: *Rhetoric* Cicero: *Rhetorica Ad Herennium* Junior Thesis | Rhetoric II Senior Thesis |
| Foreign Language | Spanish I *Destinos*, *McDougall-Littell* | Spanish II *Destinos*, *McDougall-Littell* | Hebrew-*EKS Publishing* Greek -*NT Greek Primer*, *P&R Publishing* | Greek—*NT Greek Primer*, *P&R Publishing* |
| Math | *Geometry - UCPMP*, *Scott Foresman* | *Algebra II – UCPMP*, *Scott Foresman* | *Precalculus and Discrete Mathematics -UCPMP*, *Scott Foresman* | Advanced Calculus I *Calculus Early Transcendental Functions*, Third Edition, Larson, Howard, Edwards, Veritas |
| Logic | *Anatomy & Physiology*, Thibodaux, Ninth Edition, 1992 | Advanced Biology, *Biology for Christian Schools*, 2nd ed., *BJUP*, *Pandas & People*, Houghton Publishing | Advanced Chemistry Chemistry, *BJUP*, *Chemistry for Christian Schools*, 2nd. ed., | Advanced Physics, *BJUP*, *Physics for Christian Schools*, 2nd. ed. |
| Science | Last Period | Last Period | Last Period | Last Period |
| Electives* | | | | |

# Bible Words for the Teaching and Learning Process[103]

| WORD | KEY VERSE | KEY WORD | TEACHING PROCESS | LEARNING PROCESS |
|---|---|---|---|---|
| LAMATH | Deuteronomy 5:1<br>Deuteronomy 31:13 | assimilating | not dumping information, but stimulating to imitation | create a response in action, become experienced, assimilation |
| BE-EN | Nehemiah 8:7, 8<br>Daniel 9:23 | discriminating | distinguish, draw conclusions, explain alternatives | understand, so as to apply truth learned |
| ALAPH | Proverbs 22:25 | cleaving | to adopt, to hold to truth by experience | make familiar, to hold or adopt as one's own |
| YAH-DAG | Exodus 10:2<br>Joshua 23:14 | observing | to know by experience | learn by one's own observation |
| DAH-VAR | Jeremiah 28:16 | proclaiming | speak, say, proclaim | simply learning |
| YAH-RAH | 1 Samuel 12:23 | directing | to direct by words, example | directive learning |
| ZA-HAR | Psalm 19:11 | warning | to illuminate the mind, instruction, warning | replacing darkness with light, ignorance with knowledge |
| CHAH-CHAM | Proverbs 8:33 | application | to apply instruction to practical needs of life | personal application of principles in daily life |
| SAH-CHAL | 1 Samuel 18:30 | attention | to become skilled in a subject through careful consideration | to look at attentively and gain insight |
| SHAH-NAN | Deuteronomy 6:7 | sharpening skills | to whet the appetite, to make a deep impression | gaining a deep understanding |
| RAH-AH | Proverbs 6:6 | observing carefully | see a need and make provision, provide example and illustration | learn by observation |
| DIDASKO | Ephesians 4:21<br>2 Timothy 2:2 | involving activity | the activity of teaching | ability to teach others also |
| PAIDEUO | Ephesians 6:4 | instructing | guiding by instruction and discipline | growing in maturity |
| NOUTHETEO | Colossians 1:28 | mind shaping | shaping the mind by encouragement, reproof | renewed thoughts and attitudes |
| KATEKEO | Romans 2:18 | communicating | to din into the mind, oral communication of fact | repetition (catechism), recitation |
| MATHETEUO | Matthew 28:19 | discipling | instruction in loyalty and devotion to a person and his or her beliefs | a follower who is a learner |
| OIKODOMEO | 1 Corinthians 8:1 | edifying | promote growth and maturity, learning through love | maturity |
| MANTHANO | Matthew 11:29 | experiencing | provide pattern, practice and experience | personally appropriate in personal experience |
| PARATITHEMI<br>EKTITHEMI | 1 Timothy 1:18<br>Acts 11:4 | comprehending expounding | set forth clearly and plainly | to mentally grasp |
| DIERMENEUO | Luke 24:27 | interpreting | to interpret, unfold, open up, translate spiritual truth | discovery through explanation |
| DIANOIGO | Luke 24:31 | opening | to open minds and hearts to spiritual truth | the opening of ears, eyes and heart to spiritual understanding |
| SUNIAMI | Ephesians 5:17 | understanding | to put together so as to understand | assimilate so as to apply facts |
| HODEGEO | Acts 8:31 | guiding | cause to discover practical truth, to guide or lead to understanding | understand so as to apply truth |
| ANANGELLO | John 16:13 | proclaiming | to dispense factual truth, proclaim, report, declare | to verbally respond |

---

[103] Paul A. Kienel, Litt.D., Ollie E. Gibbs, Ed.D., Sharon R. Berry, Ph.D, *Philosophy of Christian School Education* (Colorado Springs, Colorado: Association of Christian Schools International, 1995), pg 233.

# APPENDIX B

## Student Report Cards and transcripts

### Elementary Report Card

REPORT CARD

2006-2007

Student: Caleb Ellis   Grade: 4
Teacher: Mrs. Casucci
Grade Placement for Next Year: _____

| Latin Comments | | | |
|---|---|---|---|
| Q1 | Q2 | Q3 | Q4 |

## Conduct Record

**Performance Code**
S=Satisfactory  N=Needs Improvement  U=Unsatisfactory

|  | Q1 | Q2 | Q3 | Q4 |
|---|---|---|---|---|
| Conduct: |  |  |  |  |
| 1. Has a cooperative attitude |  |  |  |  |
| 2. Works independently |  |  |  |  |
| 3. Obeys class and school rules |  |  |  |  |
| 4. Follows directions |  |  |  |  |
| 5. Completes work on time |  |  |  |  |
| 6. Speaks at appropriate times |  |  |  |  |
| 7. Gets along with others |  |  |  |  |
| 8. Uses time wisely/on task |  |  |  |  |
| 9. Wears proper school attire |  |  |  |  |
| 10. Respects teachers/principal and others |  |  |  |  |

### Comments

Q1

Q2

Q3

Q4

Latin comments on reverse side

---

**Name: Caleb Ellis**  **Grade: 4**  **Year: 2006-2007**

## Attendance Record

|  | Q1 | Q2 | Q3 | Q4 |
|---|---|---|---|---|
| Days Possible |  |  |  |  |
| Days Absent |  |  |  |  |
| Times Tardy |  |  |  |  |

## Academic Record

**Performance Code**

A = 94-100  I = Incomplete
B = 85-93  / = No grade this quarter
C = 75-84  S = Satisfactory
D = 70-74  N = Needs Improvement
F = 0-69  U = Unsatisfactory

|  | Q1 | Q2 | Q3 | Q4 |
|---|---|---|---|---|
| Latin |  |  |  |  |
| History/Geography |  |  |  |  |
| Mathematics |  |  |  |  |
| Science |  |  |  |  |
| Language Arts |  |  |  |  |
| Grammar |  |  |  |  |
| Penmanship |  |  |  |  |
| Reading |  |  |  |  |
| Spelling |  |  |  |  |
| Written Expression |  |  |  |  |
| Bible |  |  |  |  |
| Art |  |  |  |  |
| Music |  |  |  |  |
| Physical Education |  |  |  |  |

Q1 _____ Parent's Signature

Q2 _____ Parent's Signature

Q3 _____ Parent's Signature

162  THE ADMINISTRATOR'S HANDBOOK

# High School Report Card

Student: _____

Class: 12

School Year: 2006/2007

## Attendance Record

|  | Q1 | Q2 | Q3 | Q4 |
|---|---|---|---|---|
| Total Days in Quarter | 43 | 39 | 46 | 43 |
| Days Absent |  |  |  |  |
| Days Tardy |  |  |  |  |

## Electives

|  | Q1 | Q2 | Q3 | Q4 |
|---|---|---|---|---|
| Adv. Conditioning |  |  |  |  |
| A.P. History Prep |  |  |  |  |
| A.P. Science Prep |  |  |  |  |
| Art |  |  |  |  |
| Computer Science |  |  |  |  |
| Debate |  |  |  |  |
| Drama |  |  |  |  |
| P.E. |  |  |  |  |
| SAT Prep |  |  |  |  |
| Study Hall |  |  |  |  |
| Yearbook |  |  |  |  |

## Academic Record

A=90-100  B=80-89  C=70-79  F=0-69  I = Incomplete

|  | Q1 | Q2 | Final Exam | 1st Sem. AVG | Q3 | Q4 | Final Exam | 2nd Sem. AVG | YEARLY AVG |
|---|---|---|---|---|---|---|---|---|---|
| Apologetics |  |  |  |  |  |  |  |  |  |
| Great Books |  |  |  |  |  |  |  |  |  |
| Rhetoric II |  |  |  |  |  |  |  |  |  |
| Greek II |  |  |  |  |  |  |  |  |  |
| Calculus |  |  |  |  |  |  |  |  |  |
| Physics |  |  |  |  |  |  |  |  |  |

## Parent Signature

Q1 _____ Parent Signature

Q2 _____ Parent Signature

Q3 _____ Parent Signature

# Student Transcript

*[Insert Student Name, School Name, Address and Logo]*

\* Denotes Honors Class: A=5, B=4, C=3    AP & ADV Classes: A=6, B=5, C=4

**Grade 9    Year: 2003 – 2004**
Term (Wks): 36
Length of class period: 1hr.
Days absent: 0

| Subject | Periods Per Week | 1st Sem. | 2nd Sem. | Yr. Avg. | Units |
|---|---|---|---|---|---|
| * Theology | 5 | A | A | A | 5.0 |
| * American Literature | 5 | A | A | A | 5.0 |
| * US History | 5 | A | A | A | 5.0 |
| * Spanish I | 5 | A | A | A | 5.0 |
| * Geometry | 5 | A | A | A | 5.0 |
| * Anatomy | 5 | A | A | A | 5.0 |
| Totals | | | | | 30 |

Credits for Year: 6    Total Credits: 6
GPA: 5.0    Total GPA:

**Grade 10**

| Subject | Periods Per Week | 1st Sem. | 2nd Sem. | Yr. Avg. | Units |
|---|---|---|---|---|---|
| * Systematic Theology | 5 | A | A | A | 5.0 |
| * Classical Literature | 5 | A | A | A | 5.0 |
| * World History | 5 | A | A | A | 5.0 |
| * Spanish II | 5 | A | A | A | 5.0 |
| * Algebra II | 5 | A | A | A | 5.0 |
| AP Biology | 5 | A | A | A | 6.0 |
| Totals | | | | | 61 |

Credits for Year: 6    Total Credits: 12
GPA: 5.17    Total GPA: 5.08

**Grade 11    Year: 2005 – 2006**
Term (Wks): 36
Length of class period: 1hr.
Days absent: 2

| Subject | Periods Per Week | 1st Sem. | 2nd Sem. | Yr. Avg. | Units |
|---|---|---|---|---|---|
| Historical Theology* | 5 | A | A | A | 5.0 |
| British Literature* | 5 | A | A | A | 5.0 |
| Rhetoric I* | 5 | A | A | A | 5.0 |
| Greek I* | 5 | A | A | A | 5.0 |
| Calculus* | 5 | A | A | A | 5.0 |
| AP Chemistry | 5 | A | A | A | 6.0 |
| Totals | | | | | 92 |

Credits for Year: 6    Total Credits: 18
GPA: 5.17    Total GPA: 5.11

**Grade 12    Year: 2006 – 2007**
Term (Wks): 36
Length of class period: 1hr.
Days absent: 1

| Subject | Periods Per Week | 1st Sem. | 2nd Sem. | Yr. Avg. | Units |
|---|---|---|---|---|---|
| Apologetics | 5 | | | | |
| Rhetoric II* | 5 | | | | |
| Great Books * | 5 | | | | |
| Greek II* | 5 | | | | |
| ADV Calculus I | 5 | | | | |
| ADV Physics | 5 | | | | |
| Totals | | | | | |

Credits for Year ____    Total Credits:____
GPA: _____    Total GPA: _____

## Electives/Extra-Curricular Activities

| Activity: | 9 | 10 | 11 | 12 | Activity: | 9 | 10 | 11 | 12 |
|---|---|---|---|---|---|---|---|---|---|
| Drama | X | X | X | | | | | | |
| Volleyball | X | X | X | | | | | | |
| Knowledge Bowl | X | X | | | | | | | |

**GRADUATION DATA:**

Year: 200X    Month: May    Day: 20th
Number in class: XX    Current GPA: _____    Class Rank: TBD

164 THE ADMINISTRATOR'S HANDBOOK

# APPENDIX C

## Parent forms

### Parental Accountability Agreement

*Parents should be asked to:*

- Foster a courteous, grateful, respectful, obedient and cooperative and forgiving attitude along with proper restraint (self-control) in thoughts, words, actions and attitudes.
- Nurture habits of punctuality, thoroughness, neatness, honesty, resourcefulness, independent reading and study.
- Expect completion of all homework daily, making sure all books and completed homework are returned to school the following day.
- Support school personnel, programs, policies and activities with prayer and communication; and serve as a volunteer in various capacities.

## Membership Pledge

I, the undersigned, having read the by-laws of (school name) printed on this application, do whole-heartedly agree with the Statement of Faith and do subscribe to the Educational and Organizational Philosophies contained therein. Furthermore, if at any time I find myself no longer able to affirm the Membership Pledge, I will, on my own accord, initiate the withdrawal of my membership in (school name).

Signature: _____ Date: _____

Signature: _____ Date: _____

# Acceptance Letter

Date
Mr. & Mrs. Smith
1234 First Street
Town, State, Zip

Dear Mr. & Mrs. Smith,

Thank you for applying for admission to *(school name)* for the 20XX-20XX school year. I am privileged to officially inform you that (child name) has been accepted into *(school name)* for *(grade)*. To accept this seat for the 20XX-20XX school year, please remit a one-time registration fee of $___. We would like to collect the registration fee within two weeks of your receipt of this letter. Please feel free, however, to give us a call if this timetable presents a problem. We will be happy to work with you.

As you know, tuition may be paid using either automatic bank draft or by full payment prior to the first day of school. If you currently pay by draft, the first of twelve tuition payments for the 20XX-20XX school year will be drafted on (date). This payment will reflect the additional monthly amount of $___ for (student) tuition.

We are committed to working with parents to develop Godly, responsible, academically prepared students. We recognize and appreciate your continued commitment to providing the best possible training and instruction for your children.

We look forward to what the Lord will accomplish in your children here at (school name) in the coming year. Thank you for continuing to partner with us in this great endeavor. If you have further questions, please feel free to contact me at ___-____.

Sincerely,



Principal

# Withdrawal from Applying for Enrollment

Date

Mr. & Mrs. Smith
1234 First Street
Town, State, Zip

Dear Mr. & Mrs. Smith,

Thank you for your thoughtful and gracious note concerning your decision to remove your children from our applicant pools here at (school name). It is our practice to partially reimburse the application fee(s) when you make the decision to withdraw from the applicant pool prior to our formally extending a seat

We respect and appreciate the time, thought, and prayer you gave toward the consideration to enroll your children at (school name). It was a blessing to spend time getting to know your family. May the Lord continue to bless you as you seek to train up your children in the light of His love and grace.


Sincerely,



Principal

# Discipline Letter

*A copy of this letter should be placed in the student's file.*
Date

Mr. & Mrs. Smith
1234 First Street
Town, State, Zip

Dear Mr. and Mrs. Smith,

Pursuant to our discipline policy on pages ___ and ___ of our Secondary Student/Parent Handbook, your child _____ has received his first office visit today for disobedience.

The Principal determined the nature of the discipline during the visit. The Principal may require restitution, janitorial work, parental attendance during the school day with their student, corporal punishment, or other measures consistent with biblical guidelines that may be appropriate.

- Incidents one through three will be handled as above.

- The fourth incident will receive an automatic 2-day suspension. Parents should meet with the Principal upon return to the school.

- The fifth incident will result in child being expelled. Parents may choose to petition the board for re-admittance into the school.

May God grant us mercy in the disciplining of our children.

In Him,


Principal

# Academic Probation Letter

Date

Mr. & Mrs. Smith
1234 First Street
Town, State, Zip

Dear Mr. & Mrs.,

We are informing you that (student) is currently on academic probation. Our policy states that secondary students are required to maintain at least a 2.0 grade point average during any two, consecutive quarters. Exceptions will be made for students who have a grade point average of less than 2.0 but have not failed any courses during the quarter in question.

Grade point averages (G.P.A.s) for each secondary student will be calculated at the end of each quarter. Elective courses and independent study courses are not included in the G.P.A. calculation. If a student's G.P.A. is at or below 2.0 (i.e. a "C" average), that student will be placed on academic probation during the following quarter. Please call the office to schedule a conference. If at the end of the next quarter the student's G.P.A (for the quarter) has not risen to at least a 2.0, that student will be expelled.

Students who are on academic probation are *ineligible to participate in extracurricular activities.*

If you have any questions regarding this policy please don't hesitate to call me at \_\_\_\_\_-_____.

Sincerely,


Administrator

# Uniform Violation Card

Date _____

Dear Parent,

This is a warning notice informing you that your child _____ has violated the school uniform policy. The (school name) parental contract states: I will fully support and abide by all school policies, including the uniform policy.

Violation #     1     2     3     4

Violation: _____

The **fifth** violation of the school uniform policy will result in an office visit.

Thank you,

_____  _____
Teacher Signature              Administrator Signature

Double sided post card mailed to parents

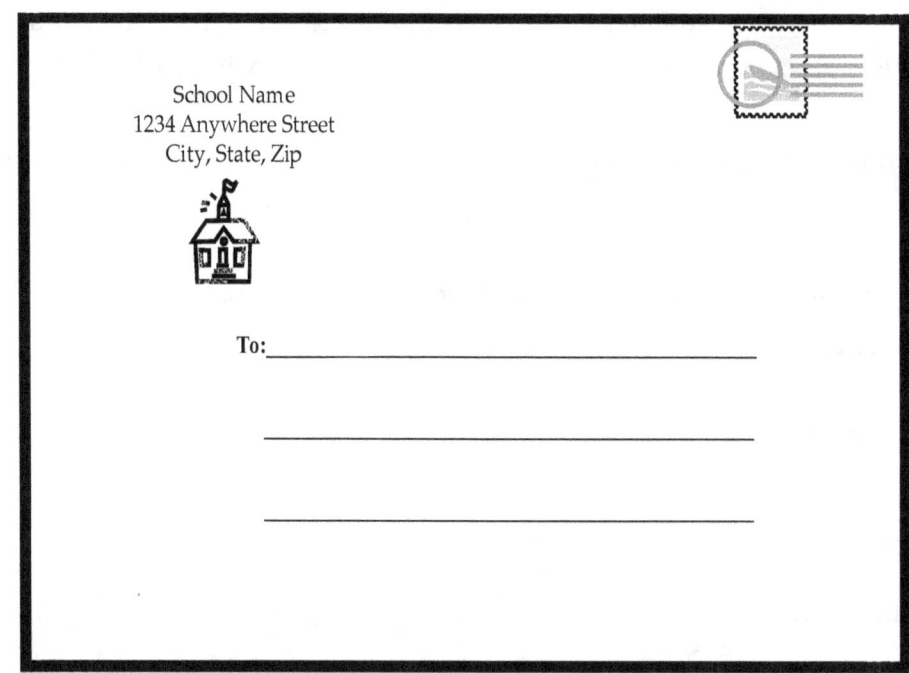

170  THE ADMINISTRATOR'S HANDBOOK

# Tardy/Absence Notice

Date

Mr. & Mrs. Smith
1234 First Street
Town, State, Zip

Dear Mr. & Mrs. Smith,

This letter is to inform you that (child's name) has accumulated (number) or more tardies since the beginning of the quarter. Our attendance policy states that <u>five tardies are equivalent to one absence</u>. In the event the total number of absences for one quarter is equal to or exceeds five days, or ten days for the semester, the student will <u>not</u> receive credit for that time period. Please review the attendance guidelines on page ___ of your student/parent handbook.

We realize various circumstances do arise, however it is important for your child to be on time to school each day and not be a disruption to other students in class. We appreciate your attention in this matter.

Please call the office should you have any questions. Thank you.

In His Service,

Principal

# Infectious Disease Parent Notification Letter

Date

Mr. & Mrs. Smith
1234 First Street
Town, State, Zip

Dear Mr. & Mrs. Smith,

This letter is to inform you that a member of the class has recently exhibited symptoms of fifth's disease. Fifth's disease is a mild, viral illness similar to chicken pox in that it may cause fever, rash, and mild flu-like symptoms in children. Symptoms appear several weeks after exposure and by the third week a red rash generally appears on the cheeks giving a "slapped face" appearance. The rash may then extend to the body and tends to fade and reappear. The patient is contagious several weeks prior to break out. Once the rash appears, the patient is actually no longer contagious. We did, however, want to make you aware of the possibility should you notice similar symptoms in your child. Pregnant women who have not previously had the illness should avoid contact with patients who have fifth's disease.

Sincerely,

Principal

# APPENDIX D

## Personnel forms

### Employment Application

Job Application

*"Providing an excellent classical education
founded upon a biblical worldview"*

*(School name) does not discriminate on the basis of race, color or national or ethnic origin in the administration of its hiring or educational policies.*

**Please complete this form legibly in ink. Each question should be answered as thoroughly as possible.**

## *PERSONAL INFORMATION*

Last Name _____ / First Name _____ / Middle Name _____ / Preferred Name _____ / Today's Date _____

| Street Address | City | State | Zip Code |
|---|---|---|---|
|  |  |  |  |

Previous addresses if less than 10 years at current address

| Street Address | City | State | Zip Code | Dates at Address |
|---|---|---|---|---|
|  |  |  |  |  |
|  |  |  |  |  |
|  |  |  |  |  |

SS# _____ Home Phone _____ Work Phone _____

Drivers License # _____ State _____ Email Address _____

Have you ever been convicted of a crime *other than* a minor traffic offense? _____ If yes, describe in detail below:

Have you ever worked or earned degrees under another name, please list below.

Last Name _____ / First Name _____ / Middle Name _____ / Dates from/to _____

**Position Desired:** _____

Date Available _____ Salary Desired _____

How did you hear about this opportunity with (School name) ? _____

## *EDUCATION AND TRAINING*

Circle *last* level of education completed:  High School 1 2 3 4   College/University 1 2 3 4   Graduate 1 2 3 4

| Education | Name and Location (City, State, and Country) | GPA | Major/Minor | Degree Earned | Date (Mo/Yr) |
|---|---|---|---|---|---|
| High School |  |  |  |  |  |
| College/ University |  |  |  |  |  |
| Graduate School |  |  |  |  |  |
| Business or Vocational |  |  |  |  |  |
| Certifications/ Training |  |  |  |  |  |
| Office Skills |  |  |  |  |  |
| Technical or Language Skills |  |  |  |  |  |

## EMPLOYMENT HISTORY

List your employment history for the last 10 years (list your most recent job first).

If you are currently employed, may we contact your employer _____ yes _____ no

**I understand that upon employment, proof of legal right to work in the United States is required.**

| Dates Employed | Starting Salary $<br>Ending Salary $ | Employer | Supervisor Name | Supervisor Title |
|---|---|---|---|---|
| Phone | Address | Your Title | Your Duties | |
| Reason for Leaving: | | | | |
| Dates Employed | Starting Salary $<br>Ending Salary $ | Employer | Supervisor Name | Supervisor Title |
| Phone | Address | Your Title | Your Duties | |
| Reason for Leaving: | | | | |
| Dates Employed | Starting Salary $<br>Ending Salary $ | Employer | Supervisor Name | Supervisor Title |
| Phone | Address | Your Title | Your Duties | |
| Reason for Leaving: | | | | |
| Dates Employed | Starting Salary $<br>Ending Salary $ | Employer | Supervisor Name | Supervisor Title |
| Phone | Address | Your Title | Your Duties | |
| Reason for Leaving: | | | | |

## REFRERENCES

List four personal references on the following Reference Release sheets. You should include a pastor, a supervisor or principal (or teacher you student-taught under, if you have no professional teaching experience), and close friends you have known for over five years.

Name        Title           Company         Relationship        Home or Work Number

_____

_____

_____

_____

♦ List any extra curricular activities with which you are willing to help (clubs, sports, etc.):

♦ Describe your personal philosophy of education and explain how it would affect your day-to-day teaching:

♦ Why do you believe you are called to teach in a Christian school?

♦ What is the most important quality you as a teacher would bring to a classroom at **(School name)**.

♦ Briefly describe your familiarity with the various approaches to discipline in a Christian School:

♦ How would you define the term classical education?

5

- How would you define the term biblical worldview?


- How often do you attend church in a typical month?
    - ☐ Every Sunday   ☐ 2 or 3 Sundays   ☐ 1 Sunday a month   ☐ Rarely, if ever
- In what ways are you currently serving in your church (Sunday school teacher, etc.)?


- What is your view of the nature of mankind?


- What is your view of the Bible?


- What is your understanding of the doctrine of the Holy Trinity?


- What is your view on the person and work of Jesus Christ?

♦ Give a detailed account of your salvation experience (how you came to know Jesus Christ as your Lord and Savior) and of your walk with the Lord up to the present:

Please list the titles and authors of five books you have read in the last twelve months:

_____
Title/Author

_____
Title/Author

_____
Title/Author

_____
Title/Author

_____
Title/Author

Any further comments:

I understand this application will be given every consideration and its receipt does not imply that I will be employed. I hereby declare that my statements on this application and on my resume or documents provided by me to -----(School name)----- are true and correct to the best of my knowledge. I acknowledge and agree that any false information may result in a decision not to hire me or if hired, may result in termination of my employment. I also authorize investigation of these statements. This investigation may include employment history, reasons for leaving previous employers, criminal record, driving record, social security number investigation, and degree verification. I hereby release Cary Christian School from all liability for any damages resulting from the information obtained.

_____ / _____
**(Applicant's Signature)**                                (Date)

*OTHER INFORMATION*

Local Church: _____

- Do you subscribe without reservation to Article III of **(School name)**'s bylaws as shown on the last page of this application? _____ If not, please explain:


- Have you read the **school's staff handbook, and do you** understand and agree to comply with its policies? _____ If not, please explain:


- List any states in which you are certified to teach:


- List any non-state organizations by which you are certified:


- List the grades you prefer to teach in order of preference:


- Have you ever been dismissed or asked to resign from a teaching position? _____
  If yes, please explain below:




- List the subjects you are most qualified to teach:



- Are you willing to take continuing adult education courses? _____ If not, please explain:

4

# Reference Form

## School Name
1234 Anywhere St.

Telephone: ___-___-_____

**TO THE APPLICANT:**
Complete the applicant section and direct this form to one of the individuals listed on your application as a reference. Ask the individual to return to you the completed form in the envelope provided, which must remain sealed until received in this office.

APPLICANT NAME:_____ City/State:_____
APPLYING FOR POSITION AS:_____
NAME OF PERSON COMPLETING THIS FORM:_____

**TO THE REFERENCING INDIVIDUAL:**
Place this completed form in an envelope and sign your name across the sealed flap. Return the sealed envelope to the applicant who will submit it with his/her application. Please respond to each of the areas below, giving your candid opinion of the applicant's qualifications for the position indicated above. Narrative comments on the back are welcome if you desire to elaborate. This information will be maintained in a separate pre-employment file and will not be made available to the employee except under subpoena or court order. Thank you for your assistance.

| Please check the level at which the applicant consistently performs. | Superior 6 | Well Above Expectations 5 | Above Expectations 4 | At Expectations 3 | Below Expectation 2 | Unsatisfactory 1 |
|---|---|---|---|---|---|---|
| Character (general conduct, ethics, morals) | | | | | | |
| Personal appearance (dress, grooming) | | | | | | |
| Energy level | | | | | | |
| Personality | | | | | | |
| Voice quality | | | | | | |
| Tact | | | | | | |
| Self-control | | | | | | |
| Enthusiasm | | | | | | |
| Willingness to accept criticism | | | | | | |
| Ability to work without close supervision | | | | | | |
| Ability to work closely with others | | | | | | |
| Dependability | | | | | | |
| Promptness and thoroughness | | | | | | |
| Overall attitude | | | | | | |
| Loyalty and cooperation | | | | | | |
| Communication skills (oral) | | | | | | |
| Communication skills (written) | | | | | | |
| Decision-making skills | | | | | | |
| Scholarship | | | | | | |
| Initiative | | | | | | |
| **PLEASE COMPLETE THE FOLLOWING ADDITIONAL INFORMATION FOR TEACHER APPLICANTS:** | | | | | | |
| Management of instructional time | | | | | | |
| Management of student behavior | | | | | | |
| Presentation of instruction | | | | | | |
| Monitoring of student performance | | | | | | |
| Evidence of planning, use of resources | | | | | | |
| Interaction with students | | | | | | |
| Interaction with co-workers | | | | | | |
| Assumption of non-instructional duties | | | | | | |
| Oral presentation skills | | | | | | |
| Evidence of professional growth | | | | | | |
| Enthusiasm for teaching | | | | | | |

(continued on reverse)

Opportunities for observing the candidate: _____
_____
_____
_____

Do you know of anything that would cause the candidate to be unfit for this position? No ____ Yes ____ (If yes please explain.) _____
_____
_____

To your knowledge, has this applicant ever been subject to any disciplinary action or asked to resign? No ____ Yes ____ (If yes please explain.) _____
_____
_____

If you were personally responsible, would you recommend the employment of this applicant? No ____ Yes ____ (If yes please explain.) _____
_____
_____
_____
_____

Additional Comments: _____
_____
_____
_____
_____

Signature: _____
Name (please print): _____
Position: _____
Company/School: _____
Address: _____
_____

Phone: _____
Date: _____

# Disclosure Form

## School Name
1234 Anywhere St.

Telephone: ___-___-_____

**DISCLOSURE, AUTHORIZATION AND RELEASE FOR BACKGROUND INFORMATION**

- I understand that in connection with my application for employment (including contracts for service), (School name) or an Agency/Agent working on behalf of (School name) School will research and verify the information I have provided on my application for employment, including my personal background, professional standing, work history and qualifications.

- I understand that (School name) or its Agent will obtain information (unless otherwise noted on the application form) it deems appropriate from various sources including, but not limited to, the following: current and past employers, criminal conviction records, Department of Motor Vehicle records, military records, school records, and professional and personal references. I authorize, without reservation, any individual, corporation or other private or public entity to furnish (School name) and its Agent all information about me. I unconditionally release and hold harmless any individual, corporation, or private or public entity from any and all causes of action that might arise from furnishing to (School name) School or its Agent information that they may request pursuant to this release.

- This authorization and release, in original, faxed or photocopied form, shall be valid for this and any future reports and updates that may be requested.

Dated: _____      _____
                            Applicant's Signature

                            _____
                            Print Name

# Pastor Reference Form

## School Name
1234 Anywhere St.
Telephone: ___-___-_____

## Pastor's Reference Form

Applicant's Name _____

Address _____

Dear Pastor,

This individual is seeking a position at (School name), an independent parent/board-run, non-denominational school. The mission of the school is to work with parents to develop godly, responsible, academically prepared students, capable of clearly articulating a Biblical worldview.

Please complete this reference form as it pertains to him/her **and return it to the applicant in a sealed envelope with your signature across the sealed flap.** All responses will be treated with complete confidentiality.

1. **Christian Commitment:** _____ evident and beyond question
   _____ no evidence of commitment

2. **Church Attendance:** _____ faithful and regular _____ occasional
   _____ infrequent _____ never

3. **Church Relationship:** _____ members in good standing
   _____ not members, but exhibit commitment
   _____ not supportive

4. Has this individual held a leadership position in the church? Please describe: _____
_____

5. Has this individual used any special talents within the church body? Please describe: _____
_____

6. Is the applicant active in the Sunday School and/or other programs of the church? _____

7. Do you consider the applicant open to spiritual instruction? _____

8. Do you recommend this applicant for employment (School name)? _____

9. How long have you known the applicant? _____ Are you related to the applicant? _____

Please use the back of this sheet for any other comments you would like to make.

Pastor's Signature _____ Date _____

Church _____ Phone _____

Church Address _____

City _____ State/Zip _____

APPENDIX D 183

# Ministry Contract

## Teaching Ministry Offer

*"Providing an Excellent Classical Christian Education Founded Upon a Biblical Worldview"*

EMPLOYEE: _____

ADDRESS: _____

SS#: _____  DATE OF BIRTH: _____

Having called upon the Lord our God for guidance, and believing ourselves led by Him, this annual good faith agreement is entered into by Cary Christian School and the above named Employee. This agreement is renewed on a yearly basis with no guarantee of a contract offer in the following year.

1. The Employee is hereby hired as a/an_____
   by ---(School name)--- . This assignment may or may not be changed by the Superintendent based on his estimation of the needs of the school as a whole.

2. ( ---(School name)--- agrees to pay the Employee a yearly salary of $_____. In the event this agreement is terminated prior to completion of the specified term, the salary will be paid on a prorated basis. {Note: payday is the last working day of the month except June and July. Preferred pay option is direct deposit.}

3. This offer covers the twelve-month period from **August 1, 2005** to **July 31, 2006** (which includes teaching days, workdays, workshops, faculty meetings, etc.). Teacher contract hours are as follows:
   - Kindergarten: 7:45 a.m. to 12:45 p.m.
   - First & Second: 7:45 a.m. to 3:15 p.m.
   - Third - Fifth: 7:30 a.m. to 3:30 p.m.
   - Sixth - Twelfth: 7:30 a.m. to 4:00 p.m.

4. The Employee agrees to maintain an exemplary Christian life and to follow the guidelines in the attached Job Description. The employee must wholeheartedly support the philosophy of a classical Christian education as described in Doug Wilson's books: <u>Recovering The Lost Tools of Learning</u> and <u>Excused Absence</u>. The employee must prescribe to the <u>Seven Laws of Teaching</u> in regards to his or her teaching techniques.

5. All employees are required to have <u>all</u> school-aged children enrolled at Cary Christian School. Not abiding by this requirement will result in termination of employment status.

6. The ---(School name)--- Board, Superintendent or the Employee may terminate this agreement at their sole discretion by providing at *least two weeks written notice.*

7. It is expected that all ---(School name)--- teachers will pursue A.C.C.S. teacher certification.

8. ---(School name)--- benefits offered will be effective as of August 1, 2005.

   **A.** *Employer Options*: (Administrative staff will check if applicable)

   \_\_\_\_ **UNUM Provident Insurance:** (30 day eligibility requirement for 20+ hours/week employment)
   - Life Insurance
   - Accidental Death and Dismemberment
   - Short Term Disability
   - Long Term Disability

   \_\_\_\_ **Medical Insurance Reimbursement:** ½ of the employee's portion of the monthly medical premium up to $100.00 per month (over a 12 month period). This is processed as a reimbursement, not a payroll deduction.

   \_\_\_\_ **Personal Leave Days**   \_\_\_\_ **Sick Leave Days**

   **B.** *Employee Options*: Check and complete the following if benefit is desired.

   \_\_\_\_ **403(B) Retirement Plan** *(participation forms available in office)*

   \_\_\_\_ **Tuition Deduction Option** *(please complete the chart below)*

   Total number of children enrolling at (School name) \_\_\_\_

|  | *Salary Amount From Front* |  | $ |
|---|---|---|---|
| Kindergarten | $4,000 x _____ (# of children) | $ |  |
| Grades 1-12 | $5,000 x _____ (# of children) | $ |  |
|  | Total Tuition | $ |  |
|  | Less FFNA grant amount (if applicable) | ($    ) |  |
|  | Total Adjusted Tuition |  | $ |
| **Compare Salary to Tuition:** |  |  |  |
| *ADJUSTED SALARY* | (If salary is greater than tuition) |  | $ |
| OR |  |  |  |
| *ADJ. TUITION DUE* | (If tuition is greater than salary) |  | $ |

THIS OFFER IS NOT VALID UNTIL SIGNED BY <u>ALL</u> THE PARTIES BELOW. (NEW EMPLOYEES: THIS EMPLOYMENT AGREEMENT IS NOT VALID UNTIL SUCCESSFUL COMPLETION OF A BACKGROUND CHECK.)

**Signed**:_____ /\_\_\_/\_\_\_   _____ /\_\_\_/\_\_\_
             Superintendent         Date                    Employee                Date

**AMENDMENTS SECTION:**

| Effective Date | Current Salary | New Salary | Comments | Superintend. Initials | Employee Initials |
|---|---|---|---|---|---|
|  |  |  |  |  |  |
|  |  |  |  |  |  |
|  |  |  |  |  |  |

Rev. 04/2005

# Employment Denial Letter

Date

Mrs. Smith
1234 First Street
Town, State, Zip

Dear Mrs. Smith:

 Thank you for your interest and time invested in pursuing employment with (school name).  We are thankful to have had such a strong pool of qualified applicants of which you were one. After thoughtful deliberation and prayer, we have filled all staff vacancies for the coming school year. Should our needs change we will contact you.  May God bless you as you continue to seek His will and perfect plan for this next year.

In Christ,


Principal

# Staff Evaluation Forms

## TEACHER OBSERVATION FORM

### Observation of (staff name) on (date)

**Chronological Overview:**

| 1:33 | Reviewing the time period before the Great Depression |
|------|-------------------------------------------------------|
| :38  | Discussing the position that Hoover held during the 1930's |
| :43  | "          " |
| :48  | "          " |
| :53  | "          " |
| :58  | "          " |

**Tools:**

| Review | Question & Answers | Media/Newspaper | Articles |
|--------|--------------------|-----------------|----------|
| Lecturing | | | |

**On Task Analysis: 97%**

| Time | Count | Notes | Scale: | (Circle) |
|------|-------|-------|--------|----------|
| 1:45 | 17/18 | Student not paying attention | | |
| :46 | 17 | "      " | | |
| :47 | 17 | "      " | 100 - | A+ |
| :48 | 17 | "      " | 95 - 99 | A |
| :49 | 17 | "      " | 94 - | A- |
| :50 | 18 | | 92 - 93 | B |
| :51 | 18 | | 90 - 91 | C |
| :52 | 18 | | 88 - 89 | D |
| :53 | 18 | | 87 and below | F |
| :54 | 18 | | | |
| | 175/180 | | | |

**Feedback:**

| Great introduction to the lesson and bringing it to application with today's events! |
|---|
| "Okay" – 29x  (Be aware of how many times you say this) |
| Good use of political cartoons. |
| |

———————— Your comments and suggestions are placed here. ————————

**OVERALL: A**

# Annual Teacher Evaluation Form

Annual Teacher Evaluation Form for Year:_____ - _____

Teacher:_____

Class/Grade_____

*The following ratings will be used to complete this evaluation:*

E = Exemplary, S = Satisfactory, N = Needs Improvement, U = Unacceptable, N/O = Not Observed

| OBJECTIVES | MARK | COMMENTS |
|---|---|---|
| **Spiritual Leadership:** | | |
| The teacher consistently exhibits love, joy, peace and spiritual maturity in his/her daily work and relationships in the school. | | |
| **Instruction:** | | |
| • Attempts to show the integration of subject matter.<br>• Demonstrates a thorough knowledge of and an interest in the subject(s).<br>• Uses valid teaching techniques that stimulate and maintain the students' active interest in the lesson.<br>• Uses clear language and vocabulary appropriate to the level of the students.<br>• Plans lessons in order to achieve curriculum goals.<br>• Checks for comprehension and does not presume on the students' understanding of new terms and concepts.<br>• Often has the student rephrase material in his own words.<br>• Begins with a review and/or what is already familiar to the students.<br>• Homework assignments are effective and appropriate.<br>• Routines and maintenance procedures are simple, but adequate. | | |
| **Classroom Management:** | | |
| • Provides an orderly teaching environment by consistently enforcing their own class rules and the school's discipline policies.<br>• Maintains a clean, attractive, well-ordered classroom. Students assist in keeping the classroom clean. | | |

| | | |
|---|---|---|
| **Lesson Planning and Grading:** | | |
| ♦ Prepares and submits weekly lesson plans for the administrator's review.<br>♦ Lesson plans implement the prescribed course objectives.<br>♦ Lessons cover all specified course objectives listed in the curriculum guide.<br>♦ Uses a variety of assignments to measure student learning.<br>♦ Keeps students, parents, and the administration adequately informed of deficiencies and gives sufficient notice of failure. | | |
| **Professional:** | | |
| ♦ Demonstrates a biblical approach to his work by his punctuality, cheerful and compliant attitude, attention to duties, appearance, etc.<br>♦ Uses acceptable English in written and oral communication. Speaks with clear articulation.<br>♦ Is working toward certification (provisional or permanent)<br>♦ Develops and maintains rapport with students, parents, and staff to promote a positive learning environment. | | |
| **Final Mark:** | | |

*Summary Comments:*

The employee's signature indicates that the employee has read and discussed the evaluation with his supervisor but does not necessarily imply agreement.

Date: _____

Employee's Signature: _____

# APPENDIX E

## Medical forms

### Emergency Medical / Contact Form

Student's Name: _____ Birthday: _____

Teacher: _____ Grade: _____

Parent(s)/Guardian Name: _____

Street Address: _____

City/State/Zip: _____ Home Phone: _____

Daytime phone (Mother): _____ Daytime phone (Father): _____

Circle one: Cellular Pager          Other Telephone Number: _____

Emergency Contacts:

Name: _____ Relationship to child: _____ Phone: _____

Name: _____ Relationship to child: _____ Phone: _____

**Medical Information:**

Is this child currently taking any medications on a regular basis? ___ If so, please list medications and possible side effects: _____
_____
_____

Does this child have any allergies? ___ If so, please list: _____
_____

Is this child currently under the care of a physician? ___ If so, please explain: _____
_____
_____

Does this child have any other on-going health considerations? _____
_____
_____

Physician's name: _____ Phone: _____

Dentist's name: _____ Phone: _____

Preferred Hospital: _____

Health Insurance Carrier: _____ Policy number: _____

In the event that I cannot be contacted, I hereby authorize (school name) to provide and/or seek emergency medical treatment for my child named above. {Note: please see permission on reverse side.}

I authorize (school name) to administer the following medications to my child during the school day. My child's age is _____ and his/her weight is approximately _____ lbs.

| Over the counter (OTC) Medicine | Dosage allowed |
|---|---|
| Acetaminophen (Tylenol) | |
| Ibuprofen (Advil) | |
| Tums | |
| Benadryl (for allergic reaction only) | |
| Topical Hydrocortisone (for allergic reaction only) | |
| Neosporin | |
| Other, please list: * | |
| Prescription Medicine | |
| Epi-pen** | |
| Inhaler** | |
| Other, please list: * | |

*Note: If you select "other under OTC or prescription drugs", please send the medication to school with a signed note stating that the (school name) staff has permission to administer this medication to your child. Please include detailed instructions. (We reserves the right to refuse the administration of certain medications.)

** For Epi-pens, inhalers, and such, the parents should provide a medical action plan. Waivers are required for Epi-pen usage.

(For Office Use Only) Action Plan On File_____ Waiver on file_____.

Signed: _____ Date: _____

*Please use blue or black ink only*          *School Year 200X-200X*

| **For Office Use Only:** |
|:---:|
| **Record of Medication Given** |

| Date | Time | Medication | Dosage | Notes |
|---|---|---|---|---|
| | | | | |
| | | | | |
| | | | | |

# Student Accident Report

| Name of Student:<br>Social Security #: | | Male  Female | Grade:<br>Date of Birth: |
|---|---|---|---|
| Date of Accident:<br>/ /<br><br>Time of Accident :<br><br>_____  ❏ AM ❏ PM | How Accident Occurred…<br>❏ Enroute to/from school<br>❏ During school session<br>❏ Practice or play of interscholastic sports<br>Name of Sport_____ MS ❏JV ❏Varsity<br>❏ Other_____ | | |
| How did accident happen? | | | |
| Details of Injury-including part of body injured: | | | |
| Name of Teacher or Coach Supervising Activity | | | |
| Statement of Parent or Guardian | | | |
| Name of Person Making this Report | | Relationship to Student | |
| Address:<br>Street/Box #<br>City          State          Zip | | Telephone:<br>Home ( ) _____<br>Work ( ) _____ | |
| Father or Guardian:<br><br>Address if different from Student: | | Occupation: | Social Security #: |
| Guardian's Employer: Name<br>City          State          Zip | | Street/Box #<br>Phone # | |
| Father or Guardian:<br><br>Address if different from Student: | | Occupation | Social Security # |
| Guardian's Employer: Name<br>City          State          Zip | | Street/Box #<br>Phone # | |
| Does either parent or guardian have Accident/Health Insurance which covers this student?<br>❏Yes ❏No<br><br>If yes, which person(s)? | | | |
| Name of Insurance Company(ies): | | Name of Policyholder(s) and policy #s: | |

# Athletic Medical and Travel Waiver

> WARNING: THIS IS AN AGREEMENT TO OBEY
> INSTRUCTIONS, RELEASE ASSUMPTION OF RISK, AND
> AGREEMENT TO HOLD HARMLESS

Both the **applicant student** and a **parent or guardian** must read carefully and sign below.

SPORT: (Student must circle all sports he or she will participate in.)

| | | | |
|---|---|---|---|
| Baseball | Cross Country | Soccer | Track and Field |
| Softball | Basketball | Football | Tennis |
| Volleyball | Gymnastics | Swimming | Cheerleading |
| Golf | Lacrosse | Other | |

STUDENT

I am aware that playing or practicing to play/participate in any sport can be dangerous in nature involving MANY RISKS OF INJURY. I understand that the dangers and risks of death, serious neck and spinal injuries which may result in complete or partial paralysis, brain damage, serious injury to virtually all bones, joints, ligaments, muscles, tendons, and other aspects of the muscular skeletal system, serious injury to virtually all internal organs, and serious injury or impairment to other aspects of my body, general health and well being. I understand that the dangers and risks of playing or practicing to play/participate in the above sport may result not only in serious injury, but in a serious impairment of my future abilities to earn a living, to engage in other business, social and recreational activities, and generally to enjoy life. Because of the dangers of participating in the above sports, I recognize the importance of following the coaches' instructions regarding playing techniques, training and other team rules, etc. and to agree to obey such instructions. In consideration of (school name) permitting me to try out for the teams circled and to engage in all activities related to the team, including, but not limited to, trying out, practicing or playing/participating in that sport. I hereby assume all the risks associated with participation and agree to hold (school name), it's employees, and volunteers harmless from any and all liability, actions, causes of action, debts, claims or demands of any kind and nature whatsoever which may arise by or in connection with my participation in any activities related to (school name) _____(indicate sport/sports) team/teams. The terms hereof shall serve as a release and assumption of risk for my heirs, estate, executor, administrator, assignees, and for all members of my family.

Date_____, 20_____  _____
                                            Signature of Student

PARENT

In consideration of (school name) permitting my son/daughter to try out for the _____team and to engage in all activities related to the team, including, but not limited to,

_____
(Indicate Sports Team(s))

trying out, practicing or playing/participating in that sport, I hereby assume all the risks of my son/daughter associated with participation and agree to hold (school name), it's employees, agents, representatives, coaches, and volunteers harmless from any and all liability, actions, causes of action, debts, claims, or demands of any kind and nature whatsoever which may arise by; or in connection with his/her participation in any activities related to (school name)

_____        _____
(Indicate Sport/Sports) team.

The terms hereof shall serve as a release and assumption of risk for my son's/daughter's heirs, estate, executor, administrator, assignees, and for all members of his/her family.

Date_____, 20_____  _____
                                  Signature of Parent or Guardian

# APPENDIX F

## Admission Applications and Re-Enrollment Forms

### Application for Student Admissions

# Application for Admission

*"Providing an excellent classical education founded upon a biblical worldview."*

## School Name
1234 Anywhere St.
Telephone: ___-___-_____
website.com • email.com

----School name----l admits students of any race, color, sex, and national or ethnic origin, to all the rights, privileges, programs, and activities generally accorded or made available to students at the school. It does not discriminate on the basis of race, color, sex, or national or ethnic origin in administration of its educational policies, admissions policies, and athletic and other school-administered programs.----School name----l does reserve the right to select students on the basis of academic performance, religious commitment, philosophical compatibility, and a willingness to cooperate with the----School name----l administration and abide by its policies.

# Application/Admission Procedure

## General Admission Standards

----School name---- ] is, in essence, an expression of the commitment of a body of parents to provide the best possible training and instruction for their children. Our mission is to instill in each student a love for truth, wisdom, discernment and learning through the use of excellent materials, in an orderly setting, founded on a growing personal knowledge of the Lord Jesus Christ. **As a discipleship school, we require that at least one parent or guardian of each applicant give a credible profession of faith in Jesus Christ as Lord and Savior, and be a regular attendee or member of a Christian church.** Students seeking admission are evaluated on the basis of their report cards, references, admission questionnaires, interviews, and potential to perform satisfactorily at ----School name---- ]. We are not equipped with the resources required to serve children who are seeking to be admitted into special educational programs. Students who seek admission directly following suspension, expulsion or behavior problems from another school will not be accepted until they prove themselves elsewhere. Students with less than a "C" average in their primary academic subjects may have difficulty in attaining a satisfactory level of academic achievement. **The first quarter is considered a trial period for all new students.**

## Application Procedures Checklist

Please keep this checklist and use it for your personal reference. It is the responsibility of the parent to be sure all application materials are completed and received by the admissions office. The admission process for your child cannot proceed until these materials are received. Your application will be processed after the following items are submitted or steps completed:

- ❑ Current corporation membership
- ❑ Completed Application for Admission
- ❑ Application fee of $150 (partially refundable if we are unable to guarantee a seat)
- ❑ Copies of standardized test scores and report cards from the past 2 years
- ❑ Pastor's reference (returned by pastor)
- ❑ Birth certificate (Kindergarten) & immunization record
- ❑ Signed Parental Contract (back page of Application for Admission)
- ❑ Student screening (schedule with school office)
- ❑ Parent/family interview (schedule with school office)

## Admission Status Decisions

<u>Approved</u>: Students approved for admission will be notified by letter. The school must receive the non-refundable registration fee of $300 for Kindergarten, or $400 for grades 1-12 within two weeks to hold the student's place. Ongoing monthly tuition payments are due beginning May 10th and occur monthly through April 10th. For students accepted after May 10th, any catch-up payments are due with registration.

<u>Denial</u>: Students not approved for admission will be notified by letter.

<u>Waiting Pool</u>: Students approved for admission, contingent upon available classroom space, will be notified by letter. The student will be placed in a waiting pool and be considered for admission when space becomes available.

**Immediately following notification of your child's acceptance, please submit:**

- ❑ Non-refundable registration fee of $300 for Kindergarten, or $400 for grades 1-12
- ❑ Completed form to authorize monthly automatic bank draft for tuition payment beginning May 10th, or payment in full **prior to the first day of school** (see Payment in Full election form for guidelines)
- ❑ The following records must be received by the first day of school. Upon receipt of registration fees, required forms will be made available to you.
  - Records from your child's previous school
  - Health form completed by child's physician (including immunization records)
  - Emergency contact form

**Please retain this form for future reference.**

# School Name
1234 Anywhere St.
Telephone: ___-___-____

## Application for Admission

**Office Use Only**
*Pre-Admission*
Application and fee rec'd _____
Corp member since _____
School forms rec'd _____
Pastor ref rec'd _____
Interview date _____
Student screening _____

*Post-Admission*
Accepted _____ Date _____
Accpt letter sent _____
Registration fee rec'd _____
Records rec'd _____
Health form _____ Birth cert _____
Immunization Record Complete _____

Applying for grade _____
Academic year _____
Application date _____

Student's Name: _____
                (Last)            (First)          (Middle)

Preferred name/nickname: _____    Social Security Number: ____-____-____

Birthdate: _____ Sex: _____ Student lives with: both parents / mother / father / guardian *(Please circle one)*

Address: _____ Telephone: _____
        (Street Address)        (City/State/Zip)

### Siblings

| Name | Age | Present School | Applying to (School) yes/no |
|------|-----|----------------|------------------------------|
|      |     |                |                              |
|      |     |                |                              |
|      |     |                |                              |

### Parent/Guardian Information

| Mother/Guardian | Father/Guardian |
|---|---|
| First/last name _____ | First/last name _____ |
| Relationship to applicant _____ | Relationship to applicant _____ |
| Home address (if different) _____ | Home address (if different) _____ |
| Cell phone _____ | Cell phone _____ |
| Work phone _____ | Work phone _____ |
| Occupation _____ | Occupation _____ |
| Employer _____ | Employer _____ |
| Email _____ | Email _____ |
| **Church Affiliation** | **Church Affiliation** |
| Home church _____ | Home church (if different) _____ |
| Church address _____ | Church address _____ |
| City, State, Zip _____ | City, State, Zip _____ |
| Pastor's name _____ | Pastor's name _____ |

# Academic Information

School background of applicant (please include preschool):

| Name of School | Address | Grade(s) | Reason for leaving |
|---|---|---|---|
|  |  |  |  |
|  |  |  |  |
|  |  |  |  |

Has your child ever failed or repeated a grade? _____ If yes, please explain: _____

_____

Has your child ever skipped a grade? _____ If yes, please explain: _____

_____

Has your child ever been suspended or expelled? _____ If yes, please state the year, school and reason:

_____

Has your child ever had discipline or attendance/tardiness problems? _____ If yes, please explain:

_____

What concerns do you have regarding your child's current progress (academic, behavioral or physical health)?

_____

_____

Has your child ever been tested, diagnosed, or enrolled in any special education program or special school (i.e. resource room, reading difficulty, learning disability, attention deficit disorder, etc.)? Please discuss the results and include a copy of the report.

_____

_____

_____

_____

Does your child have any medical condition or handicap that might affect his/her school experience? If so, explain:

_____

_____

What are your child's academic interests, abilities and strengths? _____

What are your child's current extracurricular involvements? _____

What expectations do you have of the education your child will be receiving at (School name)?

_____

_____

# Spiritual

Please use the space provided below to answer the following questions:

- What are your primary reasons for seeking to enroll your child at (School name)?
- Who, according to your understanding, is Jesus Christ?
- What do you believe concerning the death and resurrection of Jesus Christ?
- Describe your relationship to Jesus Christ.

**Father's response:**

1. 

2. 

3. 

4. 

**Mother's response:**

1. 

2. 

3. 

4.

# Parental Contract with

**I, the undersigned, do hereby commit to the following:**

- That all the information provided on this application is true, to the best of my knowledge, and that I have not intentionally withheld or misrepresented any pertinent data;
- To fulfill my financial obligations to (school name): that I am responsible for the timely payment of the full annual tuition and other fees due (school name) even if my child is voluntarily withdrawn or expelled from school.
- In the event that I decide to withdraw or choose not to reenroll my child, I will, for the school's benefit, inform the school office in writing concerning my reasons.
- That I am responsible for any and all damages incurred to school property made by my child.
- To fully support and abide by all school policies, including the uniform policy. I affirm that I have read the Student-Parent Handbook, in full.
- To include corporal punishment as a method of discipline (school name) may use with my son. (Exceptions may be granted with written documentation, dated and signed, by a parent or guardian.)
- To support school personnel, programs and activities with prayer and communication, and, when possible, to serve as a volunteer in various capacities.
- To nurture habits of punctuality, thoroughness, neatness, honesty, resourcefulness, independent reading and study. I will also expect my child to complete all homework daily and to make sure all books and completed homework are returned to school the following day.
- To allow my child to be photographed or videotaped for public relations and/or training purposes.
- To direct any grievances, concerns, or issues I may have through the proper channels, according to the principles outlined in chapter eighteen of the gospel of Matthew as summarized below:
    a. All persons are to deal with the situation at its source. This usually means initially speaking privately with the person involved in a constructive and supportive attempt to get clarification or resolution.
    b. If, after honest attempts have been made and clarification or resolution has not been satisfactorily reached, then I will proceed to the next level of authority. This generally means speaking with the principal/administrator. If satisfaction is not reached by this point, then I will proceed to the School Board by bringing the matter to the Board's attention *in writing*.

I have read the above contract and agree to abide by it while my child is enrolled as a student at (school name).

_____   _____   _____   _____
(Signature)                                          (Date)              (Joint Signature)                              (Date)

# ---(School Name)--- Guidelines Agreement
Please discuss these guidelines with your children.

**Students are expected to:**
- Maintain a courteous, grateful, respectful, obedient and cooperative attitude, to exercise restraint, and to forgive freely.
- Work responsibly and independently in the classroom without distracting others unnecessarily.
- Share, take turns, love and serve one another, refrain from teasing, name-calling, bad language, pushing, pulling, and fighting while at work or play.
- Be punctual and regular in attendance, and in all assigned work. Illness, medical appointments, family emergencies, family trips, etc., may be acceptable reasons for absence. Whenever possible, these absences should be prearranged through the school office.
- Remain in school during the entire day unless permission to leave is granted by the office.
- Remain at home in case of illness until temperature has returned to normal for a period of 24 hours and/or all signs of contagion are gone. When antibiotics are prescribed, remain at home for a full 24 hours after first dose is taken.
- Dress in compliance with the uniform policy. If found to be in violation, accept correction and consequences graciously and respectfully, and correct the error as soon as possible. Keep body clean and well groomed.

**Parents are asked to:**
- Foster a courteous, grateful, respectful, obedient and cooperative and forgiving attitude along with proper restraint (self-control) in thoughts, words, actions and attitudes.
- Nurture habits of punctuality, thoroughness, neatness, honesty, resourcefulness, independent reading and study.
- Expect completion of all homework daily, making sure all books and completed homework are returned to school the following day.
- Support school personnel, programs, policies and activities with prayer and communication; and serve as a volunteer in various capacities.

**You may expect your school to:**
- Clarify to all students our expectations, and to commend or correct as occasion demands. To the best of our ability to balance justice, mercy and faithfulness in our dealings with your child (Matt. 23:23).
- Cooperate with you in every way possible to encourage your child in the development of the above attitudes, habits, and skills.
- Communicate with you regularly concerning the growth, needs, and accomplishments of your child.

---(SCHOOL NAME)--- BY-LAWS
## ARTICLE III
## FOUNDATIONAL PRINCIPLES

This Article is not amendable in whole or in part. All corporation members, board members, and staff of ---(School name)--- must subscribe to these foundational principles by written statement.

### Section (1). Statement of Faith

The following are the foundational beliefs on which Cary Christian School, Inc. is based.

1. We believe the Bible to be the only inerrant, authoritative Word of God. (II Tim. 3:16)

2. We believe that there is one God, creator of all things, who is eternally existent in three persons: Father, Son, and Holy Spirit. (Deut. 5:4; Gen. 1:1; 1 John 5:7)

3. We believe in the deity of our Lord Jesus Christ, in His virgin birth, in His sinless life, in His miracles, in His vicarious and atoning death through His shed blood, in His bodily resurrection, in His ascension to the right hand of the Father, and in His personal return in power and glory. (John10:30; Matt. 1:18; Heb. 4:15; John 10:32; Rom. 3:25; Matt. 28:6; Rom. 8:34; Luke 21:27)

4. We believe that for the salvation of lost and sinful men, regeneration by the Holy Spirit is absolutely necessary. (John 3:3-8)

5. We believe that salvation is by grace through faith alone. (Eph. 2:8)

6. We believe that faith without works is dead. (Jam. 2:8)

7. We believe in the present ministry of the Holy Spirit by whose power the Christian is enabled to live a godly life. (Gal. 5:16)

8. We believe in the resurrection of both the saved and the lost: they that are saved to the resurrection of life and they that are lost to the resurrection of condemnation. (I Thes. 4:16,17; II Thes. 1:9)

9. We believe in the spiritual unity of all believers in our Lord Jesus Christ. (Jn 17:20-23)

### Section (2). Educational Philosophy

The Educational approach of Cary Christian School, Inc. as defined below is fundamentally different than government operated education both in philosophy and content. Cary Christian School recognizes that an excellent education is founded upon disciplined, eager attention to learning; that this discipline rests upon the student's moral character; and that this moral character can only be developed through a personal relationship with God through Jesus Christ. In support of parent's God-given responsibility for educating their children, Cary Christian School seeks to

1. Provide a clear model of Christian life through its staff and board members. (Matt. 22:37-40)

2. Encourage every student to begin and to continue to develop a relationship with God the Father through Jesus Christ. (Matt. 28:18-20)

3. Teach all subjects from a biblical worldview as parts of an integrated whole with the Scripture at the center. (II Tim. 3:6-17)

4. Provide students with a classical education, in which grammar (the fundamental facts and rules of each subject), logic (the ordered relationship of particulars in each subject) and rhetoric (the expression in speech and writing of the ideas of a subject) are emphasized in all subject areas.

5. Encourage all students to develop wisdom, discernment and a love for learning. Children will be taught how to learn for themselves and how to express what they have learned; how to think rather than simply what to think.

6. Provide an orderly and safe atmosphere conducive to attaining these goals.

Concerning the teaching of origins, we affirm that God created everything out of nothing and that He created it good. Christians have differed as to the age of the earth based upon the Genesis 1 account of creation. Various interpretations which affirm the inerrant character of Genesis 1 can be held by faithful Christians.

### Section (3). Organizational Philosophy

The mission of this organization is academic excellence within a biblical worldview. To carry out this mission ---(School name)---, Inc.,

1. Commits to operating with efficiency and excellence.

2. Maintains respect for the individual and insists upon graciousness in all interactions at every level of the organization.

3. Encourages a decentralized form of administration where decisions are made and responsibility is taken for those decisions at the lowest possible level of the organization. This organizational principle of delegation is intended to reduce administrative overhead and empower the individuals involved in a particular process to have the primary input to improve it. (Ex. 18:13-27)

4. Regards parents as customers of Cary Christian School and teachers as having board-delegated authority in the classroom.

5. Encourages parents to be active supporters of the educational process.

6. Commits to resolve disputes that arise out of or relate to its organizational documents by biblically based mediation. (Matt. 18:15-20; I Cor. 6:1-8)

If necessary, legally binding arbitration shall be in accordance with the Rule of Procedure for Christian Conciliation of *The Institute for Christian Conciliation*. These biblical methods of dispute resolution shall be the sole remedy for any controversy or claim arising out of the Articles of Incorporation or the By-Laws of Cary Christian School, Inc.

# School Name
### 1234 Anywhere St.
### Telephone: ___-___-_____

## Pastor's Reference Form

Applicant's Name _____ Grade Applying For _____

Parents _____

Dear Pastor,

This student is seeking admission to ---(School name)--- an independent parent/board-run, non-denominational school. The mission of the school is to work with parents to develop godly, responsible, academically prepared students, capable of clearly articulating a Biblical worldview.

Please complete this reference form as it pertains to this family **and return it to the school**. All responses will be treated with complete confidentiality and will be used only in serving the family as a part of our school community.

1. **Christian Commitment:**
   - _____ evident and beyond question
   - _____ no evidence of commitment

2. **Church Attendance:**
   - _____ faithful and regular
   - _____ occasional
   - _____ infrequent
   - _____ never

3. **Church Relationship:**
   - _____ members in good standing
   - _____ not members, but exhibit commitment
   - _____ not supportive

4. Have any members of the family held a leadership position in the church? Please describe: _____
   _____

5. Has the family used any special talents within the church body? Please describe: _____
   _____

6. Detail the applicant's regular involvement in church activities. _____
   _____

7. Do you consider the applicant open to spiritual instruction? _____

8. Do you recommend this applicant for admission to ---(School name)---? _____

9. How long have you known the applicant and his/her family? _____ Are you related to the applicant? _____

Please use the back of this sheet for any other comments you would like to make.

Pastor's Signature _____ Date _____

Church _____ Phone _____

Church Address _____

City _____ State/Zip _____

APPENDIX F  205

# Student Re-Enrollment Instructions

## ---(SCHOOL NAME)---
## 2006-2007 REENROLLMENT DETAILS

Every year in January we give our current families first priority for reenrolling and reserving their child's seat for the upcoming school year. **This year the reenrollment period is January 16 - 20.** If we have not received your re-enrollment paperwork with fees by January 20, 2006, we will assume your intent is not to return.

At the discretion of the appropriate principal or superintendent, a student may be refused reenrollment for the following school year. Such refusal is not considered a direct disciplinary act, requiring accumulated office visits in order to be taken. Refusal to reenroll is not the equivalent of suspension or expulsion.

**Attached Forms:**

1) (School name) Corporation Membership Application for Calendar year 2006 - Your **corporate membership must be current** to reenroll for the upcoming year. Please be sure to proofread the preprinted information for accuracy and to complete any empty fields.
2) Application for Reenrollment for 2006-2007
3) (School name) 2006-2007 School Calendar
4) (School name) Guidlines Agreement

**Please refer to the checklist of fees on the reverse side of this page.**

**Reenrollment Steps:**
1) Renew your corporation membership for calendar year 2006 (attached). **Corporate fees must be paid by a separate check. (Check #1** made payable to ___.)
2) Complete both the front and back side of the reenrollment application. **The reenrollment fee and newly enrolled sibling application fee may be combined in one check. (Check #2** made payable to ___.)
3) Return both forms with appropriate fees to the school office.

**Important Tuition Notes:**

- **Tuition for the upcoming school year will remain $4,000 for Kindergarten and $5,000 for grades 1-12.**

- **Monthly tuition payments by automatic draft will begin in May '06** and draft on the $10^{th}$ of each month, for twelve consecutive months, through April '07.

- The monthly payment plan is available only through automatic draft. Monthly payments by automatic draft are $333 for Kindergarten and $417 for grades 1-12 for **eleven** months (May '06 through March '07) with the twelfth month's payment being $337 for Kindergarten and $413 for grades 1-12.

- If you have a newly enrolled sibling, the school office will send home a student application for your completion.

- There are separate 2006-2007 Student-Parent Handbooks for Elementary (K-5) and Secondary (6-12). They are available on our website _____. If you do not have access to the website, you may request a printed copy from the appropriate school office.

- Tuition Assistance (TA) funds are available. **Those applying for TA should stop by the school office to sign for and pick up a Family Financial Needs Assessment (FFNA) application.** ___ requires you to use the "fast-back" method of processing. All applications must be submitted to FFNA in time for their response to reach ___ administration **no later than the end of the business day on February 24, 2006.** TA monies will be disbursed beginning March 1, 2006. **(Those electing to apply online must register at the school office as well.)**

Thank you for your prompt response. If you have any questions concerning reenrollment, feel free to contact (_____, during regular school hours.

# Student Re-enrollment Form

| Office Use Only |
|---|
| Rec'd _____ |
| Amt Pd _____ |
| Check # _____ |
| Corp current _____ |
| App mailed _____ |

**Application for Reenrollment for 2006-2007**

Father's Name: _____
                     (Last)                          (First)               (M.I.)

Mother's Name: _____
                     (Last)                          (First)               (M.I.)

Please reenroll the following *returning student(s)*:

_____ For grade _____
(Last)          (First)          (M.I.)          (Called)

_____ For grade _____
(Last)          (First)          (M.I.)          (Called)

_____ For grade _____
(Last)          (First)          (M.I.)          (Called)

_____ For grade _____
(Last)          (First)          (M.I.)          (Called)

Please reserve a seat for the following *newly enrolled sibling(s)*:
(The school office will send an application home with your currently enrolled student.)

_____ For grade _____
(Last)          (First)          (M.I.)          (Called)

_____ For grade _____
(Last)          (First)          (M.I.)          (Called)

_____ For grade _____
(Last)          (First)          (M.I.)          (Called)

**Please note that your Corporation Membership must be current in order for your child(ren) to be reenrolled.** If you have not renewed your membership for 2006, please submit an updated form and fees with this reenrollment application form.

New students from currently enrolled families will receive first priority in registration. All new students must submit an application for admission and be screened; however, please list them on this form to reserve their seat and assist us in planning for next year.

The reenrollment period is January 16-20, 2006. Please return this form to the school office by January 20, 2006 with a reenrollment fee of $75.00 per returning student and the appropriate application fee(s) for each new student. (Please see the checklist of fees.) Registration will be opened to corporation members on January 26, 2006.

At the discretion of the appropriate principal or superintendent, a student may be refused reenrollment for the following school year. Such refusal is not considered a direct disciplinary act, requiring accumulated office visits in order to be taken. Refusal to reenroll is not the equivalent of suspension or expulsion.

**Please read and sign the back of this form as part of the reenrollment process.**

## Parent Contract for Re-enrollment:

**I, the undersigned, do hereby commit to the following:**

- That all the information provided on this application is true, to the best of my knowledge, and that I have not intentionally withheld or misrepresented any pertinent data;
- To fulfill my financial obligations to (school name): that I am responsible for the timely payment of the full annual tuition and other fees due (school name) even if my child is voluntarily withdrawn or expelled from school.
- In the event that I decide to withdraw or choose not to reenroll my child, I will, for the school's benefit, inform the school office in writing concerning my reasons.
- That I am responsible for any and all damages incurred to school property made by my child.
- To fully support and abide by all school policies, including the uniform policy. I affirm that I have read the Student-Parent Handbook, in full.
- To include corporal punishment as a method of discipline (school name) may use with my son. (Exceptions may be granted with written documentation, dated and signed, by a parent or guardian.)
- To support school personnel, programs and activities with prayer and communication, and, when possible, to serve as a volunteer in various capacities.
- To nurture habits of punctuality, thoroughness, neatness, honesty, resourcefulness, independent reading and study. I will also expect my child to complete all homework daily and to make sure all books and completed homework are returned to school the following day.
- To allow my child to be photographed or videotaped for public relations and/or training purposes.
- To direct any grievances, concerns, or issues I may have through the proper channels, according to the principles outlined in chapter eighteen of the gospel of Matthew as summarized below:

  c. All persons are to deal with the situation at its source. This usually means initially speaking privately with the person involved in a constructive and supportive attempt to get clarification or resolution.
  d. If, after honest attempts have been made and clarification or resolution has not been satisfactorily reached, then I will proceed to the next level of authority. This generally means speaking with the principal/administrator. If satisfaction is not reached by this point, then I will proceed to the School Board by bringing the matter to the Board's attention **in writing**.

I have read the above contract and agree to abide by it while my child is enrolled as a student at (school name).

_____   _____      _____   _____
(Signature)                          (Date)                  (Joint Signature)                    (Date)

# Checklist of Fees

## Due back by January 20, 2006 to complete reenrollment process:

**Corporation Membership Renewal**  $40.00 joint
$25.00 individual                              $_____ **Check #1**

**Reenrollment Fee (returning student)**  $75.00 per child    $75.00 x_____ = $_____
                                                              (per student)

**Application Fee (newly enrolled sibling)**  $150.00 new sibling #1    Total $_____ **Check #2**
$100.00 new sibling #2    (see chart at left)
$ 50.00 new sibling #3
$  0.00 new sibling #4 or more

For newly enrolled siblings, a registration fee of $300 for Kindergarten and/or $400 for grades 1-12 will be due upon completion of the application process.

*********************************

## Tuition Notes:

Tuition for each student must be paid by one of two methods:

❖ **Automatic draft over twelve months-May, 2006 through April, 2007**

   Automatic Draft/ACH Authorization forms may be obtained from the office. If you currently pay by draft, it is <u>not</u> necessary to submit a new authorization form.

❖ **Full payment prior to the first day of school**

   If you would like to prepay tuition in full for the 2006-2007 school year, please complete and submit a Prepayment Election form (available from the office) so we will be aware of your intentions for the coming year. The required payment schedule is explained on the form.

Please call Jane Smith at (XXX) XXX-XXXX if you have any questions concerning tuition payments.

# Records Request for Student Admission

(Date)

Mr. & Mrs. Smith
1234 First Street
Town, State, Zip

Dear Mr. & Mrs. Smith:

Periodically, we review our student files to make sure we have all required documentation. In a review of (student) file, we find that we do not have her prior school records. We are enclosing a Request for Transfer of Records for you to complete and send to the last school (student) attended so that her file will be complete.

If you have any questions, please call the office at 555-555-5555. Thank you so much for your cooperation.

Sincerely,


Principal

# Transfer Request for Student Records

*(This form should be copied on your school's letterhead and given to newly accepted students)*

Student Name: _____ Date of Birth: ____/____/____

Last grade enrolled: _____ Date requested from (School): _____

Name of school last attended: _____

School address: _____

School Telephone Number: ( )_____

Please transfer all records including:

- Transcript of scholastic record (including report cards)
- Standardized test results
- Health and immunization records
- Attendance records
- Confidential records (psychological, discipline, etc.)
- Explanation of your grading system

For students transferring during the school year, please include a copy of the most current report card.

Your prompt reply will be appreciated. Records should be sent to:

School Name
Attn: Records Department
1234 First Street
City, State, Zip

I authorize the release of my child's records, as requested above, to (school name).

_____    _____
Signature of Parent/Guardian            Date

# APPENDIX G

## Classical Methodology

### "The Lost Tools of Learning"[104] by Dorothy L. Sayers

That I, whose experience of teaching is extremely limited, should presume to discuss education is a matter, surely, that calls for no apology. It is a kind of behavior to which the present climate of opinion is wholly favorable. Bishops air their opinions about economics; biologists, about metaphysics; inorganic chemists, about theology; the most irrelevant people are appointed to highly technical ministries; and plain, blunt men write to the papers to say that Epstein and Picasso do not know how to draw. Up to a certain point, and provided that the criticisms are made with a reasonable modesty, theses activities are commendable. Too much specialization is not a good thing. There is also one excellent reason why the veriest amateur may feel entitled to have an opinion about education. For if we are not all professional teachers, we have all, at some time or another, been taught. Even if we learnt nothing- perhaps in particular if we learnt nothing- our contribution to the discussion may have potential value.

I propose to deal with the subject of teaching, properly so-called. It is in the highest degree improbable that the reforms I propose will ever be carried into effect. Neither the parents, nor the training colleges, nor the examination boards, nor the board of governors, nor the ministries of education would countenance them for a moment. For they amount to this: that if we are to produce a society of educated people, fitted to preserve their intellectual freedom amid the complex pressures of our modern society, we must turn back the wheel of progress some four or five hundred years, to the point at which education began to lose sight of its true object, towards the end of the Middle Ages.

Before you dismiss me with the appropriate phrase reactionary, romantic, mediaevalist, laudator temporis acti, or whatever tag comes first to hand, I will ask you to consider one or two miscellaneous questions that hang about at the back, perhaps, of all our minds, and occasionally pop out to worry us.

*Disquieting Questions*
When we think about the remarkably early age at which the young men went up to the university in, let us say, Tudor times, and thereafter were held fit to assume responsibility for the conduct of their own affairs, are we altogether comfortable about that artificial prolongation of

---
104  Dorothy Sayers. *"The Lost Tools of Learning."* Oxford, 1947.

intellectual childhood and adolescence into the years of physical maturity which is so marked in our own day? To postpone the acceptance of responsibility to a late date brings with it a number of psychological complications, which, while they may interest the psychiatrist, are scarcely beneficial either to the individual or to society. The stock argument in favor of postponing the school-leaving age and prolonging the period of education generally is that there is now so much more to learn than there was in the middle Ages. This is partially true, but not wholly. The modern boy and girl are certainly taught more subjects but does that always mean that they actually know more?

Has it ever struck you as odd, or unfortunate, that today, when the proportion of literacy throughout Western Europe is higher that it has ever been, people should have become susceptible to the influence of advertisement and mass propaganda to an extent hitherto unheard-of and unimagined? Do you put this down to the mere mechanical fact that the press and the radio and so on have made propaganda much easier to distribute over a wide area? Or do you sometimes have an uneasy suspicion that the product might be at disentangling fact from opinion and the proven from the plausible?

Have you ever, in listening to a debate among adult and presumably responsible people, been fretted by the extraordinary inability of the average debater to speak to the question, or to meet and refute the arguments of speakers on the other side? Or have you ever pondered upon the extremely high incidence of irrelevant matter which crops up at committee meetings, and upon the very great rarity of persons capable of acting as chairmen of committees? And when you think of this, and think that most of our public affairs are settled by debates and committees, have you ever felt a certain sinking of the heart?

Have you ever followed a discussion in the newspapers or elsewhere and noticed how frequently writers fail to define the terms they use? Or how often, if one man does define his terms, another will assume in his reply that he was using the terms in precisely the opposite sense to that in which he has already defined them? Have you ever been faintly troubled by the amount of slipshod syntax going about? And if so, are you troubled because it is inelegant or because it may lead to dangerous misunderstanding?

Do you ever find that young people, when they have left school, not only forget most of what they have learnt (that is only to be expected) but forget also, or betray that they have never really known, how to tackle a new subject for themselves? Are you often bothered by coming across grown-up men and women who seem unable to distinguish between a book that is sound, scholarly, and properly documented, and one that is, to any trained eye, very conspicuously none of these things? Or who cannot handle a library catalogue? Or who, when faced with a book of reference, betray a curious inability to extract from it the passages relevant to the particular question which interests them?

Do you often come across people for whom, all their lives, a subject remains a subject, divided by watertight bulkheads from all other subjects, so that they experience very great difficulty in making an immediate mental connection between, let us say, algebra and detective fiction, sewage disposal and the piece of salmon or, more generally, between such spheres of knowledge as philosophy and economic, or chemistry and art?

Are you occasionally perturbed by the things written by adult men and women for adult men and women to read? We find a well-known biologist writing in a weekly paper to the effect that: It is an argument against the existence of a Creator (I think he put it more strongly; but since I have, most unfortunately, mislaid the reference, I will put his claim at its lowest) 'an argument against the existence of a Creator that the same kind of variations which are produced by natural selection can be produced at will by stock-breeders. One might feel tempted to say that it is rather an argument for the existence of a Creator. Actually, of course, it is neither: all it proves is that the same material causes (recombination of the chromosomes by cross-breeding and so Fourth) are sufficient to account for all observed variation just as the various combinations of the same dozen tones are materially sufficient to account for Beethoven's Moonlight Sonata and the noise the cat makes by walking on the keys. But the cat's performance neither proves nor disproves the existence of Beethoven: and all that is proved by the biologist's argument is that he was unable to distinguish between a material and a final cause.

Here is a sentence from no less academic a source than a front-page article in the Times Literary Supplement:

*The Frenchman, Alfred Epinas, pointed out that certain species (e.g., ants and wasps) can only face the horrors of life and death in association.*

I do not know what the Frenchman actually did say: what the Englishman says he said is patently meaningless, We cannot know whether life holds any horror for the ant, nor in what sense the isolated wasp which you kill upon the window-pane can be said to 'face' or not to 'face' the horrors of death. The subject of the article is mass behavior in man; and the human motives have been unobtrusively transferred from the main proposition to the supporting instance. Thus the argument, in effect, assumes what is set out to prove a fact which would become immediately apparent if it were presented in a formal syllogism. This is only a small and haphazard example of a vice, which pervades whole books particularly books written by men of science on metaphysical subjects.

Another quotation from the same issue of the TLS comes in fittingly here to wind up this random collection of disquieting thoughts this time from a review of Sir Richard Livingstone's Some Tasks for Education:

More than once the reader is reminded of the value of an intensive study of at least one subject, so as to learn the meaning of knowledge and what precision and persistence is needed to attain it. Yet there is elsewhere full recognition of the distressing fact that a man may be master in one field and show no better judgment than his neighbor anywhere else: he remembers what he has learnt, but forgets altogether how he learned it.

I would draw your attention particularly to that last sentence, which offers an explanation of what the writer rightly calls the distressing fact that the intellectual skills bestowed upon us by our education are not readily transferable to subjects other than those in which we acquired then: he remembers what he has learnt, but forgets altogether how he learned it.

*The Art of Learning*
Is not the great defect of our education today- a defect traceable through all the disquieting symptoms of trouble that I have mentioned that although we often succeed in teaching our pupils subjects, we fail lamentably on the whole in teaching them how to think: they learn everything, except the art of learning. It is as though we had taught a child, mechanically and by rule of thumb, to play the Harmonious Blacksmith upon the piano, but had never taught him the scale or how to read music; so that, having memorized the Harmonious Blacksmith, he still had not the faintest notion how to proceed from that to tackle the Last Rose of Summer: Why do I say, as though? In certain of the arts and crafts we sometimes do precisely this requiring a child to express himself in paint before we teach him how to handle the colors and the brush. There is a school of thought which believes this to be the right way to set about the job. But observe: it is not the way in which a trained craftsman will go about to teach himself a new medium. He, having learned by experience the best way to economize labor and take the thing by the right end, will start off by doodling about on an old piece of material, in order to give himself the feel of the tool.

*The Mediaeval Syllabus*
Let us now look at the mediaeval scheme of education the syllabus of the Schools. It does not matter, for the moment, whether it was devised for small children or for older students, or how long people were supposed to take over it. What matters if the light it throws upon what the men of the Middle Ages supposed to be the object and the right order of the educative process.

The syllabus was divided into two parts: the Trivium and Quadrivium. The second part the Quadrivium consisted of subjects and need not for the moment concern us. The interesting thing for us is the composition of the Trivium, which preceded the Quadrivium was the preliminary discipline for it. It consisted of three parts: Grammar, Dialectic, and Rhetoric, in that order.

Now the first thing that we notice is that two at any rate of these subjects are not what we should call subjects at all they are only methods of dealing with subjects. Grammar, indeed, is a subject in the sense that it does mean definitely learning a language at that period it meant learning Latin. But language itself is simply the medium in which thought is expressed. The whole of the Trivium was, in fact, intended to teach the pupil the proper use of the tools of learning, before he began to apply them to subjects at all. First, he learned a language; not just how to order a meal in a foreign language, but the structure of a language, and hence of language itself what it was, how it was put together, and how it worked. Secondly, he learned how to use language: how to define his terms and make accurate statements: how to construct an argument and how to detect fallacies in argument. Dialectic, that is to say, embraced Logic and Disputation. Thirdly, he learned to express himself in language how to say what he had to say elegantly and persuasively.

At the end of his course, he was required to compose a thesis upon some theme set by his masters or chosen by himself, and afterwards, to defend his thesis against the criticism of the faculty. By this time he would have learned or woe betide him not merely to write an essay on paper, but to speak audibly and intelligibly from a platform, and to use his wits quickly when heckled. There would also be questions, cogent and shrewd, from those who had already run the gauntlet of debate.

It is of course, quite true that bits and pieces of the mediaeval tradition still linger, or have been revived, in the ordinary school syllabus of today. Some knowledge of grammar is still required when learning a foreign language perhaps I should say, is again required; for during my own lifetime we passed through a phrase when the teaching of declensions and conjugations was considered rather reprehensible, and it was considered better to pick these things up as we went along. School debating societies flourish; essays are written; the necessity for self-expression is stressed, and perhaps even over-stressed. But these activities are cultivated more or less in detachment, as belonging to the special subjects in which they are pigeonholed rather than as forming one coherent scheme of mental training to which all subjects stand in a subordinate relation. Grammar belongs especially to the subject of foreign languages, and essay-writing to the subject called English, while Dialectic has become almost entirely divorced from the rest of the curriculum, and is frequently practiced unsystematically and out of school hours as a separate exercise, only very loosely related to the main business of learning. Taken by and large, the great difference of emphasis between the two conceptions holds good: modern education concentrates on teaching subjects, leaving the method of thinking, arguing, and expressing one's conclusions to be picked up by the scholar as he goes along; mediaeval education concentrated on first forging and learning to handle the tools of learning, using whatever subject came handy as a piece of material on which to doodle until the use of the tool became second nature.

Subjects of some kind there must be, of course. One cannot learn the theory of grammar without learning an actual language, or learn to argue and orate without speaking about something in particular. The debating subjects of the middle Ages were drawn largely from theology, or from the ethics and history of antiquity. Often, indeed, they became stereotyped, especially towards the end of the period, and the far-fetched and wiredrawn absurdities of Scholastic argument fretted Milton and provide food for merriment even to this day. Whether they were in themselves any more hackneyed and trivial than the usual subjects set nowadays for essay-writing I should not like to say: we may ourselves grow a little weary of A Day in My Holidays and all the rest of it. But most of the merriment is misplaced, because the aim and object of the debating thesis has by now been lost sight of.

*Angels on a Needle*

A glib speaker in the Brains Trust once entertained his audience (and reduced the late Charles Williams to helpless rage) by asserting that in the Middle Ages it was a matter of faith to know how many archangels could dance on the point of a needle. I need not say, I hope, that it never was a matter of faith; it was simply a debating exercise, whose set subject was the nature of angelic substance: were angels material, and if so, did they occupy space? The answer usually adjudged correct is, I believe, that angels are pure intelligences; not material, but limited, so that they may have location in space but not extension. An analogy might be drawn from human thought, which is similarly non-material and similarly limited. Thus, if your thought is concentrated upon one thing say, the point of a needle it is located there in there in the sense that it is not elsewhere; but although it is there, it occupies no space there, and there is nothing to prevent an infinite number of different people's thoughts being concentrated upon the same needle-point at the same time. The proper subject of the argument is thus seen to be the distinction between location and tension in space; the matter on which the argument is exercised happens to be the nature of angels (although, as we have seen, it might equally well have been something else); the practical lesson to be drawn from the argument is not to use words like there in a loose and unscientific way, without specifying whether you mean located there or occupying space there.

Scorn in plenty has been poured out upon the mediaeval passion for hair-splitting: but when we look at the shame-less abuse made, in print and on the platform, of controversial expressions with shifting and ambiguous connotations, we may feel it in our hearts to wish that every reader and hearer had been so defensively armored by his education as to be able to cry: Distinguo.

*Unarmed*

For we let our young men and women go out unarmed, in a day when armor was never so necessary. By teaching them all to read, we have left them at the mercy of the printed word.

By the invention of the film and the radio, we have made certain that no aversion to reading shall secure them from the incessant battery of words, words, words. They do not know what the words mean; they do not know how to ward them off or blunt their edge or fling them back; they are prey to words in their emotions instead of being the masters of them in their intellects. We who were scandalized in 1940 when men were sent to fight armored tanks with rifles, are not scandalized when young men and women are sent into the world to fight massed propaganda with a smattering of "subjects"; and when whole classes and whole nations become hypnotized by the arts of the spellbinder, we have the impudence to be astonished. We dole out lip-service to the importance of education lip service and, just occasionally, a little grant of money; we postpone the school-leaving age, and plan to build bigger and better schools; the teachers slave conscientiously in and out of school hours; and yet, as I believe, all this devoted effort is largely frustrated, because we have lost the tools of learning, and in their absence can only make a botched and piecemeal job of it.

What, then, are we to do? We cannot go back to the Middle Ages. That is a cry which we have become accustomed. We cannot go back or can we? Distinguo. I should like every term in that proposition defined. Does "go back" mean a retrogression in time, or the revision of an error? The first is clearly impossible per se; the second is a thing which wise men do every day. "Cannot" does this mean that our behavior is determined irreversibly, or merely that such an action would be very difficult in view of the opposition it would provoke? Obviously the twentieth century is not and cannot be the fourteenth; but if the Middle Ages is, in this context, simply a picturesque phrase denoting a particular educational theory, there seems to be no a priori reason why we should not "go back" to it with modifications as we have already "gone back", with modifications, to, let us say, the idea of playing Shakespeare's plays as he wrote them, and not in the "modernized" versions of Cibber and Garrick, which once seemed to be the latest thing in theatrical progress.

Let us amuse ourselves by imagining that such progressive retrogression is possible. Let us make a clean sweep of all educational authorities, and furnish ourselves with a nice little school of boys and girls whom we may experimentally equip for the intellectual conflict along lines chosen by ourselves. We will endow them with exceptionally docile parents; we will staff our school with teachers who are themselves perfectly familiar with the aims and methods of the Trivium; we will have our buildings and staff large enough to allow our classes to be small enough for adequate handling; and we will postulate a board of examiners willing and qualified to test the products we turn out. Thus prepared, we will attempt to sketch out a syllabus a modern Trivium with modifications; and we will see where we get to.

But first: what age shall the children be? Well, if one is to educate them on novel lines, it will be better that they should have nothing to unlearn; besides, one cannot begin a good thing too early, and the Trivium is by its nature not learning, but a preparation for learning. We will, therefore, catch em' young, requiring of our pupils only that they shall be able to read, write, and cipher.

*The Three Ages*

My views about child-psychology are, I admit, neither orthodox nor enlightened. Looking back upon myself (since I am the child I know best and the only child I can pretend to know from inside) I recognize three states of development. These, in a rough-and-ready fashion, I will call the Poll-Parrot, the Pert, and the Poetic the latter coinciding, approximately, with the onset of puberty. The Poll-Parrot stage is the one in which learning by heart is easy and, on the whole, pleasurable; whereas reasoning is difficult and, on the whole, little relished. At this age, one readily memorizes the shapes and appearances of things; one likes to recite the number-plates of cars; one rejoices in the chanting of rhymes and the rumble and thunder of unintelligible polysyllables; one enjoys the mere accumulation of things. The Pert age, which follows upon this (and, naturally, overlaps it to some extent), is characterized by contradicting, answering back, liking to catch people out (especially one's elders), and by the propounding of conundrums. Its nuisance value is extremely high. It usually sets in about the Fourth Form. The Poetic age is popularly known as the "difficult" age. It is self-centered; it yearns to express itself; it rather specializes in being misunderstood; it is restless and tries to achieve independence; and, with good luck and good guidance, it should show the beginnings of creativeness, a reaching-out towards a synthesis of what it already knows, and a deliberate eagerness to now and some one thing in preference to all others. Now it seems to me that the layout of the Trivium adapts itself with a singular appropriateness to these three ages: Grammar to the Poll-Parrot, Dialectic to the Pert, and Rhetoric to the Poetic age.

Let us begin, then, with Grammar. This, in practice, means, the grammar of some language in particular, and it must be an inflected language. The grammatical structure of an inflected language is far too analytical to be tackled by any one without previous practice in Dialectic. Moreover, the inflected languages interpret the uninflected, whereas the uninflected are of little use in interpreting the inflected. I will say at once, quite firmly, that the best grounding for education is the Latin grammar. I say this, not because Latin is traditional and mediaeval, but simply because even a rudimentary knowledge of Latin cuts down the labor and pains of learning almost any other subject by at least 50 percent. It is the key to the vocabulary and structure of all of the Romance languages and to the structure of all the Teutonic languages, as well as to the technical vocabulary of all the sciences and to the literature of the entire Mediterranean civilization, together with all its historical documents.

Those whose pedantic preference for a living language persuades them to deprive their pupils of all these advantages might substitute Russian, whose grammar is still more primitive.

Russian is, of course, helpful with the other Slav dialects. There is something also to be said for Classical Greek. But my own choice is Latin. Having thus pleased the Classicists among you, I will proceed to horrify them by adding that I do not think it either wise or necessary to cramp the ordinary pupil upon the Procrustean bed of the Augustan Age, with its highly elaborate and artificial verse forms and oratory. Post-classical and mediaeval Latin, which was a living language down to the end of the Renaissance, is easier and in some ways livelier; and a study of it helps to dispel the widespread notion that learning and literature came to a full stop when Christ was born and only woke up again at the Dissolution of the Monasteries.

Latin should be begun as early as possible at a time when inflected speech seems no more astonishing than any other phenomenon in an astonishing world; and when the chanting of Amo, Amas, Amat is as ritually agreeable to the feelings as the chanting of eeny, meeny, miney, mo.

During this age we must, of course, exercise the mind on other things besides Latin grammar. Observation and memory are the faculties most lively at this period; and if we are to learn a contemporary foreign language we should begin now, before the facial and mental muscles become rebellious to strange intonations. Spoken French or German can be practiced alongside the grammatical discipline of the Latin.

*The Use of Memory*
In English, verse and prose can be learned by heart, and the pupil's memory should be stored with stories of every kind classical myth, European legend, and so forth. I do not think that the classical stories and masterpieces of ancient literature should be made the vile bodies on which to practice the techniques of grammar - that was a fault of mediaeval education which we need not perpetuate. The stories can be enjoyed and remembered in English, and related to their origin at a subsequent stage. Recitation aloud should be practiced, individually or in chorus; for we must not forget that we are laying the groundwork for disputation and rhetoric.

The grammar of history should consist, I think, of dates, events, anecdotes, and personalities. A set of dates to which one can peg all later historical knowledge is of enormous help later on in establishing the perspective of history. It does not greatly matter which dates; those of the Kings of England will do very nicely, provided that they are accompanied by pictures of costumes, architecture, and other everyday things so that the mere mention of a date calls up a strong visual presentment of the whole period.

Geography will similarly be presented in its factual aspect, with maps, natural features, and visual presentment of customs, costumes, flora, fauna, and so on; and I believe myself that the discredited and old-fashioned memorizing of a few capital cities, rivers, mountain ranges, etc., does no harm. Stamp collecting may be encouraged.

Science, in the Poll-Parrot period, arranges itself naturally and easily round collections the identifying and naming of specimens and, in general, the kind of thing that used to be called "natural history, or, still more charmingly, "natural philosophy. To know the names and properties of things is, at this age, a satisfaction in itself; to recognize a devil's coach-horse at sight, and assure one's foolish elders that, in spite of its appearance, it does not sting; to be able to pick out Cassiopeia and the Pleiades, and perhaps even to know who Cassiopeia and Peliades were; to be aware that a whale is not a fish, and a bat not a bird all these things give a pleasant sensation of superiority; while to know a ring-snake from an adder or a poisonous from an edible toadstool is a kind of knowledge that has also a practical value.

The grammar of mathematics begins, of course, with the multiplication table, which, if not learnt now will never be learnt with pleasure; and with the recognition of the geometrical shapes and the grouping of numbers. These exercises lead naturally to the doing of simple sums in arithmetic; and if the pupil shows a bent that way, a facility acquired at this stage is all to the good. More complicated mathematical processes may, and perhaps should, be postponed, for reasons which will presently appear.

So far (except, of course, for the Latin), our curriculum contains nothing that departs very far from common practice. The difference will be felt rather in the attitude of the teachers who must look upon all these activities less as "subjects" in themselves than as a gathering-together of material for use in the next part of the Trivium. What that material is, is only of secondary importance; but it is as well that anything and everything which can usefully be committed to memory should be memorized at this period, whether it is immediately intelligible or not. The modern tendency is to try and force rational explanations on a child's mind at too early an age. Intelligent questions, spontaneously asked, should, of course, receive an immediate and rational answer; but it is a great mistake to suppose that a child cannot readily enjoy and remember things that are beyond his power to analyze - particularly if those things have a strong imaginative appeal, or an abundance of rich, resounding polysyllables.

*The Mistress Science*
This reminds me of the grammar of Theology. I shall add it to the curriculum, because theology is the mistress-science, without which the whole educational structure will necessarily lack its final synthesis. Those who disagree about this will remain content to leave their pupils' education still full of loose ends. This will matter rather less than it might, since by the time the tools of learning have been forged the student will be able to tackle theology for himself, and will probably insist upon doing so and making sense of it. Still, it is as well to have this matter also handy and ready for the reason to work upon. At the grammatical age, therefore, we should become acquainted with the story of God and man in outline, i.e. the Old and New

Testaments presented as parts of a single narrative of creation, rebellion, and redemption, and also with "the Creed, the Lord's Prayer, and the Ten Commandments." At this stage, it does not matter nearly so much that these things should be fully understood as that they should be known and remembered.

It is difficult to say at what age precisely, we should pass from the first to the second part of the Trivium. Generally speaking, the answer is, so soon as the pupil shows himself disposed to pertness and interminable argument. For as, in the first part, the master-faculties are observation and memory, so, in the second, the master-faculty is the discursive reason. In the first, the exercise to which the rest of the material was, as it were, keyed, was the Latin grammar; in the second, the key-exercise will be formal logic. It is here that our curriculum shows its first sharp divergence from modern standards. The disrepute into which formal logic has fallen is entirely unjustified; and its neglect is the root cause of nearly all those disquieting symptoms which we have noted in the modern intellectual constitution.

A secondary cause for the disfavor into which logic has fallen is the belief that it is entirely based upon universal assumptions that are either improvable or tautological. This is not true. Not all universal propositions are of this kind. But even if they were, it would make no difference, since every syllogism whose major premise is in the form "All A is B" can be recast in hypothetical form. Logic is the art of arguing correctly; "If A, then B"; the method is not invalidated by the hypothetical character of A. Indeed, the practical utility of formal logic today lies not so much in the establishment of positive conclusions as in the prompt detection and exposure of invalid inference.

*Relation to Dialectic*
Let us now quickly review our material and see how it is to be related to Dialectic. On the language side, we shall now have our vocabulary and morphology at our fingertips; henceforward we can concentrate on syntax and analysis (i.e., the logical construction of speech) and the history of language (i.e., how we came to arrange our speech as we do in order to convey our thoughts).

Our reading will proceed from narrative and lyric to essays, arguments, and criticism, and the pupil will learn to try his hand at writing this kind of thing. Many lessons - on whatever subject - will take the form of debates; and the place of individual or choral recitation will be taken by dramatic performances, with special attention to plays in which an argument is stated in dramatic form.

Mathematics - algebra, geometry, and the more advanced kinds of arithmetic - will now enter into the syllabus and take its place as what it really is; not a separate "subject", but a sub-department of logic. It is neither more or less than the rule of the syllogism in its particular application to number and measurement, and should be taught as such, instead of being, for some, a dark mystery, and, for others, a special revelation, neither illuminating nor illuminated by any other part of knowledge.

History, aided by a simple system of ethics derived from the grammar of theology, will provide much suitable material for discussion; Was the behavior of this statesman justified? What was the effect of such an enactment? What are the arguments for and against this or that form of government? We shall thus get an introduction to constitutional history - a subject meaningless to the young child, but of absorbing interest to those who are prepared to argue and debate. Theology itself will furnish material for argument about conduct and morals; and should have its scope extended by a simplified course of dogmatic theology (i.e., the rational structure of Christian thought), clarifying the relations between the dogma and the ethics, and lending itself to that application of ethical principles in particular instances which is properly called casuistry. Geography and the sciences will likewise provide material for dialectic.

*The World Around Us*
But above all, we must not neglect the material which is so abundant in the pupils' own daily life.

There is a delightful passage in Leslie Paul's The Living Hedge which tells how a number of small boys enjoyed themselves for days arguing about an extraordinary shower of rain which had fallen in their town - a shower so localized that it left one half of the main street wet and the other dry. Could one, they argued, properly say that it had rained that day on or over the town or only in the town? How many drops of water were required to constitute rain - and so on. Argument about this led on to a host of similar problems about rest and motion, sleep and waking, est and non est, and the infinitesimal division of time. The whole passage is an admirable example of the spontaneous development of the ratiocinative faculty and the natural and proper thirst of the awakening reason for definition or terms and exactness of statement. All events are food for such an appetite.

An umpire's decision; the degree to which one may transgress the spirit of a regulation without being trapped by the letter; on such questions as these, children are born casuists, and their natural propensity only needs to be developed and trained - and, especially, brought into an intelligible relationship with events in the grown-up world. The newspapers are full of good material for such exercises; legal decisions, on the one hand, in cases where the cause at issue is not to abstruse, on the other, fallacious reasoning and muddleheaded arguments, with which the correspondence columns of certain papers one could name are abundantly stocked.

*"Pert Age" Criticism*
Wherever the matter for Dialectic is found, it is, of course, highly important that attention should be focused upon the beauty and economy of a fine demonstration or a well-tuned

argument, lest veneration should wholly die. Criticism must not be merely destructive; though at the same time both teacher and pupils must be ready to detect fallacy, slipshod reasoning, ambiguity, irrelevance, and redundancy, and to pounce upon them like rats. This is the moment when précis writing may be usefully undertaken; together with such exercises as the writing of an essay, and the reduction of it, when written, by 25 or 50 percent.

It will, doubtless, be objected that to encourage young persons at the pert age to browbeat, correct, and argue with their elders will render them perfectly intolerable. My answer is that children of that age are intolerable anyhow; and that their natural argumentativeness may just as well be canalized to good purpose as allowed to run away into the sands. It may, indeed, be rather less obtrusive at home if it is disciplined in school; and, anyhow, elders who have abandoned the wholesome principle that children should be seen and not heard have no one to blame but themselves.

Once again: the contents of the syllabus at this stage may be anything you like. The "subjects" supply material; but they are all to be regarded as mere grist for the mental mill to work upon. The pupils should be encouraged to go and forage for their own information, and so guided towards the proper use of libraries and books of reference, and shown how to tell which sources are authoritative and which are not.

*Imagination*

Towards the close of this stage, the pupils will probably be beginning to discover for themselves that their knowledge and experience are insufficient, and that their trained intelligences need a great deal more material to chew upon. The imagination - usually dormant during the Pert Age - will reawaken, and prompt them to suspect the limitations of logic and reason. This means that they are passing into the Poetic Age and are ready to embark on the study of rhetoric. The doors of the storehouse of knowledge should now be thrown open for them to browse about, as they will. The things once learned by rote will be seen in new contexts; the things once coldly analyzed can now be brought together to form a new synthesis; here and there a sudden insight will bring about that most exciting of all discoveries: the realization that a truism is true.

*The Study of Rhetoric*

It is difficult to map out any general syllabus for the study rhetoric; a certain freedom is demanded. In literature, appreciation should be again allowed to take the lead over destructive criticism; and self-expression in writing can go forward, with its tools now sharpened to cut clean and observe proportion. Any child who already shows a disposition to specialize should be given his head; for, when the use of tools has been well and truly learned, it is available for study whatever. It would be well, I think, that each pupil should learn to do one, or two, subjects really well, while taking a few classes in subsidiary subjects so as to keep his mind open to the inter-relations of all knowledge. Indeed, at this stage, our difficulty will be to keep "subjects" apart; for as dialectic will have shown all branches of learning to be inter-related, so rhetoric will tend to show that all knowledge is one. To show this, show why it is so, is pre-eminently the task of the mistress-science. But whether theology is studied or not, we should at least insist that children who seem inclined to specialize on the mathematical and scientific side should be obliged to attend some lessons in the humanities and vice versa. At this stage also, the Latin grammar, having done its work, may be dropped for those who prefer to carry on their language studies on the modern side; while those who are likely never to have any great use or aptitude for mathematics might also be allowed to rest, more or less, upon their oars. Generally speaking: whatsoever is mere apparatus may now be allowed to fall into the background, while the trained mind is gradually prepared for specialization in the "subjects" which, when the Trivium is completed, it should be perfectly well equipped to tackle on its own. The final synthesis of the Trivium - the presentation and public defense of the thesis - should be restored in some form; perhaps as a kind of "leaving examination" during the last term at school.

The scope of rhetoric depends also on whether the pupil is to be turned out into the world at the age of 16 or whether he is to proceed to the university. Since, really, Rhetoric should be taken at about 14, the first category of pupil should study grammar from about 9 to 11, and dialectic from 12 to 14, his last two school years would then be devoted to rhetoric, which, in his case, would be of a fairly specialized and vocational kind, suiting him to enter immediately upon some practical career. A pupil of the second category would finish his dialectical course in his preparatory school, and take rhetoric during his first two years at his public school. At 16, he would be ready to start upon those "subjects" which are proposed for his later study at the university: and this part of his education will correspond to the mediaeval Quadrivium. What this amounts to is that the ordinary pupil, whose formal education ends at 16, will take the Trivium only; whereas scholars will take both the Trivium and the Quadrivium.

*The University at Sixteen?*
Is the trivium, then, a sufficient education for life" Properly taught, I believe that it should be. At the end of the dialectic, the children will probably seem to be far behind their coevals brought up on old-fashioned "modern" methods, so far as detailed knowledge of specific subjects is concerned. But after the age of 14 they should be able to overhaul the others hand over fist. Indeed, I am not at all sure that a pupil thoroughly proficient in the Trivium would not be fit to proceed immediately to the university at the age of 16, thus proving himself the equal of his mediaeval counterpart, whose precocity astonished us at the beginning of this discussion. This, to be sure, would make hay of the English public-school system, and disconcert the universities very much. It would, for example, make quite a different thing of the Oxford and Cambridge boat race.

But I am not here to consider the feelings of academic bodies: I am concerned only with the proper training of the mind to encounter and deal with the formidable mass of undigested problems presented to it by the modern world. For the tools of learning are the same, in any and every subject; and the person who knows how to use them will, at any age, get the mastery of a new subject in half the time and with a quarter of the effort expended by the person who has not the tools at his command. To learn six subjects without remembering how they were learnt does nothing to ease the approach to a seventh; to have learnt and remembered the art of learning makes the approach to every subject an open door.

*Educational Capital Depleted*
Before concluding these necessarily very sketchy suggestions, I ought to say why I think it necessary, in these days, to go back to a discipline which we had discarded. The truth is that for the last three hundred years or so we have been living upon our educational capital. The post-Renaissance world, bewildered and excited by the profusion of new "subjects" offered to it, broke away from the old discipline (which had, in-deed, become sadly dull and stereotyped in its practical application) and imagined that henceforward it could, as it were, disport itself happily in its new and extended Quadrivium without passing through the Trivium. But the scholastic tradition, though broken and maimed, still lingered in the public schools and universities: Milton, however much he protested against it, was formed by it - the debate of the Fallen Angels and the disputation of Abdiel with Satan have the tool-marks of the schools upon them, and might, incidentally, profitably figure as set passages for our dialectical studies. Right down to the nineteenth century, our public affairs were mostly managed, and our books and journals were for the most part written, by people brought up in homes, and trained in places, where that tradition was still alive in the memory and almost in the blood. Just so, many people today who are atheist or agnostic in religion, are governed in their conduct by a code of Christian ethics which is so rooted in their unconscious assumptions that it never occurs to them to question it.

*Forgotten Roots*
But one cannot live on capital forever. A tradition, however firmly rooted, if it is never watered, though it dies hard, yet in the end it dies. And today a great number - perhaps the majority - of the men and women who handle our affairs, write our books and our newspapers, carry out research, present our plays and our films, speak from our platforms and pulpits - yes, and who educate our young people - have never, even in a lingering traditional memory, undergone the Scholastic discipline. Less and less do the children who come to be educated bring any of that tradition with them. We have lost the tools of learning - the axe and the wedge, the hammer and the saw, the chisel and the plane - that were so adaptable to all tasks. Instead of them, we have merely a set of complicated jigs, each of which will do but one task and no more, and in using which eye and hand receive no training, so that no man ever sees the work as a whole or "looks to the end of the work."

What use is it to pile task on task and prolong the days of labor, is at the close the chief object is left unattained? It is not the fault of the teachers - they work only too hard already. The combined folly of a civilization that has forgotten its own roots is forcing them to shore up the tottering weight of an educational structure that is built upon sand. They are doing for their pupils the work which the pupils themselves ought to do. For the sole true end of education is simply this; to teach men how to learn for themselves; and whatever instruction fails to do this is effort spent in vain.

# Lost Tools Chart[105]

| PHONICS<br>(Pre-Polly) | GRAMMAR<br>(Poll-Parrot) | LOGIC<br>(Pert) | RHETORIC<br>(Poetic) |
|---|---|---|---|
| Grades K-2 | Grades 3-5 | Grades 6-8 | Grades 9-12 |
| Typical ages 4-8 | Typical ages 9-11 | Typical ages 12-14 | Typical ages 15-18 |
| *Student Characteristics:* | *Student Characteristics:* | *Student Characteristics:* | *Student Characteristics:* |
| ~ Obviously excited about learning<br>~ Enjoys games, stories, songs, projects<br>~ Short attention span<br>~ Wants to touch, taste, feel, smell, see<br>~ Imaginative, creative | ~ Excited about new, interesting facts<br>~ Likes to explain, figure out, talk<br>~ Wants to relate own experiences to topic, or just to tell a story<br>~ Likes collections, organizing items<br>~ Likes chants, clever, repetitious word sounds (e.g. Dr. Seuss)<br>~ Easily memorizes<br>~ Can assimilate other lanquages | ~ Contradicting and answering back<br>~ Likes to catch and point out the mistakes of others, especially those of elders<br>~ Enjoys academic puzzles<br>~ When not disciplined, has a high nuisance value | ~ Concerned with present events especially in own life<br>~ Interested in justice, fairness<br>~ Moving toward special interests topics<br>~ Can take on responsibility, independent work<br>~ Can do synthesis<br>~ Desires to express feelings, own ideas<br>~ Generally idealistic |
| *Teaching Methods:* | *Teaching Methods:* | *Teaching Methods:* | *Teaching Methods:* |
| ~ Guide discovering<br>~ Explore, find things<br>~ Use lots of tactile items to illustrate point<br>~ Sing, play games, chant, recite, color, draw, paint, build<br>~ Use body movements<br>~ Short, creative projects<br>~ Show and Tell, drama, hear/read/ tell stories<br>~ Field trips | ~ Lots of hands-on work, projects<br>~ Field trips, drama<br>~ Make collections, displays, models<br>~ Integrate subjects through above means<br>~ Teach and assign research projects<br>~ Recitations, memorization<br>~ Drills, games<br>~ Oral/written presentations | ~ Time lines, charts, maps (visual materials)<br>~ Debates, persuasive reports<br>~ Drama, reenactments, role-playing<br>~ Evaluate, critique (with guidelines)<br>~ Formal logic<br>~ Research projects<br>~ Oral/written presentations<br>~ Guest speakers, trips | ~ Drama, oral presentations<br>~ Guided research in major areas with goal of synthesis of ideas<br>~ Many papers, speeches, debates<br>~ Give responsi-bilities, works independently on projects<br>~ In-depth field trips, even overnight<br>~ World view discussion/written papers |

---

105 Logos School. "Logos Curriculum Guide." Moscow, Idaho.

# APPENDIX H

## Financial Samples
(School Name)

## Monthly Budget Report

| Expenses | Annual Budget | Jul-06 | Aug-06 | May-07 | Jun-07 | F.Y.T.D. | Budget % | | Total |
|---|---|---|---|---|---|---|---|---|---|
| **OPERATION DEVELOPMENT AND PROMOTION** | | 51 | 174 | 0 0 | 0 0 | 225 | 0.01 | 23,775 | 225 |
| Advertising | | 51 | 51 | 0 0 | 0 0 | 102 | 0.05 | 1,898 | 102 |
| Board expenses | | 0 | 0 | 0 0 | 0 0 | 0 | 0.00 | 18,000 | 0 |
| Consult Fees/Trav/Entert | | 0 | 0 | 0 0 | 0 0 | 0 | 0.00 | 1,000 | 0 |
| Print/Copy/Post/Supp/Newltr | | 0 | 123 | 0 0 | 0 0 | 123 | 0.04 | 2,877 | 123 |
| **EDUCATION EXPENSES** | | 13,118 | 41,655 | 0 0 | 0 0 | 54,773 | 0.28 | 137,727 | 54,773 |
| Computers | | 0 | 0 | 0 0 | 0 0 | 0 | 0.00 | 8,000 | 0 |
| Computer Support | | 2,000 | 2,000 | 0 0 | 0 0 | 4,000 | 0.15 | 22,000 | 4,000 |
| Curriculum - Consumable | | 1,689 | 24,807 | 0 0 | 0 0 | 26,496 | 0.66 | 13,504 | 26,496 |
| Curriculum - Permanent | | 4,749 | 15,666 | 0 0 | 0 0 | 20,415 | 0.51 | 19,585 | 20,415 |
| Printing/Copies | | 3,156 | 1,966 | 0 0 | 0 0 | 5,122 | 0.17 | 25,878 | 5,122 |
| Special Academic Prog. | | 0 | (5,582) | 0 0 | 0 0 | (5,582) | (0.21) | 32,582 | (5,582) |
| Teaching Supplies | | 1,523 | 2,798 | 0 0 | 0 0 | 4,321 | 0.27 | 11,679 | 4,321 |
| Testing/Miscell. | | 0 | 0 | 0 0 | 0 0 | 0 | 0.00 | 4,500 | 0 |
| **FACILITIES EXPENSE** | | 29,857 | 39,265 | 0 0 | 0 0 | 69,123 | 0.16 | 368,377 | 69,123 |
| Building/Grounds | | 133 | 2,090 | 0 0 | 0 0 | 2,224 | 0.07 | 28,776 | 2,224 |
| Cleaning/Maint/Supplies | | 4,115 | 3,610 | 0 0 | 0 0 | 7,725 | 0.15 | 43,775 | 7,725 |
| Field maintenance | | 2,035 | 1,400 | 0 0 | 0 0 | 3,435 | 0.16 | 18,565 | 3,435 |
| Furniture & equipment | | 1,606 | 95 | 0 0 | 0 0 | 1,701 | 0.11 | 13,799 | 1,701 |
| Preschool campus | | 16,901 | 17,975 | 0 0 | 0 0 | 34,876 | 0.17 | 169,124 | 34,876 |
| Utilities | | 5,067 | 14,096 | 0 0 | 0 0 | 19,163 | 0.17 | 94,337 | 19,163 |

| Expenses | Annual Budget | Jul-06 | Aug-06 | May-07 | Jun-07 | F.Y.T.D. | Budget % | | Total |
|---|---|---|---|---|---|---|---|---|---|
| **CONSTRUCT LOAN PAYMENT** | | 46,625 | 93,250 | 0 0 | 0 0 | 139,875 | 0.26 | 390,125 | 139,875 |
| **OFFICE AND ADMINISTRATIVE** | | 3,920 | 15,884 | 0 0 | 0 0 | 19,804 | 0.20 | 78,196 | 19,804 |
| Association Membership | 6,000 | 0 | 1,606 | 0 0 | 0 0 | 1,606 | 0.27 | 4,394 | 1,606 |
| Bank Charges | 500 | 0 | 0 | 0 0 | 0 0 | 0 | 0.00 | 500 | 0 |
| Computer/ADP Office | 2,000 | 25 | 2,875 | 0 0 | 0 0 | 2,900 | 1.45 | (900) | 2,900 |
| Financial Audit | 8,500 | 0 | 0 | 0 0 | 0 0 | 0 | 0.00 | 8,500 | 0 |
| Legal Services | 2,000 | 0 | 0 | 0 0 | 0 0 | 0 | 0.00 | 2,000 | 0 |
| Liability Insurance | 24,000 | 0 | 6,349 | 0 0 | 0 0 | 6,349 | 0.26 | 17,651 | 6,349 |
| Office Supplies | 24,000 | 2,729 | 3,611 | 0 0 | 0 0 | 6,340 | 0.26 | 17,660 | 6,340 |
| Postage & Delivery | 4,500 | 262 | 561 | 0 0 | 0 0 | 823 | 0.18 | 3,677 | 823 |
| Telephone / Internet | 24,500 | 904 | 883 | 0 0 | 0 0 | 1,786 | 0.07 | 22,714 | 1,786 |
| Other | 2,000 | 0 | 0 | 0 0 | 0 0 | 0 | 0.00 | 2,000 | 0 |
| **PERSONNEL EXPENSES** | 2,158,468 | 701,491 | 133,840 | 0 0 | 0 0 | 835,331 | 0.39 | 1,323,137 | 835,331 |
| Salaries | | 102,378 | 108,240 | 0 0 | 0 0 | | | | 210,619 |
| Empl'r Taxes / Wrkr's Comp | | 8,380 | 10,690 | 0 0 | 0 0 | | | | 19,070 |
| Staff Tuition Benefit | | 583,150 | 0 | 0 0 | 0 0 | | | | 583,150 |
| **TOTAL SALARY EXPENSE** | 1,995,118 | 693,908 | 118,931 | 0 0 | 0 0 | 812,839 | 0.41 | 1,182,279 | 812,839 |

| | Annual Budget | Jul-06 | Aug-06 | | | | | F.Y.T.D. | Budget % | | Total |
|---|---|---|---|---|---|---|---|---|---|---|---|
| Recruitment (intervws, relo) | 5,000 | 0 | 0 | 0 | 0 | 0 | 0 | 0 | 0.00 | 5,000 | 0 |
| Staff Incent (Hlth, Disab) | 87,000 | 7,487 | 12,381 | 0 | 0 | 0 | 0 | 19,868 | 0.23 | 67,132 | 19,868 |
| Staff Training | 2,500 | 0 | 92 | 0 | 0 | 0 | 0 | 92 | 0.04 | 2,408 | 92 |
| Other / Reserves | 68,850 | 97 | 2,436 | 0 | 0 | 0 | 0 | 2,533 | 0.04 | 66,318 | 2,533 |
| **Other Expenses** | 211,300 | 168,249 | 7,808 | 0 | 0 | 0 | 0 | 176,057 | 0.83 | 35,243 | 176,057 |
| Athletics | 31,000 | 2,375 | 4,956 | 0 | 0 | 0 | 0 | 7,331 | 0.24 | 23,669 | 7,331 |
| Band/Drama | 3,000 | 0 | 0 | 0 | 0 | 0 | 0 | 0 | 0.00 | 3,000 | 0 |
| Tuition Assistance | 165,000 | 165,000 | 0 | 0 | 0 | 0 | 0 | 165,000 | 1.00 | 0 | 165,000 |
| Vehicle Maintenance | 12,000 | 874 | 2,852 | 0 | 0 | 0 | 0 | 3,726 | 0.31 | 8,274 | 3,726 |
| Other (incl accrd, corp mtg) | 300 | 0 | 0 | 0 | 0 | 0 | 0 | 0 | 0.00 | 300 | 0 |
| **Total Expenses** | 3,651,768 | 963,311 | 331,876 | 0 | 0 | 0 | 0 | 1,295,187 | 0.35 | 2,356,581 | 1,295,187 |
| **Income** | | | | | | | | | | | |
| Tuition | 3,370,000 | 1,461,208 | 314,580 | | | | | 1,775,788 | 0.53 | (1,594,212) | 1,775,788 |

| Expenses | Annual Budget | Jul-06 | Aug-06 | | | May-07 | Jun-07 | F.Y.T.D. | Budget % | | Total |
|---|---|---|---|---|---|---|---|---|---|---|---|
| **General Fees** | | 19,575 | 885 | 0 | 0 | 0 | 0 | 20,460 | 0.37 | (34,540) | 20,460 |
| Application fees | | 2,500 | 300 | 0 | 0 | 0 | 0 | 2,800 | | 2,800 | 2,800 |
| Membership fees (Corp) | | 675 | 185 | 0 | 0 | 0 | 0 | 860 | | 860 | 860 |
| Re-enrollment fees | | 0 | 0 | 0 | 0 | 0 | 0 | 0 | | 0 | 0 |
| Registration fees | | 16,400 | 400 | 0 | 0 | 0 | 0 | 16,800 | | 16,800 | 16,800 |
| **Donations** | 45,000 | 400 | 7,750 | 0 | 0 | 0 | 0 | 8,150 | | (36,850) | 8,150 |
| Donations – | | | | | | | | | | | |
| Gen / YE / Ann | 45,000 | 400 | 2,750 | 0 | 0 | 0 | 0 | 3,150 | 0.07 | (41,850) | 3,150 |
| Donations - Restricted | | 0 | 5,000 | 0 | 0 | 0 | 0 | 5,000 | | 5,000 | 5,000 |
| **Other Income** | 182,000 | 136,815 | 2,268 | 0 | 0 | 0 | 0 | 139,083 | 0.76 | (42,917) | 139,083 |
| Interest Inc | | | | | | | | | | | |
| (CDs & MM) | 6,000 | 0 | 0 | 0 | 0 | 0 | 0 | 0 | 0.00 | (6,000) | 0 |
| Subleasing income | 41,500 | 2,300 | 2,300 | 0 | 0 | 0 | 0 | 4,600 | 0.11 | (36,900) | 4,600 |
| Other Income | 0 | 15 | (32) | 0 | 0 | 0 | 0 | (17) | | (17) | (17) |
| Surplus Carryover | 134,500 | 134,500 | 0 | 0 | 0 | 0 | 0 | 134,500 | 1.00 | 0 | 134,500 |
| **Total Income** | 3,652,000 | 1,617,998 | 325,482 | 0 | 0 | 0 | 0 | 1,943,480 | 0.53 | (1,708,520) | 1,943,480 |
| **Net Monthly Income** | 232 | 654,687 | (6,394) | 0 | 0 | 0 | 0 | --- | | | |
| **Net Cumulative Income** | 232 | 654,687 | 648,293 | 648,293 | 648,293 | 648,293 | 648,293 | 648,293 | | | |

| Bank bal @ month-end: | Opening | | |
|---|---|---|---|
| Operating Account | 888,695 | 929,146 | 1,020,472 |
| Development (Land) Acct | 91,821 | 92,944 | 97,181 |
| Money Market | 525,080 | 526,590 | 528,142 |
| CD Account | 0 | 0 | 0 |
| Lunch Account | 14,541 | 13,445 | 123,499 |
| PTF Account | 16,733 | 16,741 | 15,829 |
| Booster Club Clearing Account | 3,915 | 2,817 | 3,309 |
| (online xactn) Coastal FCU | 100 | 74 | 74 |
| (Sr. Serv. Pract.) | 3,900 | 3,900 | 3,900 |
| Misc Co. (Stock) | 0 | 0 | 0 |

# Sample Yearly Budget Report

2:54 PM
11/15/06
Cash Basis

## Profit & Loss Budget Overview
### July 2006 through June 2007

|  | Jul '06 - Jun 07 |
|---|---:|
| **Ordinary Income/Expense** | |
|   **Income** | |
|     **Donations - Operating** | |
|       Annual Fund | 45,000.00 |
|       Restricted Donations | 11,250.00 |
|     **Total Donations - Operating** | 56,250.00 |
|     **Fee Income** | |
|       **General Fees** | |
|         Application Fees | 9,000.00 |
|         Membership Fees | 10,000.00 |
|         Re-enrollment Fee | 21,000.00 |
|         Registration | 15,000.00 |
|       **Total General Fees** | 55,000.00 |
|       **Tuition Revenue** | |
|         Tuition | 3,370,000.00 |
|         Tuition Assistance | -165,000.00 |
|       **Total Tuition Revenue** | 3,205,000.00 |
|     **Total Fee Income** | 3,260,000.00 |
|     Interest Income | 6,000.00 |
|     Rental Income-Sublease | 41,500.00 |
|   **Total Income** | 3,363,750.00 |
| **Gross Profit** | 3,363,750.00 |
|   **Expense** | |
|     **Development - Operating** | |
|       Advertising - School/Operating | 2,000.00 |
|       Board Expenses | 18,000.00 |
|       Consultant Fees | 1,000.00 |
|       Print/Copy/Postage/Suppl | 3,000.00 |
|     **Total Development - Operating** | 24,000.00 |
|     **Educational Expenses** | |
|       **Classroom Computers** | |
|         Computer Support | 26,000.00 |
|         Computers-High School | 8,000.00 |
|       **Total Classroom Computers** | 34,000.00 |
|       **Curriculum** | |
|         Consumable Curriculum | 40,000.00 |
|         Permanent Curriculum | 40,000.00 |
|       **Total Curriculum** | 80,000.00 |
|       Printing & Copying | 31,000.00 |
|       Special Academic Programs | 27,000.00 |
|       Teaching Supplies | 16,000.00 |
|       Testing | 4,500.00 |
|     **Total Educational Expenses** | 192,500.00 |
|     **Facilities Expense** | |
|       Building/Grounds equip/supplies | 31,000.00 |
|       Cleaning/ Maintenance/ Supplies | 51,500.00 |
|       Field Maintenance | 22,000.00 |
|       **Furniture & Equipment** | |
|         F/Eq-new purchases | 15,500.00 |
|       **Total Furniture & Equipment** | 15,500.00 |
|       Secondary Campus | 204,000.00 |
|       Utilities | 113,500.00 |
|     **Total Facilities Expense** | 437,500.00 |
|     **Land/Property Activity** | |

# Six Year Budget

**(School Name)**
**2006/2007 Budget**

| | | | | | | |
|---|---|---|---|---|---|---|
| Enrollment | | | | | | |
| Maximum | 690 | | | | | |
| Projected Cost per Student | $5,304 | | | | | |

| | 2006-2007 Budget | 2005-2006 Budget | 2004-2005 Budget | 2003-2004 Budget | 2002-2003 Budget | 2001-2002 Budget |
|---|---|---|---|---|---|---|
| **Operations Budget** | | | | | | |
| Development & Promotion | $24,000 | $24,000 | $18,000 | $22,000 | $11,000 | $13,000 |
| Advertising | $2,000 | $2,000 | $2,000 | $6,000 | $6,000 | $6,000 |
| Consulting fees | $1,000 | $1,000 | $1,000 | $1,000 | $1,000 | $3,000 |
| Printing/Photocopying/Postal/Supplies | $3,000 | $3,000 | $3,000 | $3,000 | $2,000 | $2,000 |
| Board expenses | $18,000 | $18,000 | $12,000 | $12,000 | $2,000 | $2,000 |
| | | | | | | |
| **Facilities Expenses** | $967,500 | $953,000 | $676,300 | $338,500 | $322,353 | $149,000 |
| Cleaning services/supplies | $51,500 | $50,000 | $15,000 | $10,000 | $10,000 | $3,000 |
| Mortgage Payment | $530,000 | $530,000 | $357,500 | $10,000 | $10,000 | $3,000 |
| Peace Rent | $0 | $0 | $0 | $45,000 | $45,000 | $40,000 |
| Salem Rent | $0 | $0 | $0 | $75,000 | $85,000 | $100,000 |
| Building/Grounds equipment/materials | $31,000 | $30,000 | $32,000 | $1,500 | $1,500 | $1,500 |
| Utilities | $113,500 | $110,000 | $60,000 | $15,000 | $7,000 | $1,500 |
| Athletic field maintenance | $22,000 | $18,000 | $16,800 | $0 | $0 | $0 |
| Old Apex lease and maintenance | $204,000 | $200,000 | $180,000 | $180,000 | $147,000 | $0 |
| Furniture | $15,500 | $15,000 | $15,000 | $12,000 | $26,853 | $12,628 |
| | | | | | | |
| **Education Expenses** | $192,500 | $178,000 | $175,000 | $145,000 | $110,683 | $86,786 |
| Permanent Curriculum | $40,000 | $37,000 | $37,000 | $37,000 | $33,436 | $25,383 |
| Consumable Curriculum | $40,000 | $37,000 | $37,000 | $37,000 | $34,722 | $26,407 |
| Teaching Supplies | $16,000 | $15,000 | $15,000 | $15,000 | $13,165 | $10,794 |
| Printing/Copies | $31,000 | $30,000 | $30,000 | $24,000 | $21,088 | $17,469 |
| Computer support | $26,000 | $24,000 | $24,000 | $0 | $0 | $0 |
| Computers | $8,000 | $8,000 | $25,000 | $25,000 | $1,272 | $1,272 |
| Testing | $4,500 | $4,000 | $4,000 | $4,000 | $4,000 | $2,461 |
| Special Academic Programs/Senior proj | $27,000 | $23,000 | $3,000 | $3,000 | $3,000 | $3,000 |
| | | | | | | |
| **Office and Administrative** | $98,000 | $91,500 | $78,750 | $71,250 | $48,150 | $36,380 |
| Office Supplies | $24,000 | $23,000 | $22,000 | $22,000 | $20,000 | $12,000 |
| Postage | $4,500 | $4,000 | $3,500 | $3,000 | $2,000 | $1,750 |
| Telephone/Internet Access | $24,500 | $24,000 | $20,000 | $20,000 | $12,000 | $9,000 |
| Advertising | $0 | $0 | $0 | $0 | $150 | $30 |
| Association Membership/other members | $6,000 | $5,000 | $2,750 | $2,750 | $2,500 | $2,500 |
| Financial Audit | $8,500 | $8,000 | $6,000 | $6,000 | $5,000 | $7,000 |
| Bank Charges | $500 | $500 | $500 | $500 | $500 | $500 |
| Liability Insurance | $24,000 | $21,000 | $18,000 | $11,000 | $3,000 | $2,000 |
| Computer/ADP-Office | $2,000 | $2,000 | $2,000 | $2,000 | $1,500 | $1,000 |
| Legal Services | $2,000 | $2,000 | $2,000 | $2,000 | $500 | $500 |
| Miscellaneous | $2,000 | $2,000 | $2,000 | $2,000 | $1,000 | $100 |
| | | | | | | |
| **Personnel Expenses** | $2,166,766 | $1,914,177 | $1,709,702 | $1,562,841 | $1,373,647 | $1,210,228 |
| Teaching Staff | $1,573,466 | $1,415,876 | $1,260,313 | $1,169,539 | $1,005,355 | $880,565 |
| Administrative Staff | $429,950 | $342,851 | $314,889 | $272,802 | $261,792 | $282,163 |
| Interviews/Relocation | $5,000 | $5,000 | $5,000 | $5,000 | $5,000 | $3,000 |
| Staff Training | $2,500 | $2,500 | $2,500 | $2,500 | $2,500 | $2,500 |
| Staff Incentives (Health, Disability, Bonu | $87,000 | $80,000 | $75,000 | $66,000 | $60,000 | $42,000 |
| Reserve | $68,850 | $67,950 | $52,000 | $47,000 | $39,000 | $0 |
| | | | | | | |
| **Other Expenses** | $211,300 | $198,300 | $174,300 | $195,200 | $108,100.00 | $96,900 |
| Tuition Assistance | $165,000 | $155,000 | $145,000 | $125,900 | $100,500 | $97,000 |
| Accreditation Expenses | $0 | $0 | $1,000 | $1,000 | $1,000 | $1,000 |
| Corporation Meetings | $300 | $300 | $300 | $300 | $300 | $300 |
| Maintenance of Vehicles | $12,000 | $10,000 | $5,000 | $35,000 | $0 | $300 |
| Band/Drama | $3,000 | $3,000 | $3,000 | $3,000 | $300 | $300 |
| Tuition Refunds | $0 | $0 | $0 | $0 | $0 | $0 |
| Athletics(Officials/facilities/uniforms) | $31,000 | $30,000 | $20,000 | $30,000 | $6,000 | $0 |
| | | | | | | |
| **Total Expenses** | $3,660,066 | $3,358,977 | $2,832,052 | $2,334,791 | $1,973,933 | $1,594,294 |
| | 4.51% | 4.61% | 5.12% | 5.39% | 5.09% | 6.08% |
| Tuition Revenue | $3,370,000 | $3,062,000 | $2,713,400 | $2,295,000 | $1,946,700 | $1,559,250 |
| Annual Fund | $45,000 | $25,000 | $1,000 | $10,000 | $0 | $0 |
| General Fees | $55,000 | $50,000 | $42,500 | $42,500 | $42,300 | $42,300 |
| Subleasing preschool campus* | $41,500 | $41,500 | $10,000 | $0 | $0 | $0 |
| Surplus carry over | $134,500 | $170,000 | $0 | $0 | $0 | $0 |
| General Donations | $0 | $0 | $0 | $0 | $0 | $0 |
| Restricted Donations | $11,250 | $0 | $0 | $0 | $0 | $0 |
| Misc income-tax reimbursement | $0 | $0 | $75,000 | $0 | $0 | $0 |
| PrePay Interest | $6,000 | $4,000 | $2,000 | $4,000 | $4,000 | $4,000 |
| Total Revenue | $3,663,250 | $3,352,500 | $2,843,900 | $2,351,500 | $1,993,000 | $1,605,550 |
| | | | | | | |
| Projected Surplus/(Deficit) | $3,184 | ($6,477) | $11,848 | $16,709 | $19,067 | $11,256 |
| | $0 | $0 | $0 | $0 | $0 | $0 |
| | | | | | | |
| Remaining Operating Balance | $3,184 | -$6,477 | $11,848 | $16,709 | $19,067 | $11,256 |

# Tuition Request Letter

(Date)

Mr. & Mrs. Smith
1234 First Street
Town, State, Zip

Dear Mr. & Mrs. Smith,

In following up on (student name)'s withdrawal from (school name), we would like to remind you of the school's withdrawal policy that payment of tuition should continue uninterrupted until such time as his classroom seat has been replaced. If and when the seat is officially replaced, the school would notify you that you are then released from further tuition payments. This responsibility is stated in the student application as well as the Student-Parent Handbook and the Student Exit Procedures.

Today we received a notice from the bank indicating that your automatic draft of $_____ for _____ was returned as revoked by customer. We request a replacement payment by money order, due in the office by (date). As agreed by you in signing your child's (School name) application, continued payments of $_____ are also due on the 10th of each month until your balance is paid (usually April) or unless we can notify you otherwise.

Should you need to discuss this matter with myself or the headmaster, please call the school at ###-####.

Sincerely,


Business Manager
cc: Board of Directors

# Collection Letters

## Withdrawal/Tuition Responsibility Letter

(Date)

Mr. & Mrs. Smith
1234 First Street
Town, State, Zip

Dear Mr. & Mrs. Smith,

We would like to confirm our receipt of your notice withdrawing (student name) from enrollment for the remainder of the school year. A copy of the exit procedures is enclosed for your review.

As you know, although your child has been withdrawn from (school name), your family is still responsible for payment in full of the annual tuition until such time as another student replaces your vacated seat in a full classroom. Because we rely solely on tuition income to meet annual operating expenses, it is necessary that the financial obligations for enrollment be for the entire school year. There are no refunds allowable on any monies already paid.

In the Parental Contract section of the enrollment application which you signed, it states, "I… do hereby commit:… to fulfill my financial obligations to (school name), specifically, I understand: that I am responsible for the timely payment of the full annual tuition and other fees due (school name) even if my child is voluntarily withdrawn or expelled from school."

We will notify you right away if this seat is formally replaced and if you are released from further auto draft payments. In the meantime, should you have any questions, please do not hesitate to call. We will be glad to help in any way we can. We wish you the best as you endeavor to provide excellent education for your children.

Sincere regards,

Business Manager
cc: Administrator

# Non-Sufficient Funds Letter

(Date)

Mr. & Mrs. Smith
1234 First Street
Town, State, Zip

Dear Mr. & Mrs. Smith,

We just wanted to inform you that your check #_____, dated _____ and covering application fees for $_____, was returned from the bank non-sufficient funds. There is also a bank charge of $5.00. Please remit a replacement check for $_____ to the school office within two weeks from the date of this letter. A copy of our returned check policy is enclosed for your information.

Thanks! Feel free to call me if you have any questions.

Sincerely,


Business Manager
cc: Administrator

# Collection Letter

VIA RETURN RECEIPT
(Date)

Mr. & Mrs. Smith
1234 First Street
Town, State, Zip

Dear Mr. & Mrs. Smith,

It has been thirty days since our last correspondence to you. Just to reiterate, the contract you signed with the school states that full annual payment of tuition is still due even upon a child's withdrawal from the school.

To date we have not received any payment from you toward the remainder of your child's tuition, which is still due unless and until the class seat can be replaced. We would like to advise you that, if we do not receive your payment within the next two weeks, we will be forced to submit your account to a collection agency. You should note that if your account is sent to a collection agency, your full outstanding balance will become due and payable immediately, and we will no longer be able to honor the seat replacement policy.

The full amount due as of today is $_____ for January and February, and we must receive payment no later than the afternoon of _____.

Sincerely,


Business Manager
cc: Board of Directors and Administrator

# Year End Pledge Letter

(Date)

Mr. & Mrs. Smith
1234 First Street
Town, State, Zip

Dear Mr. & Mrs. Smith,

Greetings to you this most glorious Christmas season! May the gift of the incarnation be your hope and joy as you celebrate with family and loved ones.

As we reflect upon this year, it's impossible to ignore the fact that God has blessed the (school name) community beyond what we deserve. Every day we are reminded of His goodness to us as we drive onto our campus. The columned academic building and grounds are a monument to God's faithfulness. The school has also experienced tremendous growth. We began the academic year with xxx students, representing the largest enrollment increase in the history of the school! Significant additions to the student population have required additional teaching staff, and God has certainly met our need by bringing to the school gifted teachers who love the Lord. God's kindness to us is truly humbling.

As Director of Development, I am pleased to announce that financial gifts to the school have increased significantly this academic year. Donations to the (school fund name) currently stand at $xxxxx. We are also encouraged by the number of families who have made new pledge commitments to the (type of campaign). Your continued gifts have helped to make the dream of (school name) a reality. We thank you for your prayers and participation in this endeavor.

Tax receipts will be mailed after the end of this calendar year. If you have not fulfilled your 20XX pledge commitment, please consider doing so during the next few weeks. Your attention to this matter is greatly appreciated.

Remember that all tax deductible payments must be received in our office by December 31st if you wish to claim this gift on your 20XX tax return.

Should you have any questions regarding the enclosed statement or payment methods, please do not hesitate to call. Again, we are grateful for your support.

Have a blessed Christmas!

In Christ,
Director of Development
(School Name)

# APPENDIX I

## Athletic samples

### Head Coach Job Description

Responsibilities: Within the framework of the entire athletic program, the Head Coach is required to provide leadership in the ongoing development and improvement of his coaching area through coordination, planning, evaluation, and implementation of programs.

Responsible to: Athletic Director

Functions: Assist in the coordination of all sports programs (6-12)

*During the season:*
- Implement athletic standards as outlined in Athletic Handbook
- Provide information for transportation, officials and game management
- Assume responsibility for constant care of equipment and facilities being used
- Assume supervisory control over all phases of teams in his program
- Organize and schedule practice sessions on a regular basis with the idea of developing the athlete's greatest potential
- Apply discipline in a firm and positive manner as outlined in the Athletic Handbook
- See that building regulations are understood and enforced
- Emphasize safety precautions and be aware of best training and injury procedures
- Conduct himself and his teams in an ethical manner during practice and contests
- Report a summary of all contests and provide any publicity information that would aid this program and his athletes
- Instruct players concerning rules and rule changes, new knowledge, and innovative ideas and techniques
- Communicate to parents (in writing) all travel plans: game times, locations, directions, departure and return times

*End of season:*
- Arrange for the systematic return of all school equipment and hold the athlete responsible for all equipment not returned
- Arrange for the issuance of letters and special awards
- Arrange for cleaning, sorting and inventory of all equipment
- Be concerned with the care and maintenance of the facility by making recommendations concerning additions and improvements
- Recommend concerning equipment needed to be purchased or repaired
- Maintain records of team and individual accomplishments

# Application for Paid Coaching Position

## Contact Information

Name: _____

Address: _____

Social Security #:_____ Phone: _____ Date:_____

## EDUCATIONAL BACKGROUND

Name and Location                                                Graduation Date

High School_____     _____

College_____     _____

_____     _____

College Major(s)_____ College Minor(s)_____

Other Education:_____

## SPORTS EXPERIENCE AND PARTICIPATION

Name and Location                                                Year(s) Letter

High School_____ _____ ____

Other:_____ _____ ____

_____ _____ ____

List any related activities and/or experiences: (Include sports, community and recreational work, etc.) _____

_____

List any additional information that you would like to be considered as we review your application: _____

REFERENCES (one must be from your pastor)

Name, Title, Address, Phone Number

1._____

2._____

3._____

PLEASE ANSWER ALL OF THE FOLLOWING QUESTIONS:

Do you hold a valid state health certificate?_____

Do you hold a valid state teaching certificate?_____

What is your citizenship?_____

Are you 18 years of age or older?_____

Are you available for an interview?_____

Most convenient time for interview?_____

Are you a member of a Protestant Church?_____

# Seasonal Evaluation of Coach

NAME: _____ POSITION: _____

For the _____ Season     Date of this Evaluation ___/___/____

S = Satisfactory     U = Unsatisfactory     NI = Needs Improvement

| INTERPERSONAL AND PROFESSIONAL RELATIONSHIPS: | S | U | NI |
|---|---|---|---|
| 1. With students | | | |
| 2. With faculty | | | |
| 3. With parents and community | | | |
| 4. With principal | | | |
| 5. With athletic director | | | |
| 6. With team manager | | | |
| 7. With game officials | | | |
| 8. With opposing coaches and teams | | | |
| COACHING ABILITIES AND RELATED AREAS: | | | |
| 1. Instructional techniques | | | |
| 2. Motivational techniques | | | |
| 3. Adherence to league and district policies | | | |
| 4. Organization of staff and support personnel | | | |
| 5. Evidence of pre-planning | | | |
| 6. Teaching of fundamentals | | | |
| 7. Maintenance of discipline | | | |
| 8. Evidence of professional growth (learning) | | | |
| 9. Supervision of participants (including injuries) | | | |
| 10. Ability to motivate | | | |
| 11. Public relations and promotions | | | |

COMMENTS: _____

_____

OBSERVER: _____ COACH: _____

# Coaches Checklist

1. Roster for grade checks (eligibility) to be submitted to the Athletic Director one day after turnouts.

2. Forms required to be filled out and filed with the coach. Forms to be submitted to Athletic Director at end of the season.

    ___Parent Authorization for Travel with attachment

3. Coaches/parent meeting scheduled no later than 1 week prior to first game. For library usage, reservations must be made with (name) at the main office.

4. Official team roster with all pertinent information submitted to Athletic Director two weeks prior to the first game played.

5. Accident report forms to be filled out immediately and submitted to the school official.

6. Scores reported weekly to: conference webmaster, school webmaster; game summaries reported on day after event to local new media.

7. Hold athletes accountable for cleanliness of changing rooms; gym/field and school vans.

8. Complete and return coaches information sheet prior to first match.

9. End of season requirements: Due no later than two weeks after the end of the season.

| Complete: | |
|---|---|
| | Athletic inventory |
| | Athletic request for next year |
| | Athletic awards list |
| | Recommendations for following year |
| | Physical cards |
| | Return of all keys signed out |
| | Season end evaluation meeting with athletic director |
| | Return of uniforms: cleaned, folded and submitted by the coaches |

# Volunteer Coaching Application

Name: _____

Address: _____

Position applying for: _____

High School attended: _____ Yrs_____

**List high school sports participation record:**

| Sports Participation | Years | Letters Earned |
|---|---|---|
| _____ | _____ | _____ |
| _____ | _____ | _____ |
| _____ | _____ | _____ |
| _____ | _____ | _____ |

College attended: _____
Major_____Minor_____Yrs. _____

| College Sports Participation | Years | Letters Earned |
|---|---|---|
| _____ | _____ | _____ |
| _____ | _____ | _____ |
| _____ | _____ | _____ |
| _____ | _____ | _____ |

| Sports Participation other than college | Years |
|---|---|
| _____ | _____ |
| _____ | _____ |
| _____ | _____ |

List any paid experiences in sports, recreation or physical activities   Years
_____   _____
_____   _____

Do you have a valid First Aid Certificate?_____ If so, date_____ #____

REFERENCES: Give name and address. (School district certified personnel preferred)
_____
_____

*Return to: Director of Athletics*

# Drivers License Guidelines

## -----(SCHOOL NAME)----- LICENSE CHECK GUIDELINES

In order for an individual to drive a van on behalf of (School), he/she must first complete the Driver's Application Form, which allows (School) to do a driver license records check. Once the Motor Vehicle Report is obtained for the prospective driver, the record will be evaluated based on the following criteria. This is to ensure the safety and well being of our students and others traveling in the school vans, whether owned by (School) or borrowed or leased from another organization.

An individual will be permitted to drive provided they receive an *Excellent* or *Acceptable* rating based on the last three years of their driving history. Those with a *Borderline* rating will be allowed to drive only if the record reflects one or fewer violations per year during the three-year history. ---(School name)--- reserves the right to revoke an individual's driving privilege at any time. Drivers must submit a new application every three years as long as they desire to continue driving on behalf of the school.

RATING CRITERIA:

Based on prior three year history:

| # Minor Violations | # of At-Fault Accidents: | | | |
|---|---|---|---|---|
| | 0 | 1 | 2 | 3 |
| 0 | Excellent | Acceptable | Borderline | Poor |
| 1 | Acceptable | Acceptable | Borderline | Poor |
| 2 | Acceptable | Borderline | Poor | Poor |
| 3 | Borderline | Poor | Poor | Poor |
| 4 | Poor | Poor | Poor | Poor |

Based on entire history:

| 6 points | Poor | Poor | Poor | Poor |
|---|---|---|---|---|
| Any Major Violation | Poor | Poor | Poor | Poor |

Minor Violations:

Any moving violation other than a major violation *except*:
- * Motor vehicle equipment, load or size requirement violations
- * Improper failure to display license plates or vehicle registration
- * Failure to have a driver's license in possession

Major Violations:

An individual with a major violation on his/her record *at any time* will not be allowed to drive.

- * Reckless driving
- * Railroad crossing violations
- * DUI/DWI
- * Driving while license is suspended or revoked
- * Failure to stop and report an accident
- * At fault in a fatal accident

*Revision 09/01/2005*

# Driver's Application Form

**(SCHOOL) VANS MAY NOT BE DRIVEN PRIOR TO COMPLETION OF D. L. VERIFICATION BELOW.**

**(SCHOOL) VEHICLES: DRIVER'S APPLICATION FORM**
Driver must agree to guidelines on the back, and complete and sign the front of this form.

*\*\*\*Please attach a back & front copy of your license to this form.\*\*\**

Name: _____ Today's Date: _____

Social Security #: _____ Birthdate: _____ Birthplace: _____

Have you ever used name(s) other than the one above (including maiden name)? If yes, please list:
_____

Current address: _____

If at current address less than 6 months, please list previous address:
_____

Current phone: (H) _____ (W) _____ (Cell) _____

Current insurance?   YES   NO   Name of company: _____

Do you have a commercial driver's license? _____ License number: _____ State issued: _____

Please list all traffic violations in the last 3 years (Include date/type/result):
_____
_____

Have you ever been convicted or plead guilty to a criminal offense?   YES   NO

---

I hereby request Total Information Systems (Agency) to release information to ---(School name)--- that pertains to driving records researched or in any criminal or motor vehicle file researched/maintained on me whether local, state, or national. I hereby release the Agency from any and all liability resulting from such disclosure. I declare that the information given on this application is true and correct to the best of my knowledge. I also agree to implement the (School) transportation policy listed on the reverse side of this form.

**Signature:** _____  **Date:** _____

## DRIVER LICENSE VERIFICATION/VALIDATION

*Please SHOW YOUR LICENSE for Administration to record the following:*

Is license valid?   YES   NO

License number: _____ State issued: _____ Exp. date: _____

Classes/restrictions listed on license: _____
_____

**Verified by:**

Admin Signature: _____  Date: _____

APPENDIX I

# Transportation Policy

**-----(SCHOOL NAME)-----  TRANSPORTATION POLICY**

The following safety precautions **must** be implemented while driving or using any of the (School) vehicles, particularly the 15-passenger vans, to ensure safety of passengers and drivers. Anyone violating this policy will no longer be allowed to drive on behalf of (School)

---

**Be aware:** Because 15-passenger vans are substantially longer and wider than cars:
- They require more space and additional reliance on side-view mirrors for changing lanes. Always use a 'spotter' when backing up.
- They do not respond as well to abrupt steering maneuvers.
- They require additional braking time.

---

**ALL PASSENGERS AND DRIVERS IN (School) VEHICLES MUST ADHERE TO THE FOLLOWING:**

---

1. **All drivers must be over the age of 25.**
2. **All drivers must maintain an active license.** If your license becomes suspended or revoked after verification, you will immediately notify Administration and cease driving any school vehicle.
3. **Seatbelts must be worn at all times.**
4. Van passengers must be **seated from front to back.** Never allow more than 15 people to ride in the vans.
5. **Never drive over 60 mph** in the vans. Drive responsibly, cautiously and conservatively.
6. **No disruptive activity** will be permitted while the vehicle is moving.
7. **All windows must be kept clear** of objects that may obstruct the driver's view.
8. Absolutely **NO cell phone use by the driver** while driving. Pull safely off of the road before using the cell phone.
9. In case of an accident or **emergency**, stop and only exit the vehicle if necessary, and only on the sidewalk or shoulder side of the vehicle, never on the traffic side.
10. Any accident should be reported immediately to (School) Administration.

I have read, understand and will comply with the rules stated in this policy during the entire trip.

Name: _____  Date: _____

# Permission to Transport Students

I, _____, parent/guardian of _____,

give permission to (school name) to transport my child from (school or other location) to

_____to participate in the

_____on the _____day of _____,

20XX. I understand that students will be leaving the school at about _____ (a.m./p.m.) and returning at about _____ (a.m./p.m.). I understand that travel will be in either a school or parent owned vehicle, where all safety rules are abided by and appropriate restraint devices are utilized.

Signed:_____ Date: _____

Emergency Contact Name:_____Number:_____

# WORKS CITED

R.L. Dabney. *On Secular Education*. Moscow, Idaho: Ransom Press, 1989.

David Feddes, "Christianity and Education," *Banner of Truth: Biblical Christianity Through Literature*, http://www.banneroftruth.org/pages/articles/article_detail.php?152/ (accessed November 18, 2006).

John Milton Gregory. *The Seven Laws of Teaching*. Grand Rapids, Michigan: Baker Book House, 1884.

Logos School. *Logos Curriculum Guide*. Moscow, Idaho: Canon Press.

Bruce N. Shortt. *The Harsh Truth About Public Schools*. Vallecito, California: Chalcedon Foundation, 2004.

Charles F. Potter. *Humanism: A New Religion*. New York: New York, 1930.

Paul A. Kienel, Litt.D., Ollie E. Gibbs, Ed.D., Sharon R. Berry, Ph.D. *Philosophy of Christian School Education*. Colorado Springs, Colorado: Association of Christian Schools International, 1995.

Law Academy for Independent School Leaders. *Senate Bill 226 - Administration of Medication*. Raleigh: Schwartz and Shaw, P.L.L.C, 2005.

Logos School. "Logos Curriculum Guide.". Moscow, Idaho.

Roy W. Lowrie, Jr. and R. Leon Lowrie. *Serving God on the Christian School Board*. : Association Christian Schools International, [Rev. ed.] edition (1998).

Dennis W. Mills, Ph.D. "Classroom Discipline: A Management Guide for Christian School Teachers." *available from http://www.csrnet.org/csrnet/articles/classroom-discipline.html*, http://www.csrnet.org/csrnet/articles/classroom-discipline.html. (accessed October 1, 2006).

National Federation of State High School Associations. *National Federation of State High School Association 2006-2007 Handbook*. http://www.nfhs.org/web/2004/01/nfhs_sports_publications.aspx:.

North Carolina Independent Schools Athletic Association. *North Carolina Independent Schools Athletic Association Athletic Handbook*.

Claudius Ptolemy. *Almagest*. New York: Springer-Verlag, 1984.

Dorothy Sayers. *Essay, "The Lost Tools of Learning"*. Oxford, 1947.

Douglas Wilson. *Excused Absence: Should Christian kids leave public schools?*. Mission Viejo, CA: Crux Press, Inc, 2001.

www.ingramcontent.com/pod-product-compliance
Lightning Source LLC
Chambersburg PA
CBHW082226010526
44111CB00040BA/2905